Eduard Batalov

THE AMERICAN

utopia

Progress Publishers
Moscow

Translated from the Russian by *Dmitry Belyavsky*
Designed by *Vladimir Bisengaliev*

Э. Я. Баталов
Американская утопия
На английском языке

Printed in the Union of Soviet Socialist Republics

Б $\dfrac{05\,06000000\text{-}666}{014\,(01)\text{-}85}$ 35-85

CONTENTS

This book is about the American utopia. The reader may well wonder what, in our age of realism, can prompt a historian or a philosopher to tackle the subject of the social utopia—to all intents and purposes, a theme quite far from reality.

Paradoxically, it is only taking into consideration phenomena "far from reality" such as the social utopia or the social myth that one can construct a model of actual social consciousness and of actual culture, whether at the national or global level.

Indeed, to grasp the mentality of a nation (or of an individual) one must examine all dimensions of its (or his) awareness, including illusions and dreams, especially those represented definitively as an integral element of national culture. To achieve this, one has to enter the realm of utopia where a person with an open mind will be able to unravel many mysteries inherent in this awareness.

The reason is that utopias are coded expressions of social ideals and actual interests of classes, groups and individuals, interests which manifest themselves both in everyday political behavior and in the ideological struggle within this or that country or on the international scene. And so, decoding utopias can aid in ensuring a more profound understanding of people's attitude to the existing society, of their convictions, expectations, concepts of the future and social ideals.

Besides, the historical record shows that utopias are far from indifferent to actual historical developments. Marx's famous words about ideas becoming a great material force when they permeate the masses are perfectly applicable to utopias. Utopian ideas often become widespread in mass consciousness and demonstrate enviable resilience.

As to the American utopian tradition, a Marxist historian has quite adequate reasons to turn to this particular subject. The traditional picture of America is that of a country whose national consciousness, distinctly hostile to any visionary ideas, is rooted in pragmatism and clear, sober thinking; in other words, it is based on realism in theory and practice and rules out, either completely or largely, any utopian schemes.

This picture is only partly true. Yes, the conditions of America's colonization and subsequent development did breed shrewdness in practical matters, a sober-minded attitude to life and similar traits in Americans. The distinctive features displayed by the development of capitalism in the United States also promoted the spread of empiricism; this was reflected clearly in national culture. But, objectively, those same conditions prodded the shaping of utopian consciousness in American society. The conviction that the riches of the new continent were inexhaustible and that personal initiative would not encounter any rigid obstacles, the impression of economic, political and religious freedom, together with the Manifest Destiny and American exceptionalism concepts gradually took shape, combined to provide fertile soil for libertarianism in both theory and practice, for the development of the sociological imagination and the emergence of social and political schemes which were often utopian to a considerable degree and bold to the point of adventurism. It appeared that in the new country nothing was impossible: even the least feasible of dreams could be translated into reality, any type of resistance by objective reality could be eventually broken if only one was vigorous enough and confident in one's own abilities. That was how the American Dream was born, how American utopian consciousness and the American social utopia were shaped.

Of course, the American contribution to utopian literature is much smaller than the British, French, German or Italian. The New World failed to produce great utopians such as More, Fourier or Owen. But one must not lose sight of the fact that there was one aspect in which the United States played a great role which has not been appreciated properly to this day. I refer to utopian experiments, conducted in America on a scale unprecedented in other countries. The United States was the proving ground for testing, with different degrees of success, projects designed in the "laboratories" of Cabet, Owen, Fourier and other European—and, later, American—utopian theorists. It would be no exaggeration to say that a careful and all-round examination of these experiments and their comparison with similar undertakings in other countries can contribute to our knowledge not only of America's intellectual and political historical development but also of the overall laws guiding the realization of ideas in sociopolitical practice.

I am fully aware that I am not the first to attempt a study of the American utopia. The works of V. L. Parrington, V. L. Parrington, Jr., Glenn Negley and J. Max Patrick, H. W. Morgan, Kenneth Roemer, Arthur Bestor, Mark Holloway, Charles Nordhoff and John H. Noyes, to name but a few, and of my Soviet colleagues Eduard Arab-Ogly, M. Zakharova, M. Avdeyeva and other historians and philosophers have done much to ensure a proper understanding of the question. At the same time, I do not believe I am the last one to tackle this theme. And so, without attempting to offer an exhaustive treatment of an inexhaustible subject, I propose to trace the principal stages in the development of utopian consciousness in the United States and single out the main types of social utopias which have sprung from American soil. My aim is to try and show how, as social and political conditions connected with the development of the nation and American capitalism evolved, the utopian tradition evolved too; how one type of utopia ousted another or absorbed a new content; how utopian ideals transformed; and finally, how the role of utopia changed in social and political affairs.

Since a number of issues examined in the book give rise to differences of opinion (including the question of utopia's nature, essence and functions), I deemed it necessary to preface the specific historical analysis with a chapter on theory and methodology to determine the scope and content of the key concepts used throughout the book. By discussing questions of methodology and identifying the links of utopias to society's material functions we are clearing the way towards understanding the phenomenon of social utopia in the U.S.A. and, on a broader plane, American social consciousness.

Chapter I

————◆◆✕◆◆————

THE AMERICAN UTOPIA AND
THE AMERICAN DREAM

1. The Social Utopia: Genesis, Essence, Forms

In the autumn of 1516 Sir Thomas More published *A Fruteful and Pleasaunt Worke of the Best State of a Publyque Weale, and of the Newe Yle Called Utopia*—by today's standards, a longish and somewhat ornate title for a treatise but at that time, quite usual in style. And so the word "utopia" was born, to enter many languages and to become the subject of heated debates among philosophers, sociologists, political scientists and generally all those who tried either to design the "best state of public weal" themselves or to see what others were doing in this field.

The very etymology of the word coined by More gave rise to different interpretations. It was clear that "utopia" was a combination of two Greek elements but unclear which components precisely made it up. If these should be "ou" (not) and "topos" (place), then "utopia" meant "land of nowhere"; if the first elements should be "eu" (good) instead of "ou", it meant a "blessed, good land". Since the book was written in Latin and Greek words were presented in transcription, More's intent remains unclear. There is a school of thought claiming that More deliberately used a play on words. In any case, the mystery remained a mystery.

But the real difficulties started when in describing their imaginary "islands", "lands", "planets" and so forth, different authors imitated More and called them "utopias"; when people began discussing "utopian consciousness" or "utopian thinking", "utopian projects" and "utopian ideals"; when it became clear that experts interpreted the concept of utopia absolutely differently.

Let us quote an academic assessing the situation. "The words 'utopia' and 'utopian'," George Kateb writes in *The*

Encyclopedia of Philosophy, "have been put to many uses besides the one suggested by More's book. Common to all uses is reference to either the imaginary or the ideal or to both. But sometimes the words are used as terms of derision and sometimes with a vagueness that robs them of any genuine usefulness. For example, a proposal that is farfetched or implausible is often condemned as 'utopian', whether or not the proposal has any idealistic content. In another, closely related pejorative use, 'utopian' designates that which is unacceptably different from the customary or is radical in its demands.... Almost any kind of thoroughgoing idealism—a view of the good life, a statement of fundamental political principles, a plea for major reform—can earn for itself the title 'utopian'. Furthermore, all literary depictions of imaginary societies are called 'utopian', even if they represent some totalitarian or fiendish horror or are primarily futuristic speculations about technical and scientific possibilities that have no important connection to any idealism."[1]

It should be noted that the differences in the interpretation of the term and the very phenomenon of utopia are largely rooted in the fact that different scholars approach it from different angles. Many—and this can be deduced from the above quotation—see utopia's primary meaning in its impracticability, the illusory nature of the ideals it proclaims. This view is reflected in the word's colloquial usage: "utopian" means fantastic, whether in society, science, technology or everyday life.

This serves merely to obscure the real meaning of utopia. History tells us that many utopian projects proved to be feasible within a broad time framework, and many schemes that remained unrealized had nothing to do with utopia.

Karl Mannheim, a German sociologist who undertook, in the 1920s and 1930s, an analysis of the utopian phenomenon (to apply it to sociology of knowledge he was working on) and whose concepts are popular in the West to this day, sees utopia as a manifestation of a certain type of consciousness. This consciousness, he maintains, is opposite to so-called ideological consciousness (or simply "ideology");

[1] *The Encyclopedia of Philosophy*, Vol. 7 and 8, the Macmillan Company & the Free Press, New York, Collier-Macmillan Publishers, London, 1972, pp. 212, 213.

it is "incongruous with the state of reality within which it occurs". "This incongruence is always evident in the fact that such a state of mind in experience, in thought, and in practice, is oriented towards objects which do not exist in the actual situation."[1] Mannheim goes on to explain that this state of mind is "transcendent" in relation to reality, "alien to reality" and "unreal". It cannot be realized in the actual conditions and it is impossible to act according to it.[2]

It turns out, however, that Mannheim extends the same characteristics to ideology—according to him, the opposite of utopia. Ideology, too, is a "transcendent" and "unreal" state of mind. The only difference is that utopia and ideology are "blind" to different elements of social reality, that they record different phenomena and, consequently, discharge opposite social functions. The German sociologist emphasizes that the utopian state of mind is critical consciousness. It distinguishes only those elements in the reality which aid in the undermining of the existing order. "It turns its back on everything which would shake its belief or paralyse its desire to change things."[3] By contrast, the ideological state of mind is apologetic consciousness, aimed at perpetuating the status quo and at unconsciously concealing those elements of the situation which destroy the existing social order.

Mannheim believes that the utopian state of mind is "blind" (as is the ideological state of mind) and sees only certain elements within a certain framework of social reality, and that this is rooted in the distinctive features of social existence manifested in the social status of the group to which the subject of utopian consciousness belongs. He insists that group social being is "inadequate"—but this is the natural, inevitable inadequacy of a specific, historically conditioned social status which makes it impossible, given that the subject remain within the framework of the given social being, to grasp social reality in its entirety. In other words, the subject of utopian (and ideological) consciousness sees (and cannot help seeing) reality not quite the way it actually is or the way those immersed in a

[1] Karl Mannheim, *Ideology and Utopia. An Introduction to the Sociology of Knowledge*, Routledge and Kegan Paul, Ltd., London, 1968, p. 173.

[2] *Ibid.*, pp. 173-175.

[3] *Ibid.*, p. 36.

different reality see it. Therefore, utopian consciousness can be viewed as the reality code of the subject of consciousness or—and this is essentially the same thing—as a state of mind inadequate to the given reality and aimed at its destruction. Such is the stand taken by the German sociologist Karl Mannheim and his numerous followers in Europe and the United States.

It is easy to see that Mannheim deduces utopia's substantive characteristics from the role which it plays in society and which, in turn, is determined by its social functions. But here a very important question remains unanswered: how does utopia take shape in creative consciousness and what characteristics should it possess to discharge these functions effectively. It follows that the essence of the utopian phenomenon remains unclear too.

It appears that in examining this essence, we should—according to the principles of Marx's analysis of consciousness—proceed not from utopia's role in society and not from its functions but from the mode in which our consciousness shapes it. One can unravel the essence of utopia as a phenomenon of consciousness and of culture, a phenomenon possessing certain structural and functional characteristics and playing a certain role in social developments, only through a comparative analysis of the ways used to construct works such as Plato's *Republic* and *Laws*, More's *Utopia*, Campanella's *City of the Sun*, Harrington's *Oceana*, Cabet's *A Voyage to Icaria*, Bellamy's *Looking Backward*, several treatises on the "best state of public weal" by Saint-Simon, Fourier and Owen, and a number of other obviously utopian works.

It is generally accepted that human activity, object- and purpose-oriented, is shaped in accordance with an ideal postulated in the consciousness of the subject of activity. But the ideal underlying this activity and serving as its goal can be postulated in different ways. This is of primary importance for understanding the nature and essence of utopia.

The subject may postulate his ideal in accordance with objective laws and trends, as conceived, at a given time, by science—by philosophy, sociology, history and other disciplines dealing with the laws of social development. Marx, one might recall, said repeatedly that the social ideal people striving to really transform the world looked up to must be earthly in its background. In other words, this ideal should not be simply thought up, even by a good thinker, but deduced from the actual historical development of society. Besides, the ideal should not only express society's actual needs perceived by certain classes or groups but also conform to the emergent trends of sociohistorical development which have, at a certain stage, become necessary. In other words, Marx sees the social ideal not as the image of the desirable state of society but as the image of its necessary state (which may, of course, coincide with the desirable), arising from the solution of the existing contradictions and from the natural transition of one social stage to the next. This ideal is the fruit of specific sociological analysis dealing with the state of the social organism taken in its historical motion.

Still, the history of culture knows another way of postulating the ideal, when it is shaped by the free play of the imagination—that is, when the consciousness producing it strives to mentally throw off the tyranny of necessity, to rise above time and history. Dostoyevsky had this to say when he explained his understanding of "dreams" (which figured prominently in his works): "It appears that it is not reason but will, not the mind but the heart which is the motive force of dreams.... You skip over space and time and over laws of reality and reason, stopping only at points of which the heart is dreaming."[1] But the dreams of Dostoyevsky's protagonists are nothing less than utopias, and the quotation describing their characteristics reflects substantive features of utopia.

Indeed, free play of the imagination in the construction of an ideal is the basis of a utopian's creative effort. He shapes his project by purely speculative methods. He invents and composes his ideals, guided not so much by his mind as by his heart—and does not agonize intellectually over whether the world he is creating in his imagination conforms to the laws of social development.

True, the utopian's free-wheeling has its limits. True, he cannot break completely away from either his time or his society, even though he may strive to do so. But if one wants to grasp the essence of utopia, one must postulate that the utopian's subjective logics is arbitrary, for he—in Thore-

[1] Fedor Dostoyevsky, *Complete Works*, Vol. 25, Leningrad, 1983, pp. 108, 110 (in Russian).

au's wise words—wants us to "so live as to secure all the advantage without suffering any of the disadvantage."[1]

The utopian sees the real world as a diversity of fragments unconnected by any organic links, not as a system. It is a world of sharply contrasting elements, of "plus" and "minus", without any diffused gradations of color; a world in which objects and even time are truly out of joint. However, while breaking the world as an integral whole into "positive" and "negative" elements, the utopian also feels the need to do the reverse, to synthesize, from an arbitrary arrangement of these elements, a new world his heart longs to see.

The result is the image (idea) of a world-construct functioning according to its own laws which may only coincide with the actual laws purely by accident. Such are the worlds constructed in the imagination of Plato, More, Harrington and all other utopians, great and small: in this respect, they are all equal, they are all social inventors, although some are more gifted than others.

It is easily demonstrable that any utopian project has social roots. However, this does not at all mean that utopia must—according to Mannheim's logic—be traced directly to a rigidly interpreted social "situation" associated with a critical approach to the existing social relations. Marx's methodology produces much more fruitful results: the product of consciousness is derived not only, and not so much, from the negation or support of the existing social structures (although the attitude of the subject of consciousness to them must be taken into account) but from the entire system of social relations into which the subject is "entwined", from those objectively recorded tensions which are inherent in the system and which determine the subject's functioning within the given system.

While recognizing that utopia is socially determined, one should also see it as the product of the subject's cognitive activity. As man perceives the world, he inevitably subjects it to ideal transformation by taking it apart mentally, deleting some elements and disrupting links among objects. An object's copy (image, idea) which eventually

[1] Henry David Thoreau, *Walden or, Life in the Woods and On the Duty of Civil Disobedience*, A Signet Classic, New York, 1960, p. 26.

12

takes shape in man's consciousness can, under certain conditions, be an arbitrary form in relation to the actual
world—becase in certain situations, the subject of knowledge sees only what he wants to see in the object under
examination and does not see that which, for this or that
reason (whether known or unknown to him), he does not
wish his consciousness to record. This process does not at all
have to be linked rigidly to the subject's social situation,
that is, to his social status and conscious attitude to the
existing order. Of importance here are factors like the
overall level of society, the cultural level of the individual,
the psychological characteristics of the subject, and his
direct everyday concerns.

The Marxist interpretation of utopia does not deny
the latter's transcendental and critical qualities, the ones
stressed by Mannheim, but it does not view them as representing the essence of utopia. Ideology (as viewed by Mannheim) is transcendental too, which he acknowledges, and
many types of consciousness far from utopia have critical
traits. One can be radically critical of the institutions in
power but plan one's actions according to the social development laws known in science. One can also—since we are
dealing with transcendental matters—act counting on
essentially new institutions and values that do not yet exist,
but again not be a utopian, if consciousness constructs these
institutions and values proceeding from identified trends of
social evolution and not from the free play of the imagination. On the other hand, one can advocate retention of the
existing social structures and still be a utopian. As Georgi
Plekhanov, the well-known Russian Marxist, wrote, "one may
laugh at any kind of 'music of the future', one may be firmly convinced that the existing social order we have the good
fortune to live under is the best of all possible social orders
and, in spite of it all, view the 'structure and life of the social
body' from the very angle the utopians viewed them."[1]

Indeed, there are many utopias picturing the "ideal
society" as a somewhat modified present or an imaginary
Golden Age long past, associated with the slaveowning, feu-
dal or early capitalist stage. One should, generally, note that
"incongruity with the state of reality" is inherent, to dif-

---

[1] *Plekhanov's Literary Heritage*, Collection VIII, Part I, Moscow,
1940, p. 157 (in Russian).

ferent degrees, in different types of consciousness, since in some respects they are ahead of the given reality and in others, inevitably lag behind it. The heart of the matter is not incongruity as such but its nature.

To sum up: if one assumes that the essence of any utopian project is determined by the mode of its construction, then utopia is an image (ideal) of the desired (and in this sense, perfect) human commonwealth, environment, be it a community, city, country, planet or cosmos; and this image is postulated arbitrarily by consciousness.

In accordance with this definition, consciousness manifested in the social utopia (i.e., utopian consciousness) can be described as oriented on a break with the objective laws governing the operation and development of nature and society, and on arbitrary construction of an ideal. And although this type of consciousness finds its fullest and most consistent expression precisely in the social utopia, it is by no means confined to the latter; it is a universal— that is, existing in different spheres of the creative effort— and relatively stable type of consciousness manifested in literature, art, architecture, science and political theory.

Naturally, utopian consciousness *per se* is merely an analytical construct (it can, for the sake of clarity, be compared to Max Weber's "ideal types") which exists, in its pure form, only in the mind of the philosopher. As any other type of consciousness, it enters real, actually functioning polyphonic chorus of consciousness as a definite orientation— in this case, orientation on the utopian mode of perception and construction of an ideal object.

But, turning back to the specific utopian projects constructed over the past 25 centuries and representing a huge layer of world culture, it is easy to see that they differ from one another, and sometimes quite substantially, not only in content but also in aspects of form which, together with other parameters, should be taken into account in classifying utopias.

To begin with, utopias emerge at different social levels and serve different social groups. A. L. Morton, A. I. Klibanov and other Marxist scholars have demonstrated that historically, the first form of utopia on which "poets, prophets and philosophers" drew as authors of utopian works, was the folk utopia. In the words of A. L. Morton, "It is the first in time, the most universally current and the most enduring, and it gives us a standard of values against which all its successors can be judged."[1]

The folk utopia expresses the ideas of the lower social strata, peasants and town-dwellers, of a "just" social order, whether God-given, established by a just king (the "king of the people") or created by their own efforts in the struggle against oppressors. This utopia is part of the culture of different social structures. The folk utopia exists wherever there are lower and higher strata, wherever there is social antagonism.

The folk utopia has many layers. As a rule, it comprises a broad range of social ideals, from the petty-bourgeois to elements of the proletarian ideal. Their common denominator is their opposition to the dominant social relations and to the official establishment. This opposition alternates between covert and openly polemic forms.

The folk utopian ideal is expressed in different literary genres—in epic poems, legends, fairy tales, songs and pamphlets, whether secular or religious.

Aside from the folk utopia, a society divided into opposing classes also has a different utopia, more or less pronounced as an independently functioning type. It is the official utopia, designed as a mass market product and constructed at the top either by professional ideologists working to fulfill a social order of the officialdom or as a result of the creative effort undertaken by statesmen themselves who express their own ideal. The building blocks of an official utopia may include products of work by philosophers, authors or politicians, as well as elements of folk utopias appropriately arranged in social, political or stylistic terms.

One cannot rigidly classify any official utopia as deception of the people or a deliberate lie the establishment uses to consolidate its domination of society and to manipulate the masses. No doubt, such manipulation does take place, just as there is a conscious desire to implant in the masses a notion of the interests and objectives of the ruling class favorable to the latter. Aside from this, however, the official utopia usually also expresses the ruling elite's actual conception of the prospects and main goals of the given society (or of the world as a whole), the vision which

[1] A. L. Morton, *The English Utopia*, Lawrence and Wishart, London, 1952, pp. 15, 16.

reflects the elite's distinct social status and is therefore one-sided, incomplete and utopian in its orientation.

Besides the folk and the official utopia each society has literary and theoretical utopias which are produced by cultural figures and which do not directly express either the hopes of the lower classes or the demands of the higher ones—although these utopias do essentially reflect the interests of this or that social group at any level of the hierarchy. These works, whose authors are, as a rule, easily identifiable, make up the bulk of utopian literature. And, while most of the many hundreds or even thousands of the literary and theoretical utopias created over two millenia and a half were products of mediocre writers, great authors—Plato, Dostoyevsky, Shakespeare, Tolstoy, Rabelais—and philosophers—Saint-Simon, Fourier, Owen, Fedorov, Sir Francis Bacon—also produced utopian works.

Utopias differ in the form in which the utopian ideal is articulated—in other words, in the genres of works in which it is expressed. Fiction is the commonest form here: it can be a novel, a story, a poem, travel notes and the like. The utopian ideal may be incorporated into a nonutopian context. This technique was used by Dostoyevsky and also by Rabelais: the latter included the thoroughly utopian story of the Thélème L'Abbey in his far from utopian *Gargantua and Pantagruel.*

The social, political or economic treatise (or a series of treatises) is an equally common form in which utopian ideals have been expressed, notably, by many British, French and American utopian socialists. Some authors used both these forms and their works were a sort of synthesis of fiction and the sociopolitical treatise. One of them was Edward Bellamy, a well-known American utopian of the 19th century (more about him later), whose *Equality*, a sequel to his utopian novel *Looking Backward*, was a cross between a novel and a treatise.

The political or social document—a declaration, manifesto, program and the like—is another familiar form used to express a utopian ideal. These documents are produced in quantity by mass movements, and are especially numerous during social revolutions. In this case, too, a utopian ideal may be incorporated into a generally non-utopian work. Such was the type of the many documents produced by the bourgeois revolutions of the 18th and 19th centuries, including the French Declaration of the Rights of Man and Citizen and the American Declaration of Independence. Obviously, neither of these documents can be classed as utopian. Nevertheless, their analysis shows that some of the ideas recorded in them (those expressing the social ideal expounded by the progressive wing of the bourgeoisie and by working people whose interests and demands had to be taken into account in a revolutionary era) were essentially utopian: these were expressions of the principles and purposes sharply at variance with the objective trends of capitalist development and with the actual capabilities of the bourgeois class.

The folk utopia has a distinctive form of expressing its ideals through folklore—mostly legends (for example, the famous legend of the Land of Cockaigne), parables, sagas, fairy tales and folk songs.

Yet another form of expressing socioutopian ideals is the experiment, far from always based on a theoretical program or at least a theoretically substantiated plan of action. This was a sort of ideal-in-action which sometimes affected considerably the shaping of public consciousness. All these forms of expressing a utopian ideal are connected with appropriate spheres in which utopian consciousness is formed: literature, art, sociopolitical theory and sociopolitical practice.

Utopias also differ in the type of their social ideal which can be viewed from different angles. For example, proceeding from the social, class content of the ideal, utopias can be divided into bourgeois, peasant, petty-bourgeois and the like. Examined from the standpoint of the ideal's sociopolitical content and thrust, these same utopias can be described as socialist, liberal bourgeois, anarchist, fascist, etc.—depending on what relations and institutions they are designed to construct.

The researcher may proceed from the sociocultural content of the ideal, that is, from the nature of the cultural values and the mechanism for regulating social relations in the imaginary society. By applying this criterion, romantic, technocratic and other utopias can be singled out, although their political orientation may differ.

Finally, it is important to note the position of a utopian ideal on the historical time scale. In this case, one would be justified to divide utopias into reactionary (oriented on reviving historically obsolete social forms), conservative (aimed at preserving historically no longer viable and therefore disappearing social forms) and progressive (designed to elaborate new forms geared to ensure further social progress).

Naturally, the large body of research into utopia offers other criteria for distinguishing and, consequently, classifying different types of utopian works. Utopias can be classified by how plausible they are ("utopias", "semi-utopias" and "quasiutopias" of Fred L. Polak); by how they express the critical spirit (Lewis Mumford's "utopias of escape" and "utopias of reconstruction"); by the way the ideal is localized (F. E. Manuel's "utopias" and "uchronias") and so on.

Apparently, each of the listed aspects of a utopian ideal can highlight some of its new dimensions, more or less substantive and more or less typical of this or that utopian tradition. The task of a researcher analyzing a given tradition is to find precisely the angle which would make it possible to produce an adequate understanding of the nature of the utopias shaped within the framework of this tradition, to determine their role in the emergence and evolution of national consciousness and identity, to trace the impact of utopian precepts on the behaviour of individuals, groups, classes or even the entire nation.

2. Utopia's Main Functions

For all their differences, utopias inevitably share certain common functions—above all, no doubt, the *critical* function. While it does not exhaust, as Mannheim maintains, the essence of utopia, it is nevertheless important. A utopian is always a critic, a rebel, sometimes a heretic who refuses to even theoretically accept his destiny, the destiny of his society or even of all mankind.

But criticism can be different in its objectives, intensity and form. It can be passive and contemplative; it can be active, aimed at radically transforming society. This was the criterion the U.S. sociologist and historian Lewis Mumford used to divide all the utopias he knew into two large groups, each with a distinctly expressed critical function. "One of these functions," he wrote in his *Story of Utopias*, "is escape or compensation, it seeks an immediate release from the difficulties or frustrations of our lot. The other attempts to provide a condition for our release in the future. The utopias that correspond to these two functions I shall call the utopias of escape and the utopias of reconstruction. The first leaves the external world the way it is, the second seeks to change it so that one may have intercourse with it on one's own terms."[1]

Obviously, the division Mumford suggests is relative, all the more so since many utopias combine both a trend toward escape and a desire of reconstruction. Generally, however, this pattern does describe the simplest ways of rejecting actual reality.

Utopian criticism may be conducted from different positions. A utopian may criticize the existing social order as a "perversion" or "profanation" of past ideals dear to his heart and cherish the hope that the past, symbolically embodied in his concept of the Golden Age, would return. In other words, he may build the image of the desired reality according to ideals of the past, thus operating from historically reactionary positions.

Utopian rejection may also be aimed at the shape of things to come, at a future threatening to destroy the status quo so dear to the heart of the conservative. In this case the utopia is the somewhat improved and preserved present. Plato's position is a classic example of a combination of reactionary and conservative utopianism. As the Soviet philosopher Aleksei Losev aptly remarked, "Plato's utopia combined elements of different social and government forms which had already existed in the past... Plato was an ideologue advocating the revival of obsolete forms of government based on slaveowning relations, although in his utopia these once real sociopolitical forms were subjected to a peculiar and complex transformation. His revivalist plans were largely vague. The only thing that mattered was to fall out of step with the decaying Greek society of his time."[2]

Utopian criticism can also be progressive, that is, aimed

[1] Lewis Mumford, *The Story of Utopias*, Boni and Liveright Publishers, New York, 1922, p. 15.

[2] A. F. Losev, "Plato's Life and Work" in: *Plato's Works in Three Volumes*, Vol. 1, Moscow, 1968, p. 25 (in Russian).

at the destruction of the institutions, relations and values which have outlived their creative usefulness and become a dead weight hampering social development. This was the stand taken by the utopian socialists of the first half of the 19th century who rejected bourgeois civilization and planned a new social system in their imagination.

A utopia's critical thrust may be directed at different objects. A utopian may rebel not only against social and political precepts or the dominant morals but also against laws of nature and against death itself. This rebellion is expressed poetically in many religious doctrines and folk utopias. In time, the idea of mastering nature and attaining immortality assumes the form of projects—for example, in the so-called cosmic utopia of Nikolai Fedorov, a 19th-century Russian philosopher. This author of a peculiar socio-cosmic utopia dreamed of a world in which man had conquered death and extended his power beyond Earth (see N. F. Fedorov, *Works*, Moscow, 1982). And, while Fedorov did not directly attack the existing social order the way Owen or Bellamy did (*Looking Backward* was the subject of Fedorov's critical remarks), it is clear from his principal work entitled *The Philosophy of the Common Cause* that he saw victory over death as possible only after a radical—patriarchic—transformation of the society he lived in.

Naturally, a utopia's mission is not confined to criticism of the existing sociopolitical structures or laws of nature. As a rule, utopian criticism is indirect or even covert; it serves merely as a sort of background against which the utopian projects his picture of an alternative world based on his concepts of the social, political, moral or aesthetic ideal. In constructing the ideal, utopia discharges a *normative* function.

Since human activity postulates and is oriented on an object, man invariably looks for an ideal as the perfect image of the object at which his activity is aimed. In this respect, ideals differ not only from era to era but also within individual eras, reflecting the interests of different social classes and groups.

The social utopia postulates the main parameters of the ideal which are finite in the utopian's consciousness. However, history tells us that these limits may be situated at different distances from the boundaries of the existing society.

Immanuel Kant was the first to formulate and try to

substantiate an orientation on a utopian ideal as a limit situated as far as possible from the boundaries of the existing society. "The Platonic Republic," he wrote in his *Critique of Pure Reason*, "has become proverbial as an example—and a striking one—of imaginary perfection, such as can exist only in the brain of the idle thinker; and Brucker ridicules the philosopher for maintaining that a prince can never govern well, unless he is participant in *the ideas*. But we should do better to follow up this thought and, where this admirable thinker leaves us without assistance, employ new efforts to place it in clearer light, rather than carelessly fling it aside as useless, under the very miserable and pernicious pretext of impracticability.... Now although a perfect state may never exist, the idea is not on that account the less just, which holds up this *maximum* as the archetype or standard of a constitution, in order to bring legislative government always nearer and nearer to the greatest possible perfection. For at what precise degree human nature must stop in its progress, and how wide must be the chasm which must necessarily exist between the idea and its realization, are problems which no one can or ought to determine—and for this reason, that it is the destination of freedom to overstep all assigned limits between itself and the idea."[1]

Therefore, the more impractical a utopian ideal appears and the closer it is to the conceivable maximum, to the absolute, the higher its degree of possible practical effect. In other words, according to the Kantian logic, the closer a utopia's ideal is to the maximum, the more valuable it is in practical terms and the better it serves social progress.

One must, however, note that this was precisely what intuitively motivated many utopians, including the authors of folk utopias, as well as Plato, More, Campanella, Cabet, Fourier, Bellamy, Morris and many others. They dreamed of a Golden Age, of an earthly paradise, of a perfect society.

Still, history demonstrates that the limit recorded in a utopia can be transcendental to different degrees, that is, it can be positioned at different distances from the boundaries of the actual society. Depending on the historical situation, this limit alternates between approaching the

---

[1] Immanuel Kant, *The Critique of Pure Reason*, William Benton Publisher, Chicago, London, etc., 1952, p. 114.

near reaches of the existing world (one might call this the "minimum ideal") and moving infinitely far away from it (the "maximum ideal"). And so, always involving a limit from the viewpoint of the utopian, that is, embodying the specific limit of his sociological imagination, the utopian ideal is relative in its actual content. Here, a distinct regularity is present. The maximum utopia is usually born in a period dominated by historical optimism and ideas of social progress. When optimism and the faith of the given class (or of society as a whole) in social progress give way to skepticism and pessimism, more modest (and at the same time closer to reality) and essentially reformist utopian ideals emerge, pushing the maximum ideal to the background.

This type of situation is often described as a "decline" or "end" of utopia; but this is hardly adequate to reflect the essence of the matter. Naturally, orientation on the minimum ideal, readiness to be content with little can be seen as an indication that the civilization which produced it and the social class whose expectations it expresses are decaying. Nevertheless, utopia as such does not disappear; it continues to exist as the fruit and embodiment of a certain type of consciousness, of a certain form of perceiving reality and shaping a social alternative.

As a result, in each historical era a nation's social consciousness comprises a more or less broad range of utopian ideals embodied in different forms and situated at different distances from the boundaries of the existing society.

The advancement of science inevitably restricts utopia's normative function: the scientifically substantiated ideal is pushing the utopian ideal aside. Still, the latter persists and continues to be reproduced both in the consciousness of professional intellectuals and in mass consciousness too.

The reproduction of the utopian ideal in mass and theoretical consciousness is also stimulated, as will be demonstrated later, by man's urge to gain knowledge. This urge, coupled with practical interests, prompts man to go beyond the field mastered by science and to intellectually turn to frontiers which are still closed to precise science and can therefore be mastered only in extrascientific forms, in particular by building utopian constructs. Yet, to avoid misunderstanding, one should note that "extrascientific", that is, outside the realm of science, does not equal "antiscientific", that is, antagonistically opposed to science, denying its legitimate rights and actual capabilities. Extrascientific forms of mastering the world may lack an antiscientific content if they complement scientific forms the way, say, art organically complements science.

The turning to utopia is also connected with the fact that consciousness needs a future-oriented system of social, aesthetic and moral values not limited by the achievements and possibilities of science. Usually, as man acts, he mentally reproduces himself and the world around him in different spatial and temporal coordinates, that is, he lives, as it were, in the past, present and future simultaneously, picturing them in different "versions". This means that it is not enough for man to imagine what the existing world may be like in the future. He feels the urge to imagine what he himself would like to become and what he would like society, the world and the universe to become today, tomorrow or in three hundred years. In other words, in order to act successfully in today's world, he has to form a picture of the imaginary limit which different nations in different ages expressed in concepts of the "Golden Age", "earthly paradise", "great millenium", "harmonious society" and the like. Nikolai Konrad, an eminent Soviet historian, wrote that "whatever shape the concept of that limit took, it never left mankind and inspired it in the struggle against that which hampers the attainment of the ideal state of society worthy of man. The Russian author Dostoyevsky put it brilliantly and forcefully: 'The Golden Age is the most impossible of all dreams that ever existed but for which people gave their entire lives and all their efforts, for which prophets died and were killed, without which nations do not want to live and cannot even die.'"[1] This is where utopia comes in.

And so, man always lives in a world of ideals which differ not only in their social content and political thrust but also in their genesis. Some ideals take form within the mainstream of scientific knowledge and, "cleansed" of value elements, record the parameters of the images of a possible future world in this or that aspect. Others appear within the mainstream of utopia and record the subject's value orientation, needs and wishes in their arbitrary and often extrem-

[1] Nikolai Konrad, "On the Meaning of History" in: *East-West,* Moscow, 1966, p. 512 (in Russian).

ist expression. And, while at each new spiral of social development science wins more and more ground from utopia and ensures the implementation of newer utopian ideals, it not only refrains from blocking utopian endeavors but even stimulates them, as it were, by setting new and great tasks for mankind, and "crazy" ideas become an imperative for the success of science itself.

Here we approach another, *cognitive* function of utopia. The fact is that what is not true in a given sociohistorical context may prove true as a "moment" in the dialectical process of knowledge. As Engels noted, "what formally may be economically incorrect, may all the same be correct from the point of view of world history."[1] This "transformation" is expressed above all in the fact that as history progresses, the implausibility of utopias proves to be relative, and projects impracticable at a given stage of social development become feasible within a broader historical framework. Functioning as a delusion, as a manifestation of "inadequate" consciousness, utopia nevertheless distinctively records both the contradictory nature of the very social development which gave birth to the utopia in question and the actual fact of its ideal, intellectual perception. One might recall in this connection that Hegel was the first modern European philosopher to found the tradition of rejecting a crudely metaphysical opposition of delusion to truth. (Since "error is a Positive as an opinion affirming that which is not in and for itself, an opinion which knows itself and asserts itself",[2] that is, since error traces the outlines of positive knowledge, it is therefore an organic integral part, in a canceled form, of truth.)

As science advances, extrascientific forms of the ideal perception of the world, including utopia, retain their practical usefulness. At each specific stage of scientific development the possibilities of scientific knowledge and scientific methods are limited; meanwhile, the increasing role of the "factor of the future" virtually in every sphere of human activity and the exacerbation of ideological struggle over the issue of the prospects facing man and society call

[1] Frederick Engels, "Preface to the First German Edition" of *The Poverty of Philosophy* by Karl Marx, Progress Publishers, Moscow, 1975, p. 13.

[2] G. Hegel, *Science of Logic*, Vol. 2, George Allen & Unwin Ltd., London, 1929, p. 65.

for a more vigorous search of forms and methods of "mastering the future". Assuming the function of tentatively probing the limits of the possible (as applied to the cosmos, to society as a whole or to its individual institutions) and forming value attitudes, utopia complements scientific knowledge about the world with extrascientific hypotheses and ideas which pave the way for future scientific advances and anticipate truths which science may discover and substantiate tomorrow.

It is apparently no accident that the twentieth century, and especially its latter half, is the period in which social science fiction, this sublimated form of utopia, has risen to unprecedented heights and become extremely popular. Nor is it an accident that while remaining firmly anchored in science proper, many scientists nevertheless turn simultaneously to utopia and science fiction, fields which remove obstacles from the path of their fertile imagination. Konstantin Tsiolkovsky, the founder of the theory of space flight, wrote several utopian[1] and science fiction[2] works. Today this tradition is upheld by Dennis Gabor, Burrhus Skinner and other recognized experts in natural sciences and technology. Another notable fact is that many science fiction authors have had a science education and important scientific works to their credit—people like Arthur Clarke, Isaac Asimov or Ivan Yefremov.

Of course, relations between science and utopia are not always smooth, especially since the latter lacks proper critical selfreflection and, unconscious (or insufficiently conscious) of its utopian nature, sometimes tends to claim the role of a social and political imperative. Nevertheless, it would be naive to suggest, on these grounds, that our knowledge (and consciousness) be "cleansed" once and for all of utopian elements or of every value-oriented element. A student of knowledge has noted that "the complex re-

[1] K. Tsiolkovsky, *Nirvana,* Kaluga, 1914; *Woe and Genius*, Kaluga, 1916; *Mind and Passions*, Kaluga, 1928 (all in Russian).

[2] K. Tsiolkovsky, *The Road to the Stars,* Moscow, 1960 (in Russian). *Khimiya i zhizn* (*Chemistry and Life* magazine) No. 1, 1977, featured a previously unpublished transcript of a talk between Tsiolkovsky and Alexander Chizhevsky, another prominent Russian natural scientist. Elaborating on his ideas of man mastering outer space, Tsiolkovsky spoke about the evolution of the human species and said that there might come a time when man became "immortal in time and infinite in space".

lations between theoretical and practical knowledge produce intermediate forms of perceiving social reality, where elements of a theoretical approach may be combined with the assertion of certain value-oriented components. Apparently, the task is not to try and eliminate these forms from contemporary social knowledge but to take a clear-cut reflective stand which makes it possible to tell scientific elements from myth-making, utopian and similar elements."[1]

Obviously, a "clear-cut reflective" position vis-a-vis utopias is not always easy to take, especially if, for some external reasons, theoretical elements in a system of knowledge are ousted by value-oriented elements and utopian constructs are elevated to the level of official ideology. However, since "intermediate" (including utopian) forms of perceiving reality are independent of our will, the task is to try and correctly assess the cognitive value of this or that specific utopia.

The cognitive value of utopia is not confined to the fact that it helps to delve into the essence of the objective world. Utopia also contains certain information about the subject himself who expresses his concept of the desired world in a utopian ideal. This ideal (though sometimes coded) is especially valuable to the historian and the sociologist who, by examining it in a sociohistorical context, can glean additional information about the values on which the subject is oriented, the degree to which his class consciousness is developed, his attitude to official culture and a number of other parameters which, in turn, shed light on the consciousness of his time.

The role of utopia in learning about social phenomena is also determined by the fact that throughout its history, it has played the part of a distinctive form of *social forecasting*. To a certain degree, utopia retains this role even today, when futurology exists—a discipline claiming to shape, in consciousness, images of things to come.

Strictly speaking, there is a substantial difference between forecast and utopia. The direct purpose of forecasting is to identify the actual possibilities of a society

<hr />

[1] V. S. Shvyrev, "On the Problem of the Distinctive Features of Social Knowledge" in: *Voprosy Filosofii (Philosophical Problems)*, No. 3, 1972, p. 127.

(or of a given particular system inherent in it) at a certain stage of its evolution, depending on the time range of the forecast, and to assess the probability of each of these possibilities. Here, the more a forecast relies on objective laws of social development and the better it is cleansed of any subjective, value-oriented elements, the more accurate and effective it is. On the contrary, a utopia draws the picture of a desired, not possible or probable, society. Naturally, this desired and ideal (perfect, in the eyes of the utopian) social order may coincide with the possible and even the most probable in a given historical situation. But the need for such a coincidence is not inherent in utopia: the utopian acts noι as a scholar but rather as an artistic free agent who, even if he does see through the screen concealing the future from the present, does it mostly by intuition.

Still, frequently the desired order pictured by a utopian coincides both with the possible and with the probable, that is, fulfills the role of a spontaneous social forecast (which becomes clear after the fact). This prompted Lenin to say that great utopians "anticipated innumerable things, the correctness of which is now being scientifically proved by us"[1].

Modern social theory firmly believes that the images of the future which take shape in social consciousness are far from neutral in relation to this future, especially when these images are consciously used as a basis for programs of action. According to A. Bauer, a German Marxist philosopher, "the decisive point of forecasting is its active feedback impact on social practice. The decisive function of social forecasts should be viewed within the framework of their feedback function."[2]

Obviously, one cannot consider all conceivable images of an alternative world equally feasible (and effective in their feedback) simply because they are equally conceivable. Still, history tells us that many utopian projects have proved to be an active and effective constructive social force. Apparently, the explanation is above all that history

[1] V. I. Lenin, "What Is to Be Done?", *Collected Works*, Vol. 5, Progress Publishers, Moscow, 1977, p. 371.

[2] A. Bauer, "Topical Problems of Scientific Management of Social Processes" in: *Historical Materialism as the Theory of Social Knowledge and Practice*, Moscow, 1972, p. 147 (in Russian).

is made not by an abstract rational subject who is above emotion and to whom the dialectics of history presents no mysteries, but by real people with their hopes, illusions, errors and determination to make the world a better place to live in, with their faith or conviction that this is possible. Since historical necessity does not exist as something posited *a priori* but emerges from a clash of different historical trends and since the subject of a historical creative effort is free in his social choice, the very act of choosing a historical alternative and turning it into a direct objective of practical action (be that alternative scientifically valid or utopian) determines, to a certain degree, the direction and nature of social change.

The utopian nature of an alternative which has become a program of action will, of course, make itself felt sooner or later: in all probability, this program will not be implemented fully, definitively or adequately. But even in this case, it may make a noticeable impact on the course of the sociohistorical process. A utopian project may, for instance, be implemented in part or temporarily, the end result, as it has happened many times, being either a restoration of the status quo or the emergence of a hybrid structure. And finally, attempts at making a utopia a reality may produce results which neither the masses nor their leaders have expected. For example, this is what happened to the European utopian movements of the 16th and 17th centuries: instead of helping build a just social order, the dream of their participants, they aided in the emergence of capitalist society.

Utopia affects the sociohistorical process in different ways. It may be a direct impact, when a utopian project serves as a program or even plan of action for large and small groups. For example, Owen and Cabet tried, together with their followers, to reshape existing society according to the principles of their doctrines. There is another, indirect way, when a utopian ideal inspires or stimulates the subject of history to action. Many mass movements of modern history were rooted in the desire to either find the "promised land" which allegedly existed but was hidden, or transform the world in accordance with the principles of "justice", "truth", "good" and so on. As Lewis Mumford said aptly in this connection, "the Icarians who lived only in the mind of Etienne Cabet, or the Freelanders who

dwelt within the imagination of a dry little Austrian econo-
mist [Theodor Hertzka, the author of *Freeland*], have had
more influence upon the lives of our contemporaries than
the Etruscan people who once dwelt in Italy, although the
Etruscans belong to what we call the real world, and the
Freelanders and Icarians inhabited—Nowhere."[1]

Utopian ideas exert particular influence on public and
political figures involved in the drafting of history-making
documents. The impact of James Harrington's *Oceana*
on the American Founding Fathers' concepts of the best
possible political organization of society is a typical example. "No one who has studied Harrington's writings," the
U.S. historian Ivan Doig wrote, "can help being struck by
the resemblance between the political ideas expressed
there and those that have been successfully put into practice
in America. Again and again one is tempted to substitute
the name America for Oceana and spell his new England
with a capital N."[2]

Some researchers single out yet another function of utopia; it can be described as *compensatory* or, if you will,
psychotherapeutic. To a man who faces an unjust, evil and
grim world and finds it impossible to actually transform
it, utopia offers perhaps the only consolation, a buttress in
an unequal struggle. To this man, the Golden Age described in a utopia is the only light of hope. When this light
goes out, life becomes unbearable.

Maxim Gorky repeatedly tackled the question of the
place an ideal held in man's life. His famous play *The
Lower Depths* features a monologue in which the idea of
the consolatory nature of the ideal underlying utopia is
especially pronounced:

"*Luka*: Once, for instance, there was a case like this:
a certain man I knew believed in a true-righteous land.

"'There ought to be,' says he, 'a true-righteous land in
this world....' He was a poor man and had a hard life. Sometimes things got so bad it looked as if there was nothing left
for him to do but lie down and die. But he didn't give up.
He would just smile to himself and say: 'That's all right,
I can bear it. I'll wait just a little longer and then I'll quit

[1] Lewis Mumford, *op. cit.*, p. 24.

[2] Ivan Doig, *Utopian America: Dreams and Realities*, Hayden Book
Company, Inc., Rochelle Park, 1976, p. 139.

this life and go to the true-righteous land.' That was his only joy in life—his faith in the true-righteous land.

"...And then to the village ... they exiled a very learned man.... And this poor man says to the man of learning, he says: 'Be so kind as to tell me where this true-righteous land lies and how to get there.' Then and there the learned one gets out his books and opens up his charts and looks and looks, but he can't find the true-righteous land anywhere. Everything is in its place, all the lands are on the charts, but the true-righteous land is nowhere to be found!

"The man can't believe it. 'It must be somewhere,' says he. 'Take a better look, because if there's no true-righteous land, then all your charts and books are of no account.' The learned one doesn't like this. 'My charts,' says he, 'are the very best, but there's no such place as your true-righteous land.' That makes the poor one furious. 'What's that?' says he. 'Here I've gone on living and bearing it all these years just because I was sure there was such a place, and now according to the charts it turns out there isn't any such place! A swindle, that's what it is!' And he says to the learned one: 'You wretch! It's a rascal you are, and not a man of learning!' And he gives him a whack over the ear— bang! Then another one—bang! And after that he goes home and hangs himself."[1]

However, this function is not confined to pure consolation. A utopia fills out, as it were, the gaps which exist in an imperfect world by making it possible to imagine that which cannot be acquired or done in real life. A. L. Morton illustrates this very well by citing the example of a 17th-century British utopia—*The Description of a New World, Called the Blazing World* by Margaret Cavendish, Duchess of Newcastle, in which she described how quickly she won the hearts of the inhabitants of the Blazing World and became their Empress—that is, how she attained everything she failed to achieve in real life. "Just because of its complete simplicity," Morton writes, "the role of fantasy as compensation for defeat is seen at its clearest. Margaret Cavendish, in exile, consumed with pride in her and her husband's family, her wealth vanished, contemptuous of the victorious Commonwealth, ridiculed by the raffish bankrupt

[1] Maxim Gorky, *The Lower Depths*, Act III, Progress Publishers, Moscow.

Court that surrounded Charles abroad as an eccentric, frumpish bluestocking, crowned herself Empress of a Never-Never World, covered herself with a blaze of diamonds and mocked or exiled all those whom she hated or could not understand. Here, but for the Grace of Genius, goes Jonathan Swift!"[1] One can add many more such examples. A. L. Morton recalls that William Morris wrote his *News from Nowhere* "to hearten and inspire his comrades by a reminder of the positive goal towards which their efforts were leading."[2] One can cite the examples of today's authors resorting to utopia in order to soothe the alarmed man in the street and convince him (and themselves too) that the future promises to be bright, that the existing civilization opens boundless vistas, that eventually, a "happy end" is guaranteed. Active in the comforting business are also some futurologists and artists. Hollywood used to be called a "dreams factory" for a reason. And in his analysis of the "semifantastic and completely fantastic" cities of the future discussed in the West in the 1960s and 1970s, the Soviet architect Andrei Ikonnikov says that their images "have become a sort of social tranquilizer, a source of vague but somehow comforting hopes for the mystical and mysterious year 2000."[3]

The critical, normative, cognitive, constructive and compensatory functions of utopia hardly represent all of its potential. But I believe that they determine the role of the utopian ideal in social and political developments. I shall only add that although these functions are manifest in close interrelationship and interaction with one another, their order of priority and hierarchy are not constant. Depending on specific conditions and on priority tasks, one function assumes temporary primacy, only to surrender it later to another.

[1] A. L. Morton, *op. cit.*, p. 129.

[2] *Ibid.*, p. 213.

[3] A. V. Ikonnikov, *On Modern Bourgeois Aesthetics*, Moscow, 1976, p. 104 (in Russian).

3. The Emergence of the Utopian Tradition in the United States

The history of the American utopia begins with the history of American society. Virtually since the time the news of its discovery spread in Europe, people in the Old World pictured the new continent as a unique land in which "worldly social salvation"[1] could be achieved and the boldest utopian dreams realized. The Renaissance Europe of the time saw the discovery of America as the long-awaited discovery of the Promised Land; this largely molded the attitude to it both from outside, from across the ocean, and from within, on the part of the settlers themselves.

Subsequent developments have shown that Americans have always been convinced that they are unique. And, while this conviction clearly exaggerated the actual distinctive features of the development of the United States, it also reflected a perfectly real aspect: America proved to be very, even exceptionally, fertile for utopian consciousness, a land where utopian beliefs and experiments tangibly affected the social, political and cultural fabric. "America," Michael Harrington remarked in this regard, "was indeed an exceptional capitalist society. Its utopian tradition was deeper than that of any European country, which made the practical work of transforming the existing order all the more difficult."[2]

One can, of course, argue over where utopian traditions were deeper—in America or in Europe, or perhaps in Asia, or, more precisely, in the East. A general history of utopia is yet to be written, and different civilizations may cite sufficiently convincing arguments to prove that their utopian traditions have particularly deep and firm roots.

After all, Plato's *Republic* and *Laws* may well be called utopian classics which inspire and serve as examples to many authors of utopias to this day. Plato's works, Euhemerus's *Sacred History* and Iambulus's *Islands of the Sun* present the first systematic attempts at a rationalist interpretation of the Golden Age myths and at the construc-

[1] Michael Fellman, *The Unbounded Frame*, Greenwood Press, Inc., Westport, 1973, p. XI.

[2] Michael Harrington, *Socialism*, Saturday Review Press, New York, 1970, p. 250.

tion of images of a better world. It is clear from ancient Greek utopias that their authors were striving to offer a radical solution—which would satisfy all nations at all times—to a broad range of social problems which were to remain topical for many utopians over the next two millenia; these problems concerned the principles of government, the organization of work and leisure, man's moral and physical development, the structure and principles of marriage and family relations, the system of education, international relations and the like.

The utopian tradition founded by the ancient Greek civilization was later, and especially during the bourgeois revolutions of the 17th to 19th centuries, developed in the culture of many European countries, primarily Britain, Italy, France and Germany. The names of Thomas More, author of *Utopia*, Tommasso Campanella who wrote *City of the Sun*, Françis Bacon and his *New Atlantis*, of the utopian socialists Henri Saint-Simon, Charles Fourier and Robert Owen with their numerous utopian treatises, of Harrington, Morris, Vairase, Dostoyevsky and many others who dreamed of a happy future for their countries and for all mankind are part and parcel of the history of utopian thought.

However, from the very beginning the utopian tradition developed as an international phenomenon, as an element of both Western and Eastern culture. "The entire East, although to different degrees, was shaken by these upheavals [emergent social utopias and attempts to implement them by mass movements] generated deep inside society and aimed against the injustices of social systems."[1] Today it is clear that the world history of utopia would be incomplete without the names of Meng-zi, Lao-zi , al-Farabi, Ibn Rushd and many other Eastern thinkers.

In short, the assertion that the American utopian tradition was "deeper than that of any European country" may encounter valid objections. Still, in some respects Harrington is right. More than any other country, America stimulated utopian hopes and favored the conduct of utopian experiments. This was rooted above all in the specific

[1] Jean Chesneaux, "Egalitarian and Utopian Traditions in the East" in: *Narody Asii i Afriki (Peoples of Asia and Africa)* No. 5, 1968, p. 56.

conditions under which American culture developed, in what is sometimes called the "historical destiny of nation".

America possessed huge material resources, and this was important for its subsequent development and the outcome of the emerging social contradictions. Much more important, however, was that the country was free of many of the restrictions which capitalist Europe had inherited from feudalism and which hampered the development of social relations. Marx and Engels noted that repeatedly. It his article "The Labor Movement in America", Engels wrote about the "more favored soil of America, where no medieval ruins bar the way, where history begins with the elements of modern bourgeois society as evolved in the seventeenth century."[1] Engels also wrote about this in his letter to N. F. Danielson of October 17, 1893 and to Friedrich Sorge of December 31, 1892, and in several other works. Addressing President Lincoln, Marx described the United States as the country "where hardly a century ago the idea of one great Democratic Republic had first sprung up, whence the first Declaration of the Rights of Man was issued, and the first impulse given to the European revolution of the eighteenth century."[2]

The conditions in which American capitalism developed were favorable for the realization of many of the social ideals which had been virtually impractical in the Old World. This bred exaggerated assessments of the opportunities America offered. Having left Europe with its burden of social prejudice and restrictions, with its cumbersome legacy of ages past which, embodied in cultural traditions, both stimulated and hampered progress, the ex-European found himself in a country he saw as "open". He tended to believe that this country's salient feature was the "absence of the past", of an integral historical tradition which shaped the sociopolitical ways of its citizens. He could, of course, know or have an inkling of the fact that the new country had a history of its own. But this concerned him little, for this history neither directly affected his freedom nor placed any significant restrictions on his activity.

[1] Frederick Engels, "The Labour Movement in America" in: Marx and Engels, *On the United States*, Progress Publishers, Moscow, 1949, p. 284.

[2] Karl Marx, "To Abraham Lincoln, President of the United States of America" in: Marx and Engels, *On the United States*, p. 168.

The feeling of "freedom from the past" evoked a feeling of unlimited freedom which made it possible to choose from what was now a foreign legacy (European or originating elsewhere) all that was "useful", rejecting all that was not—in other words, to see this legacy as a mass of building materials from which, given a will to do so, one could construct almost any social system one's heart or mind desired. "Our Revolution commenced on more favorable ground," Thomas Jefferson wrote to Major John Cartwright on June 5, 1824. "It presented us an album on which we were free to write what we pleased. We had no occasion to search into musty records, to hunt up royal parchments, or to investigate the laws and institutions of a semi-barbarous ancestry. We appealed to those of nature, and found them engraved in our hearts."[1]

But this was not only the Americans' view. This was also the opinion of many Europeans who visited the United States. In his famous and still important *Democracy in America*, Alexis de Tocqueville saw the salient features of America's historical development in that "the emigrants who colonized the shores of America in the beginning of the seventeenth century somehow separated the democratic principle from all the principles that it had to contend with in the old communities of Europe, and transplanted it alone to the New World."[2]

Obviously, one cannot say that American life in Colonial times, severely Puritan and regimented, even though more democratic than in Europe, opened broad vistas for the imagination and aided in the conduct of social experiments. Still, as the Colonies developed, as the revolution drew nearer and theocratic control weakened, conditions for creative initiative and social experiment became increasingly favorable. Besides, as those colonists who "failed to make it" lost their utopian illusions, new ones were constantly reproduced—in the minds of new waves of immigrants and of new generations of Americans.

Of special importance in the emergence and development of American utopian consciousness in the 19th century was

[1] *Basic Writings of Thomas Jefferson*, Ed. by Philip S. Foner, Willey Book Company, New York, 1944, p. 788.

[2] Alexis de Tocqueville, *Democracy in America*, Vol. 1, New York, Alfred A. Knopf, 1945, p. 13.

the so-called frontier—the boundary of the newly settled lands which was constantly moving farther and farther West, toward the Pacific. This gave rise to the belief that there, on lands out West, one could again and again try one's luck and work to put one's social ideals into practice.

The U.S. historian Harold Rhodes, author of *Utopia in American Political Thought*, divides all utopias into three large groups—upward, inward and outward—and regards the latter as images of a perfect society that "exists now—somewhere—but not here".[1] To reach this type of utopia, there is no need to restructure the existing society; it is enough to simply leave it and move to that utopian "somewhere". "Thus for Jefferson, utopia could be realized by moving from the seaport town to the interior country where man could mix his talents and energies with the soil in order to realize the benefits of a virtuous and serene life."[2]

Harold Rhodes believes that the concept of the frontier advanced by Frederick Jackson Turner actually offers the same pattern of attaining utopia. According to Turner, "the existence of the American frontier offered a genuine option to the discontent and depression which afflicted the man living in the nation's more crowded areas.... 'So long as free land exists, the opportunity for a competency exists.'"[3]

One might note in passing that generally, the concept of the frontier is very important for utopian consciousness. For, taken in its broadest sense, utopian thinking is precisely an act of surpassing a spatial or temporal boundary, of going beyond the confines of the usual or that accepted by law or custom. Most frequently, utopian consciousness becomes widespread either when the "frontier" is too narrowly outlined and it becomes imperative to cross it to ensure further progress, or when it moves further and further away, thereby as if vanishing into nonexistence and producing the illusion of a boundless field of human activity.

Much has been written about Turner's concept both in America and abroad. It has been noted, and quite justly, that the attempts to explain almost all distinctive features of U.S. history by the existence of the frontier are clearly

---

[1] Harold V. Rhodes, *Utopia in American Political Thought*, University of Arizona Press, Tucson, 1967, p. 17.

[2] *Ibid.*, p. 19.

[3] *Ibid.*

untenable. But this sober assessment does not at all belittle the role the availability of "free lands" and the westward drift of the country's border which continued up to the last third of the 19th century played in the emergence and development of national utopian consciousness. To be sure, here, the American's mentality displayed the same aberration which shaped his belief in his country's "absence of history". America's lands were not vacant; there was indigenous population there; but in the minds of the white men who were spreading through the country, that was as though they were really vacant.

The concepts the frontier notion bred were, of course, illusory in many respects. They clearly overrated the freedom the settlers enjoyed on the new lands and the actual opportunities for building their lives according to utopia. As Ray Billington wrote, "In the West, according to the frontier myth, a veritable Garden of the World awaited to transform newcomers into superior beings. There, where nature's abundance stifled the competitive instinct, men lived together in peace and contentment, freed of the jealousies and meanness inevitable in the crowded East."[1]

Still, for decades, the "frontier myth" remained a tangible factor in the formation of utopian consciousness in the United States. This was enhanced considerably by the constant influx of immigrants, especially in the latter half of the 19th century. Like their forerunners, these people came to America in the hope of breaking free of the past and starting a new life.

But American utopian consciousness did not stem solely from the belief in the "boundless opportunities" open to the people of the New World. It was also stimulated by directly opposite ideas about restrictions on actual opportunities encountered, especially in crisis situations, by members of various social groups—above all by industrial workers, farmers, urban petty bourgeoisie and national minorities.

Fervent social criticism, a powerful incentive in the development of utopian consciousness, permeates American history. The way to the American Revolution itself was, to a certain extent, paved by increasingly critical

[1] Ray Allen Billington, *The American Frontier*, Publication No. 8, Service Center for Teachers of History, Washington, D. C., 1958, p. 23.

attitudes and socioutopian endeavor. "Colonists began as British subjects with rather common political grievances. As these complaints continued unattended, however, the colonists began to imagine a society more nearly ideal than any in Europe. This vision, based on freedom, abundant land, and the chance to avoid institutionalized error, expressed itself in essays, declarations, and constitutions. Albeit most revolutionaries of 1776 simply opposed British rule, some clearly held in their minds the idea of a model society."[1]

The existence of "boundaries", in economic, political and social terms, became especially manifest in the latter half of the 19th century, when American capitalism put on pace following the victory of the North over the Southern Confederacy in the Civil War. Few areas demonstrated such sharp and intense contradictions of capitalism straining the class and ethnic relations as the 19th century America. And though throughout the period since, the United States has never approached a revolutionary situation, this was due not to an absence of mass discontent and the ensuing protest eruptions, not to any lack of desire to restructure American society, but primarily to the lack of political prerequisites for revolution.

But revolutions which have failed to materialize—and sometimes those that have occurred—often give an impetus to utopian consciousness. Generally, no matter what national tradition we take, the history of utopian thought displays a feature which may be described as "pulsation". During some periods, utopian thought appears to be extinguished—only to flare up again later, perhaps with even greater intensity than before.

Most often, utopian thought flourishes during radical social, political, cultural and scientific upheavals, when sociohistorical catastrophes occur, when old institutions, relations and values collapse and new ones spring up. At such times of expectation and tragedy, of hope and despair, people, especially those particularly sensitive to social issues, burn with the desire to rise above the times, to affect history either by urging it onward or by reversing it.

[1] *The Reform Spirit in America*, Ed. with introductions by Robert H. Walker, G. P. Putnam's Sons, New York, 1976, p. 503.

Such upheavals stimulate utopia. Besides, utopian consciousness becomes active not only directly during a revolution but also prior to it, when many future participants in revolutionary battles are full of hope. "France in the eighteenth century, when the bourgeois revolution was maturing, produced a whole crop of utopias at a time when in England this form had temporarily almost disappeared. Here the bourgeois revolution had been accomplished, and the question of its successor had not been raised."[1]

Utopia's pulsation is clear not only from the fact that it fades and then surges up again but also from the change in the priorities of utopia's functions and in the degree to which the utopian ideal is transcendental. As a rule, reformist utopian projects proclaiming an ideal which the subject of the revolutionary change sees as feasible either immediately or in the near future, move to the foreground in prerevolutionary or revolutionary periods. Besides, the euphoria the social upheaval induces in the masses usually leads them to see revolutionaries as virtually omnipotent miracle workers—especially when a revolution uses religious slogans or is directed by religious forces.

The American bourgeois revolution was no exception. Liberation from the British Crown generated enthusiasm in various strata of the colonists; they believed that now great prospects were open for realizing the boldest projects and the most radical ideas. And still, when subsequent developments demonstrated that these hopes were illusory, the ideas and ideals of the American Revolution frequently inspired critics of the existing order, including those who proceeded from utopian positions.

In short, throughout its history, U.S. capitalism has periodically reproduced utopian consciousness which stemmed from a feeling of both power and impotence, of constraint and unlimited freedom, of hope and despair. As an independent nation, America has gone through at least four stages of a utopian revival of sorts; three of them coincided with periods when the traditional sociopolitical institutions were suffering from more or less serious malfunctions and an intensive search was under way for new values and institutional structures.

[1] A. L. Morton, *op. cit.*, pp. 126-27.

The first such phase occurred from the 1820s to the 1840s, the time of an exacerbation of social contradictions and of the first major economic crisis. Naturally, in that period the issue was not replacement of the existing institutions with new ones; the foremost objective was to make the existing institutions, still not quite established, conform to the principles of "Life, Liberty and the pursuit of Happiness" proclaimed in the Declaration of Independence. That was the time of romantic quests and hopes, the Golden Age of American utopia, as many historians described it. That was when utopian ideals became visible clearly, or at least in general outline—the ideals which spread, developed and evolved throughout the 19th century and, to a certain extent, in the first half of the 20th century.

Between the 1820s and 1840s American Romanticism reached its peak. James Fenimore Cooper, Herman Melville, Henry David Thoreau, Nathaniel Hawthorne and their fellow authors molded the national romantic utopian tradition which still exists to this day. Simultaneously, Americans studied European socialist utopian doctrines (those of Owen, Fourier and Saint-Simon) and produced the first socialist utopias of their own (Thomas Skidmore). Jeffersonian utopian ideals which formed the basis of the so-called farmer utopias (more about this later) were also making headway. Finally—and this is a substantial element of the national utopian tradition too—it was in these decades that American involvement in experimental utopian communities was at its highest.

The last quarter of the 19th century, when it became clear that American capitalism generated crisis phenomena, was the second stage in the development of utopian consciousness. Supported by industrial workers, mass action by farmers against monopolies destroying the illusion of equal opportunity were coupled with the increasingly tense relations between the trusts and the government (the latter feeling that the laissez-faire policy was tying its hands). This made the question of America's future again topical both for the lower classes and for the elite. Utopian projects (advanced by Grangers, Greenbackers, farmers' unions, the People's Party, nationalists and other movements, trends and groups) had never before been so numerous. Never before had utopian novels appeared in such great quantities as in the 1880s and 1890s (Edward Bellamy, Ignatius Donnelly, William Dean Howells); this prompted U.S. historians to refer to this period as the "utopian era". According to V. L. Parrington, Jr., over 50 utopian novels were published in the United States from 1887 to 1900. Subsequent research by Kenneth Roemer paints an even more impressive picture: from 1888 to 1900, some 160 utopian works appeared (including what Roemer calls "partial" utopias.[1]

In these years, the two sides to the struggle were partisans of the American farmers' utopia which obviously had to be renovated and revised, and those advocating a petty-bourgeois image of a socialist America.

The third stage in the evolution of U.S. utopian consciousness was connected with the crisis of the 1920s and 1930s and with the New Deal. America was again at a crossroads. "Suspended between past and future, the nation drifted as on a dark sea of unreality. It knew only a sense of premonition and of change; but the shape of the future was as baffling as the memory of the past,"[2] Arthur Schlesinger, Jr. wrote many years later.

The choice of a future was indeed hard. Radically different sociopolitical alternatives were clashing. Besides, now America had an opportunity to watch two actually functioning models tackle the contradictions of capitalism—in Germany where fascism was established and in Soviet Russia which embarked on building socialism. True, there were forces in America which were ready to push the nation toward fascism—witness Sinclair Lewis's *It Can't Happen Here*. But there were also those who saw socialist change as the only radical way out of the crisis (although sometimes they interpreted socialism in a rather peculiar way). Some historians called the period from the late 1920s to the late 1930s a "Red" decade. "It was Red in the sense that the center of political gravity swung sharply to the Left, and millions of jobless, war veternas, and mass industry workers took to the streets in demonstrations or 'seized' factories in sit-down strikes. It was Red in tone, mood, flavor as thousands of artists, intellectuals, movie stars, and lit-

[1] Kenneth M. Roemer, *The Obsolete Necessity: America in Utopian Writings, 1888-1900*, Kent State University Press, Kent 1976.

[2] Arthur M. Schlesinger, *The Age of Roosevelt*, Vol. I, *The Crisis of the Old Order, 1919-1933*, Houghton Mifflin Co., Boston, 1957, p. 456.

erary figures found an emotional haven with various radical parties."[1] That period gave rise not only to powerful movements of social protest but also to various socialist utopian projects.

American utopian socialism, quite prominent in the 1930s, was represented, among others, by the followers of the nationalists' tradition with the colorful figure of Upton Sinclair at the head. Often cited as a typical example of the impact made by the nationalists' ideas and of the radical wishful thinking of the 1930s is the movement initiated by Upton Sinclair in 1933 and designed to implement the EPIC Plan. The plan was devised to reinvolve the unemployed in the production process at cooperative enterprises free from the immoral pursuit of profit and thus restructure the entire society according to cooperative principles.

On the other hand, it was in that period that a new type of the social utopia appeared, subsequently to become a key element in the national utopian tradition—the technocratic utopia. The official utopia was changing considerably. And, finally, science fiction, a new literary genre not quite identical with but in many respects close to utopia, was coming into the limelight.

The latest, fourth stage in the development of American utopian consciousness occurred in the 1960s and 1970s. The great advances in science and technology, coupled with radical sociopolitical changes (the emergence of the world socialist system and the restructuring of world economic relations, the increasing prominence of the government in America, the changing role of the United States in world affairs, etc.) inevitably produced changes in social consciousness and transformed what different social groups saw as their social ideal. A new view of utopia as such and of its role in the functioning and development of society was taking shape. A new, massive body of utopian thought was arising, calling for an independent examination, an important element of the contemporary political field which affected the movements, groups and individuals within it.

Although most American utopias share certain characteristics determined by the distinctive conditions in which

[1] Sidney Lens, *Radicalism in America*, Thomas Y. Crowell Company, New York, 1966, p. 297.

the national utopian tradition developed (orientation on practical feasibility, on the use of legitimate political institutions, etc.), nevertheless they do not, just like in other countries, form a single mainstream which could erase their social and political dividing lines.

The differences in the positions and ideals of social classes are reflected in utopia too. This is clear from a comparison, say, of the projects advanced by John Eliot and Thomas Skidmore, Thoreau and Bellamy, Henry George and Skinner. To emphasize the inherently contradictory nature of the American utopian tradition, Vernon Parrington, Jr., writes that American utopians "have in common only their interest in outlining a different government, or a better way of life. Some of them were wise, some were foolish, and a few simply ignorant.... Their prescriptions for economic, political, social, intellectual and religious change have differed widely. Each generation has worked out formulas which seemed to solve the problems of the day. Each generation has looked for reassurance and been satisfied by different promises."[1]

As in other countries, in the United States the classes and groups turning to utopia were mostly those which either possessed no real power or were facing a real threat of losing it. For this reason, an overwhelming majority of the utopian projects which arose in the United States in the 19th and the first half of the 20th centuries were petty-bourgeois—from the viewpoint of their social content and the nature of the social forces they expressed. It was only later that utopia became the permanent intellectual refuge of the bourgeoisie concerned with retaining its own power and stabilizing the existing sociopolitical structures.

And now to the reasons behind the evolution of the utopian tradition in general and of the American tradition in particular. The great body of literature which analyzes the utopian phenomenon offers different explanations. The evolution of utopian thinking is attributed either to the distinctive conditions of economic development, or to the evolution of theoretical and artistic thought, or to the

---

[1] Vernon Louis Parrington, Jr., *American Dreams. A Study of American Utopias*, Brown University, Providence, Rhode Island, 1947, p. VII.

dynamics of the political process, or to some other material or ideal factors or their combinations.

Apparently, the reasons in question can only be traced with the help of the methodology Marx used to analyze the results of spiritual production. According to this methodology, the evolution of the utopian tradition should be viewed as a distinct form of a reflection of the social reality which cannot be reduced either to a mechanistically interpreted combination of different material factors or to any of these factors taken individually. What determines the actual existence of a utopian tradition anywhere, including the United States, is the change of the social reality seen as the material conditions in which a social entity exists.

While on the subject of social consciousness as the "reflection" of social being, the following point should be made to prevent any crude misinterpretation of Marxist precepts. Marx has demonstrated that each socioeconomic formation as a system of social acitivity, and each of its stages generate a consciousness which, while reflecting a given system, is also its inner, organic element, a necessary condition enabling the reflected system of activity and its products—spiritual values, institutions, etc.—to function and evolve.

As Marx shows in *Capital*, a definite mode of production is the key to the understanding of specific forms of the social reality. Here, one should also take into consideration the changes that occur within one and the same mode of production, i.e., within one and the same socioeconomic system.

The two centuries of American capitalism demonstrate that the evolution of the utopian tradition and of national social consciousness as a whole is largely shaped by the nature of the mechanisms which regulate social production and reproduction—that is, by the market and the state. At all stages of its development, capitalism needs both these mechanisms, but their roles and functions in both material and spiritual matters of society change depending on the stage in question.

The hegemony of a self-regulating market with its basis of free competition, the primacy of small-scale over large-scale private property, of rural over urban population and the like imply, through a chain of mediation factors, the hegemony of definite types of consciousness and social ideals, including utopian ones, which operate in the given conditions. The evolution of free enterprise capitalism into state-monopoly capitalism, the increasingly prominent role of the state which assumes a number of functions the market used to play in the past, the growing influence of the monopolies in all social spheres, and the related changes in the social fabric—all this inevitably leads to a restructuring of the existing types of social consciousness and social ideals, including the field of utopia.

One can easily see that all the listed upsurges of utopian consciousness in the United States have coincided not simply with periods of exacerbation in the socioeconomic and political contradictions of American imperialism, but with periods of transformation in the mechanisms regulating reproduction of social processes, more specifically, with times when the role of the state increased. Notably, each stage in the growth of the state's role has been accompanied by similar reactions on the part of social consciousness and generated similar utopian ideals (different, of course, in their immediate content).

This book focuses on three types of utopian ideals, especially pronounced and especially strong in their social impact. These are, first, *romantic* ideals which reflect an apologia of market-generated relations, institutions and values and are more or less clearly aimed against the state. Romantic opposition to the state was, of course, relative. Each subsequent stage made new concessions to the state, rejecting only its new claims and attempts at attaining "hegemony". Second, *positivist* or *scientist-technocratic* ideals which stem from an exaggerated opinion of the ability of the state (and of the members of the technocratic elite operating within the state) to effectively and promptly tackle the problems facing society and which link this ability to advances in science and technology. Third, *socialist* ideals which, for all their diversity (and heterogeneity of their social base), are oriented, on the one hand, on eliminating (or severely restricting) market mechanisms and, on the other, on changing the very nature of the state, transferring the socioeconomic regulatory function to it.

Obviously, when speaking about similar reactions of utopian consciousness we simplify the actual developments somewhat. Yet, it is a productive simplification. It helps one to grasp both the essence of the past stages in the evolution of American utopia and the possible directions U.S. utopian consciousness may take in the future.

However, before we raise the question of the future, or discuss the current stage, or examine the development of the U.S. utopian tradition in the 19th and the first half of the 20th centuries, we've got to unravel a rather tangled question connected with the nature of this tradition and its distinctive features.

4. The American Dream: Utopia or Myth?

Any student who has decided to trace the main stages in the emergence of the utopian tradition in the United States inevitably runs into the question of the so-called *American Dream* and its relation to utopia.

The American Dream is widely regarded to be utopian in nature. Moreover, some authors see it as all but the epitome of all the utopian ideals the United States has ever produced.[1] Now, is this indeed the case? Is the American Dream synonymous with American utopia?

Practically every student of the phenomenon has complained about the difficulties involved in defining its essence and scope. "It should be noted at the outset," V. P. Shestakov, a Soviet author, writes, "that the 'American Dream' is a concept very difficult to define. Some U.S. researchers believe that its precise meaning simply cannot be formulated; they claim that it is not a notion of logic but an irrational collective hope."[2] To support his view, Shestakov quotes the American literary critic Frederic Carpenter: "'The American Dream' has never been defined exactly, and probably never can be. It is both too various and too vague: many men have meant many different things by it."[3]

True, although, as is generally recognized, the American Dream has always been an important factor in the emergence of national social consciousness and a specific form in

[1] Stewart H. Holbrook, *Dreamers of the American Dream*, Doubleday and Company, Inc., New York, 1957.

[2] V. P. Shestakov, "The 'American Dream' and the Moral Crisis" in: *USA: Economy, Politics, Ideology*, No. 2, 1979, p. 25 (in Russian).

[3] Frederic I. Carpenter, *American Literature and the Dream*, Philosophical Library, New York, 1955, p. 3.

46

which it has been expressing itself, and although it embodies the belief in the opportunity of "climbing to the top", of realizing one's innermost hopes, its interpretation in specific terms invariably gives rise to difficulties and debate. One can endlessly list the attributes of the American Dream, examine its countless interpretations, and still fail to clearly define the scope of its content. Just as it is easy to define its essence—a happy person in a happy world (more precisely, the person in question is an American and the world, America)—it is difficult to divide this intellectual construct into autonomous, rationally substantiated elements which could be described as parts of a definite whole. This is not accidental: although the American Dream does contain utopian ideals, it cannot be reduced to them; a careful analysis will identify typical elements of a different phenomenon—the *social myth* in its modern version. But what is the social myth, how does it differ from and relate to utopia?

The French anarcho-syndicalist Georges Sorel was among the first to raise and try to solve this theoretical question. Popular in the West, his concept, together with the ideas of Karl Mannheim who studied the relationship between ideology and utopia, formed the theoretical basis used to this day by many Western philosophers and sociologists studying the so-called transformed forms of consciousness, including utopia and the myth.

As a politician and social practitioner, Sorel was interested in contemporary manifestations of mythological consciousness—and in real life, in politics, not in literature. For this reason he dealt not with the myth in general but with the social myth, seeing a classic example of the latter in the "idea of the general strike". "The general strike," he wrote, "is exactly what I refer to: a *myth* which embodies socialism, an organization of images capable of evoking instinctively all sentiments corresponding to the various manifestations of the war socialism is waging against modern society.... We thus acquire an intuitive understanding of socialism which the language cannot give us with perfect clarity."[1]

As a theoretician and practitioner of anarcho-syndical-

[1] Georges Sorel, *Réflexions sur la violence*, Librairie de "Pages libres", Paris, 1908, pp. 95-96.

ism inspired by his desire to find an effective method of revolutionary mobilization of the masses, Sorel opposes the myth—a direct, unreflected upon and therefore inherently indivisible expression by the masses of their innermost wishes and interests—to utopia which, in Sorel's view, differs radically from the myth. "Utopia," he wrote in a letter to Daniel Halévy, "is the product of an intellectual labor; it is the work of theoreticians who, after observing and discussing the facts, strive to construct a model against which one could compare the existing societies in order to measure the good or evil they embody (1); this is a totality of imaginary institutions which, however, represent a sufficient analogy with the real institutions for the jurist to be able to contemplate them.... A myth cannot be refuted because, essentially, it is identical with the convictions of a group, because it expresses these convictions in the language of movement and for this reason cannot be broken into parts to be tackled on the plane of historical descriptions. On the contrary, utopia can be discussed as any social construct ... it can be refuted by demonstrating that the economy on which it is based is incompatible with the necessities of actual production."[1]

No doubt, the French anarcho-syndicalist had good reason to speak about the impressive role the myth played in mass sociopolitical movements and popular revolutions, especially those that developed on a nonproletarian basis, and about the mobilizing functions of the myth in historical processes involving the masses. However, Sorel obviously overrated this role, especially in relation to the socialist revolution which he arbitrarily interpreted as an anarchic revolt occurring and developing on an irrational basis. At the same time, he clearly underestimated the role of the social utopia in mass movements and claimed, without proper justification, that it was elitist and conformist.

There indeed are substantial differences between utopia and the myth, and Sorel does grasp some of them. The myth, which expresses, in its images and overall emotional and psychological makeup, a view of an integral, indivisible cosmos, is itself integral and indivisible. It springs from an intuitive feeling that there is unity and indissoluble interrelationship between man and man, man and society,

[1] *Ibid.*, pp. XXXV-XXXVI.

man and nature. Besides, mythological consciousness holds that this unity is blessed by some sort of a supreme and suprahuman force. As to utopia, it is generated by the collapse of mythological consciousness, by the disintegration of the view of the cosmos as something indivisible. Fred Polak is essentially right when he notes that "the utopia may in fact be considered as one of the oldest and purest examples of *de-mythologizing*."[1] Utopian thinking is a type of consciousness which has perceived the contradictory nature of society, the alienation of people from one another and from nature, and the inner conflict of man. It is a consciousness which strives to bridge this gap and put the cosmos, falling apart in the imagination, together again.

The myth is a product and embodiment of rigid determinism which rules out any arbitrary or violent action in relation to the predetermined order of things. On the contrary, utopia stems from a desire to break away from determinism and advocates arbitrary and violent action aimed at the laws of social development.

Mythological consciousness is preanalytical and irrational. As the embodiment of the consciousness of an unestranged subject, it lacks a critical dimension, recording a conformist (if not fatalistic) attitude of man (not the individual but the species, for it does not recognize the individual as an autonomous subject of activity) to the social cosmos. It is entirely a mass, "collective" consciousness. By contrast, utopian consciousness is an expression of man's confidence in his own abilities and intellect, multiplied by his desire to apply these abilities to tasks of practical transformation. Any utopia is essentially a rejection, a rebellion, a heresy—even if it is merely a heresy of consciousness in self-imposed exile.

But, while recording substantial differences between utopia and the myth, Sorel ignores the important fact that in the actual sociohistorical process, in the political creative effort utopia and the myth are closely intertwined, that they interact with and complement each other, that the first impression of their polarity is by no means completely true.

It is difficult to accept the argument that unlike the

---

[1] F. L. Polak, *The Image of the Future*, Vol. 1, Oceana Publications, New York, 1961, p. 419.

myth, utopia is elitist, that it is the product of "philoso-phizing" ideologists who are above the masses—compared to the myth, which is born spontaneously in their midst. Both the myth and utopia have common, popular roots. They are the products of collective creative efforts; they are the basis for structures arranged by ideologists and profes-sional mythmakers.

Neither can we agree that, unlike the myth, utopia is incapable of discharging a socially mobilizing function since it allegedly appeals not so much to the emotions as to reason and therefore cannot fire the masses. History offers a wealth of cases when it was precisely the image of a desired world and not an intuitively grasped idea that motivated popular movements.

In the 19th and the first half of the 20th centuries, having been subjected to a disintegrating influence on the part of utopia, the myth incorporated in itself certain utopian elements and even assumed, at least in part, the form of utopia. In turn, utopia may assume certain mytho-logical characteristics and even transform itself into a myth should the utopian project lose its erstwhile functions, be-come petrified and simply express an abstract idea used by one of the rival classes in its own political interests. In short, utopia and the myth do not simply coexist; they need each other, they are mutually complementary, and each ex-presses itself through the other. Taking into account the turbulent history of the first half of the 20th century, one cannot agree that "where the myth dominates, utopia has no chance".[1]

This mutual need and interrelationship are evident in the American Dream. The latter includes a social ideal, the image of a desired society. But it "includes" and is not "reduced to"; therefore, it cannot be regarded as a syno-nym of utopia, as a type of utopian thinking. American utopia and the American Dream are concepts of a differ-ent scope: as a myth, the Dream is not fully integrated in utopia; utopia covers it only in part because the Dream comprises values, orientations and attitudes completely de-void of utopian content.

Had there existed an archeology of consciousness, it could have demonstrated that the building blocks of the

[1] *Ibid.*

American Dream, which began to take shape as early as the colonial period and which is still being built and rebuilt in the course of the spontaneous collective creative effort (but aided, of course, by the mass media and the socio-cultural and political forces behind them), include whole monoliths and debris of social utopias. Some of these were brought to America by the first settlers from the Old World, others were conceived on American soil. For its part, like the myth which needs no proof or rational substantiation and exists as a fact of mass consciousness, the American Dream serves as an incentive to and basis for a social utopia which, proceeding from logical, rational precepts, proves, justifies and develops the postulates of the Dream, embodies them in specific images tied to the historical situation and the requirements of the times, links them to the activities of social, political and cultural institutions and transforms them into specific items in programs of action.

Chapter II

AMERICAN UTOPIA IN THE 19th AND THE FIRST HALF
OF THE 20th CENTURIES

1. Official and Folk Utopias

A historical analysis of American utopian thought identifies three major levels in it—and these are present in other national utopian traditions too. These are the *official utopia* level, the *folk utopia* level and the *literary and socio-theoretical utopia* level.

The American official utopia and American statehood were born simultaneously, although the social ideals which formed the first, fundamental layer of this utopia had been in preparation long before the Colonies attained independence. Here, much of the credit should go to figures of the American Enlightenment; many of these wanted to build a brave new world on the new continent. As Thomas Paine wrote in his *Common Sense*, the creation of a new world was in the hands of the Americans. Debate about the nature of the future social system in America was especially heated in the last prerevolutionary decade. Thomas Paine expressed the left-wing position on this question in his *Common Sense*. John Adams, at that time already a well-known public figure, set forth his *Thoughts on Government*, and Thomas Jefferson advanced certain considerations with regard to the future government system. Numerous anonymous pamphlets appeared, also expounding models for new government. In this connection it is important to note that the ideas and ideals of the American Enlightenment were not simply transplanted European Enlightenment constructs; they were the crystallized expression of the sociopolitical experience of at least three generations of Americans, of practical expertise gained by different political and social groups.

However, although the type of utopia under consideration had begun to form long before the American Revolution, it assumed the shape of an *official utopia*, that is, of a system of social ideals advanced by the authorities, only with the appearance of the official documents which proclaimed the independence of the American Colonies and laid down the principle of American statehood—first and foremost, the 1776 Declaration of Independence.

For all its brevity, the Declaration is a complex and many-sided document, compressing the main principles of the American Enlightenment into a single coherent whole. Although it had a clearly defined political objective—to justify the political break of the American Colonies with the British Crown (this largely determined its wording)—it went far beyond the confines of a purely political document and represented a manifesto which determined some of the important social parameters of American society, the social ideal and legal principles of independence of the free commonwealth as imagined by progressive representatives of the ascending class.

No doubt, it would be stretching the matter to describe this extremely important political document as a social utopia in any sense of the word. A number of the Declaration's provisions reflected objective trends in America's political and social development and identified certain abilities and intentions of the young American bourgeoisie to remove obstacles to free enterprise, individualism and freedom from tutelage by the state.

But it is equally impossible to ignore the fact that the Declaration of Independence possessed pronounced utopian features: the image it projected was not of the America which was to develop subsequently (in accordance with the historical trends which made themselves felt at the time of independence) but of an America as pictured by progressive representatives of the rising bourgeois class, that is, an arbitrarily constructed (although far from detailed) social ideal which conformed neither to the laws of capitalist development nor to the actual abilities (and, in the final analysis, interests) of the American bourgeoisie.

The authors of the Declaration had a vision of a free society whose citizens enjoyed political sovereignty and had a right and ability to liberate themselves—through revolution—from any government incapable of ensuring self-evident civil rights. It was a society based on the recognition of human equality: "We hold these truths to be self-evident: that all men are created equal, that they are endowed by their Creator with certain inalienable Rights, that among these are Life, Liberty and the pursuit of Happiness." The realization of these rights was to ensure, eventually, the independence of the entire nation.

Notably, in Locke's formula, taken here as the basis (life, liberty and property) the last element is replaced with "pursuit of happiness"—an ideal which lacks a specific content and has a clearly utopian ring to it.

According to the Declaration, relations between the people and the government and the exercise of power are to be guided by democratic principles—governments "deriving their just Powers from the consent of the governed". The basis of a free society is not the state but the private individual, the citizen. And so, the foundation of new forms of society is not a national, state or social entity but its autonomous part, the individual.

However, the 200 years of American history have shown that most of the ideals proclaimed in the Declaration of Independence (and some other documents of the American Revolution) have failed to be implemented fully or consistently. "The sincere aspirations of the founders of the American republic," the Soviet scholar Konstantin Fedorov concludes, "were negated by the subsequent economic and social development."[1] This happened not only and not so much because the bourgeoisie abandoned what it used to proclaim earlier (although this, too, played its part) but above all because the Founding Fathers were looking up to ideals which were generally inconsistent with the logic of capitalist development.

The ruling class firmly established the social ideals proclaimed in the basic documents of the American republic as part of its rhetoric and upheld them publicly even after the advance of American capitalism and the collapse of the initial democratic illusions had seriously disfigured the bourgeois social ideal. Moreover, virtually throughout American history these ideas served as the foundation on which the edifice of official American utopia was being further built and rebuilt.

This building and rebuilding, connected with the changes

[1] K. G. Fedorov, *History of the State and Law in Foreign Countries*, Leningrad, 1977, p. 191 (in Russian).

occurring both in the material sphere and in the field of social consciousness, was effected by adding to the basic layer of official utopian ideals and by their different interpretation depending on the specific needs of the moment. It would be no exaggeration to say that throughout the two centuries of American history, almost every President contributed something to the interpretation of the fundamental ideals and added his own emphasis to the official utopia.

Indeed, conducting his election campaign or formulating the chief objectives of his work during the forthcoming 4-year period, the President of the United States usually does not limit himself to merely stating the main principles he intends to observe but advances an entire program, a set of national objectives linked, as a rule, to the original and fundamental ideals of the nation proclaimed by the American Revolution and formalized in the documents adopted at the time of independence.

It would, of course, be naive to include any of American Presidents among the utopians. They have never been that kind, just as their statements, programs and other documents have on the whole not been utopias. Yet it is all the more important to point out that these pieces of prose did contain more or less distinct elements of utopianism. Of course, the most radical, qualitative changes in the official utopia are connected only with outstanding political figures who were usually active during crises or at turning points in American history.

One such turning point was the so-called Second American Revolution brought about by the Civil War between the Union and the Confederacy. It was a war of "two social systems",[1] and the victory of the North was not simply a victory of one of the parties to a war but the victory of a "system of free labor" with its underlying system of social values and ideals—those proclaimed, albeit in abstract terms, by the First American Revolution. Now these ideals were to be specified and expanded; that mission fell to Abraham Lincoln who, having confirmed his commitment to the

[1] "The present struggle between the South and North is ... nothing but a struggle between two social systems, the system of slavery and the system of free labor." (Karl Marx, "The Civil War in the United States" in: Marx and Engels *On the United States*, Progress Publishers, Moscow, 1979, p. 99.)

traditions of Thomas Jefferson and Andrew Jackson, formulated the ideal of a "government by the people". "Fourscore and seven years ago," Lincoln said in his Gettysburg Address of November 19, 1863, "our fathers brought forth upon this continent a new nation, conceived in liberty, and dedicated to the proposition that all men are created equal.... The nation shall, under God, have a new birth of freedom, and ... the government of the people, by the people, and for the people, shall not perish from the earth."

It was Lincoln who, having stressed that "this government cannot endure permanently half slave and half free", formulated at the official level the ideal of racial equality, formalized in the Emancipation Proclamation of 1863 and subsequently in the Thirteenth, Fourteenth and Fifteenth Amendments to the Constitution. At the same time it was Lincoln who, with a clearer vision than his predecessors, connected the ideal of "equal opportunity" and the fundamental principles of the Declaration of Independence and the Constitution with the domination of capitalist social relations based on individual enterprise and competition. "While we don't propose any war upon capital," Lincoln said, "we do wish to allow the humblest man an equal chance to get rich with anybody else. When one starts poor, as most do in the race of life, free society is such that he knows he can better his condition; he knows that there is no fixed condition of labor for his whole life.... I want every man to have a chance—and I believe a black man is entitled to it."[1]

Lincoln's ideal of a society which, while capitalist and based on the principle of free enterprise, would be ruled by a government of and by the people to ensure universal equality, was a modified version of the official utopia which remained in force up to the turn of the century and into the early 20th century, when U.S. capitalism entered the new, imperialist stage of development. That was when the official utopia had to be adjusted and corrected; eventually, this was accomplished in the fullest and most consistent form by Franklin D. Roosevelt and his administration.

Naturally, like Abraham Lincoln before him, Roosevelt relied on the achievements of his predecessors—in this

[1] Quoted in: V. L. Parrington, *Main Currents in American Thought*, Harcourt, Brace and Company, New York, 1930, p. 154.

case, Theodore Roosevelt, Woodrow Wilson and Herbert Hoover—and in some respects, simply continued their policies and brought them to their logical culmination; his course was geared to the new historical conditions, to the new needs and interests of the American bourgeoisie. But it fell to Franklin Roosevelt to impart radically new qualities to the official utopia and predetermine its future shape for several decades to come.

Like most of his precursors in the office of the President of the United States, Roosevelt was a realistic politician. But, first, he had to promptly tackle complex strategic political problems with many unknowns. Second, he was perfectly aware of the rules of the game any prominent politician had to observe. These rules had appeared long before his time; all Presidents had complied with them more or less skillfully; and those who had brought him to power—both at the top and at the bottom—expected him to abide by them. In other words, Roosevelt knew that the President was not only to formulate a practical program of action of his administration but, first of all, to outline the social ideal his work was supposed to be aimed at. This ideal had to conform to the expectations of the voters, to their opinion of what America should be like and how the President should shape it. This sort of game had long become an integral part of the political process accompanying the emergence of each new U.S. President on the historical scene; it made it imperative for any, and even the most realistic, political program to include purely utopian elements which thus appeared as a factor of big politics.

Essentially, the official credo proclaimed by Roosevelt had no elements at variance with the fundamental ideas of the official utopia as it had developed over the 150 years of American history. Franklin Roosevelt had no intention replacing the ideal of bourgeois democracy with the ideal of either fascist dictatorship or socialism—the charges that his political opponents sometimes leveled at him. His assurances that his main goal was to uphold the "old ideals and original purposes"[1] of democracy formulated many decades before him did generally reflect his actual purposes and intentions. He emphasized repeatedly that he was

[1] *F. D. R. His Personal Letters. 1928-1945*, Vol. I, Ed. by Elliott Roosevelt, Duell, Sloan and Pearce, New York, 1950, p. 119.

striving to create a society in which the independent businessman would have reliable safeguards against the oligarchy, the overall number of stockholders would increase, social justice based on a more equitable distribution of public wealth would prevail, and poverty would be banished. It was to be a society without the sweatshop system, unjust competition, shameful trade practices, etc.

The problem was that in the new conditions, upholding the "old ideals and original purposes" (that is, protecting U.S. capitalism) called for new means which were bound to eventually modify the ends themselves. That was why the policy speeches and documents which laid the foundations of the New Deal featured motifs and ideals which made up a new facet of the official utopia. These included, first and foremost, the ideal of social harmony based on "collectivism without communism", i.e., the collectivism of private property holders. Many Presidents before Roosevelt had spoken of social harmony, but none connected its establishment in America with any form of collectivism. On the contrary, the officially sanctified image was that of an individualist-oriented society of small and medium property holders, each forging his own career, each master of his own destiny who could not and should not rely on the state.

Franklin Roosevelt articulated a new ideal which, in its formal aspects, was consonant with the slogans of the mass democratic movements of the late 19th century but which was essentially the only feasible way of saving American capitalism in conditions of the 1920s and 1930s: a strong state which has assumed the function of regulating private enterprise and some other functions previously discharged by the free market. Roosevelt emphasized that American society must be made more manageable, that Americans could attain "social justice" only through "social action". "The philosophy of 'letting things alone' has resulted in the days of the cave man, and in the days of the automobile—has resulted in the jungle law of the survival of the so-called fittest. But this philosophy of social action results in the protection of humanity and the fitting of as many human beings as possible into the scheme of surviving."[1]

[1] Quoted in: *The Reform Spirit in America*, p. 218.

And so, as laissez-faire capitalism transformed itself into monopoly and state-monopoly capitalism, certain changes occurred in the American official utopia. To the image of a society which accords priority to the individual, the citizen, was added the image of a society which stressed the importance of the whole, of society, the nation, the state.

Also evolving was the foreign policy aspect of the official utopia—that is, the officially expressed view of what place the United States should hold in the world community of nations and what role it should play in human history. Although the Founding Fathers had considered America a chosen land, a unique society whose exceptional destiny was divinely preordained (this was subsequently reflected in the concepts of "American exceptionalism" and "Manifest Destiny"), the image of the United States as a country standing above and imposing its will on other nations was virtually absent from the official utopia throughout the first half of the 19th century. The foreign policy doctrine proclaimed by President Monroe in 1823 and stipulating that "the American continents are no longer subjects for any new European colonial establishments" was still devoid of the aggressive meaning officially adopted several decades later.

The growth of American expansionism made its impact felt here too. The interpretation of the Monroe Doctrine and the Manifest Destiny concept changed: America was not simply "exceptional" compared to other nations; it was to guide them and assume the burden of world leadership. In the late 19th and early 20th centuries this image of America as the world's shepherd (easily transformable now into that of the world's policeman, now the moral arbiter) became a stable element of the official utopia and retained this status throughout the first half of the 20th century, irrespective of whether the actual foreign policy pursued by the United States tilted toward isolationism or toward vigorous participation in world affairs.

Marx's well-known precept about the ideology of the ruling class being the ruling ideology is perfectly applicable to the U.S. official utopia. In other words, this utopia can be regarded as an expression of the utopian social ideals of the American bourgeoisie, and its evolution—as an important aspect of the evolution of the social ideals held by the U.S. ruling class. But there is another point which should be taken into consideration. An official utopia can discharge its integrating function only if it reflects, to a certain degree, the ideals, objectives, illusions and orientations of the "common folk"—that is, if it echoes, at least in some way, the folk utopia.

Originally, the American folk utopia arose *outside America* and *prior to its discovery*; this, incidentally, is also true of the American Dream. "As a state of mind and a dream, America had existed long before its discovery. Ever since the early days of Western civilization, peoples had dreamed of a lost Paradise, of a Golden Age characterized by abundance, absence of war, and absence of toil. With the first accounts of the New World it was felt that these dreams and yearnings had become a fact, a geographical reality fraught with unlimited possibilities.... Thomas More in 1516 set a precedent followed by countless imitators in locating his ideal state of Utopia in the newly discovered world.... America as an idea was already at work pointing the way in the neverending and hitherto chimerical quest of happiness."[1]

The American folk utopia was initially American only in name, or rather, in the name of the geographical region with which folk consciousness connected the long-awaited realization of the utopian ideals born on European (above all, English and French) soil, of the contradictions of European society and of European culture. For some time, these concepts remained unchanged—until they were corrected, developed, complemented or ousted by new concepts which were a direct product of the local conditions and were recorded both by Americans and by such observant European authors as Tocqueville and Crèvecoeur.

In the modern age, the European folk utopia sprang from the contradictions of late feudalism and early capitalism, from the working masses' desire, constantly reproduced by the actual social relations, to put an end to the existing order of things and create—even though in the imagination only—a *different* social reality in many respects *opposite* to the actual.

In the real world, wearisome toil reigns supreme; in uto-

1 *Literary History of the United States,* Macmillan, New York, 1957, pp. 192-93.

pia, all is *idleness and play*. Social, political and economic inequality dominates the real world; in the world of utopia, all barriers separating classes, estates and castes are broken down and complete *equality* is established. As it exists in actual fact, society is plagued by shortages of material goods and shaken by famine and epidemics; but utopia means *abundance, wealth and prosperity*. In the real world, man is oppressed and downtrodden; in utopia he is *free*. To sum up, the society constructed by folk utopian consciousness is the embodiment of *justice and social harmony*, a world which rules out hostility among men, where there is *no war*, a world of *peace and universal brotherhood forever*.

These ideals were what formed the original foundation of the American utopia. Anticipating a little, let us note that they never disappeared completely from America's folk utopian consciousness, for at every stage of its development American society deprived sizable masses of their property-oriented illusions and dumped them at the foot of the social ladder—a process which intensified in the latter half of the 19th and the early 20th centuries. This was connected with the growth of the working class, the mass pauperization of farmers and the end of the frontier. This explains why, throughout this period, American folklore featured ideals and images traceable to the European folk utopia of the modern age.

But the salient features of America's historical development introduced corrections both into the content and into the form of the folk utopian ideals, giving rise to concepts connected with the American Dream. In the Europe of the modern age, the folk utopia reflected the aspirations of the lower classes, above all of peasants and artisans who saw no real chance of changing their social status. These peasants and artisans saw America, where they fled from "European feudalism in order to establish a purely bourgeois society",[1] in a different light. Most early immigrants represented the groups in which the European folk utopia had taken firm root. The enclosures in Britain drove a great deal of tenant farmers and agricultural laborers

[1] "Engels to N. F. Danielson in St. Petersburg" in: K. Marx, F. Engels, *Selected Works* in three volumes, , Vol. 3, Progress Publishers, Moscow, 1973, p. 500.

off the land. Unemployment, already in evidence in the cities, made it difficult for British industry to absorb them. Another group of people English capitalism deprived of their means of livelihood included petty artisans, skilled workers and apprentices from small workshops. They formed the bulk of the first wave of immigration. Broke at home, they were ready to try their luck across the Atlantic. Here, as they became small property owners, they broke free of the bonds which had hogtied them in Europe; they often thought they were becoming masters of their destiny. True, in the New World many immigrants found themselves in a situation which was almost as difficult as in the old country. But in America, they kept up the hope that they would get a lucky break and that things would change for the better. Even those forced to accept a period of work in bondage (as so-called contract laborers) hoped to purchase a farm or start a business of their own once the contract term was over.

The new social forms inevitably transformed the psychology of the hard-working immigrant and, eventually, his social ideals too. Describing this transformation, Hector St. John de Crèvecoeur wrote in *More Letters from an American Farmer* that upon a European's arrival in America, "he begins to forget his former servitude and dependence, his heart involuntarily swells and glows, this first swell inspires him with those new thoughts which constitute an American... From nothing to start into being, to become a free man, invested with lands, to which every municipal blessing is annexed! What a change indeed! It is in consequence of that change that he becomes an American."[1]

For all the heterogeneity and inner contradictions of the European folk utopia of the modern age, it clearly displayed a socialist or, to be more precise, communist trend (this was a crudely egalitarian communism). Naturally, the American folk utopia of the 18th and 19th centuries did incorporate more or less pronounced elements of this trend. Still, dominating this utopia was the petty-bourgeois, property-oriented tendency which colored its main ideals.

Central to the American folk utopian tradition of the period in question was the ideal of *equality*, interpreted

[1] Quoted in V. L. Parrington, *op. cit.*, p. 143.

not so much in the spirit of equality in consumption and property as in the spirit of *equality of opportunity* open to every citizen. Besides, this opportunity applied not only to the economic but also to the political and legal dimensions. The ideal, therefore, was that of equal rights, of equal participation in political affairs, in other words, of the people's sovereignty. "The people are the Government"[1] was the ideal which was firmly established in America's folk utopian consciousness and which largely determined the course of action taken by participants in the American mass movements arising throughout the 18th and 19th centuries.

Strictly speaking, the traditional American term "equal opportunity" denotes equality of the conditions in which individuals are placed and which make their actual opportunities unequal since, as a rule, their abilities, strength, skills in adapting to their environment, let alone their property, are unequal. America created more favorable conditions for European immigrants than other countries, but it was never a society of equal opportunity.

The orientation on equality of opportunity and the people's sovereignty also predetermined the interpretation of freedom; aside from a negative aspect (freedom from exploitation, from oppression) it also acquired a well-articulated positive value (freedom of enterprise, freedom to take decisions having a bearing on one's life).

As American society developed and capitalist contradictions intensified, the folk utopia found and absorbed new ideals, socialist in spirit and content—*the ideals of public property in the means of production, elimination of class differences and exploitation*, etc. Some U.S. labor organizations had adopted these ideals in a rather vague form as early as the 1830s.[2] However, these notions spread widely only in the last three decades of the 19th century, during the upsurge of the labor and farmer movement. After the publication in 1888 of Edward Bellamy's *Looking Backward* with its utopian socialist program, the so-called nationalist clubs sprang up in several states, aimed at actually implementing its provisions. Nevertheless, socialist ideals

[1] Philip S. Foner, *History of the Labor Movement in the United States*, Vol. I, International Publishers, New York, 1978, p. 89.
[2] *Ibid.*, pp. 169-70.

failed to acquire the dominant role in the American folk utopia. Even in the late 1880s and early 1890s when, in the words of a contemporary author, "the books of Henry George, Bellamy, and other economic writers were bought as fast as the dealers could supply them ... bought to be read greedily",[1] Grangers, Greenbackers and Populists put forward slogans and political programs advocating ideals which were not so much socialist as traditionally bourgeois-democratic—equality of all before the law and government by the people.

Not only farmers but also a large part of the working class shared these ideals. One of the reasons, Engels noted, was the uneven development of the United States. "America is the world's *youngest* but also *oldest* country," he wrote to Friedrich Sorge. "Just as you see antiquated furniture types side-by-side with those you have invented yourselves, just as in Boston, the droshky I last saw in London in 1838 and stage coaches out of the 17th century in the mountains exist side-by-side with Pullman Cars, so you preserve the old spiritual garments long discarded in Europe. Everything that has outlived itself here can last in America for one or two more generations.... This happens, on the one hand, because America is only beginning to find the time not only for its pursuit of material production and wealth but also for free spiritual work and the basic education this requires; on the other hand, this also stems from the dual nature of the way America is developing. On the one hand it is still tackling the first task: developing the enormous tracts of wild land, and on the other, it already has to compete for the first place in industrial production. Hence the ups and downs depending on what gains the upper hand in the mind of the average American—the consciousness of an industrial worker or that of a farmer tilling virgin land."[2]

The Great Depression, naturally, made an impact on American utopian consciousness, including the folk utopia which had to respond in some way to the increased concern

[1] John D. Hicks, *The Populist Revolt. The History of the Farmers' Alliance and the People's Party*, The University of Minnesota Press, Minneapolis, 1931, p. 132.

[2] "Engels an Friedrich Adolph Sorge. 16. Januar 1895", Karl Marx, Friedrich Engels, *Werke*, Vol. 39, Dietz Verlag, Berlin, 1968, pp. 385-86.

about socioeconomic and political problems among ordinary people. According to V. L. Parrington, Jr., in those years "social planning was more frequently discussed than baseball or liquor laws. More than ever before, the radio became a political force". But, as before, "in the public consciousness it was always the simple solutions",[1] a cure-all—some sort of a clever monetary or tax reform—that would put things right at once. Hence the broad support generated by the utopian projects of Francis Townsend, Huey Long, Howard Scott and others who declared they had found a simple key to complex problems, a key which would not only help lead the nation out of the crisis but also ensure unheard-of prosperity. For the same reason, Franklin Roosevelt's New Deal (in his speeches he reduced it to simple slogans any American could understand, presenting these, too, as a key to every problem) eventually also won mass support.

The trend toward reliance on the state present in folk utopian consciousness and expressed in the ideal of a "strong state" taking care of the people and upholding their interests, was clearly articulated during the Roosevelt Administration and persisted into the postwar times. Moreover, in the period of the state-monopoly capitalism of the 1950s and 1960s it consolidated its position, aggravating the crisis of bourgeois individualism and producing new images of the human ideal and of human relations in an "organized society".

Still, despite all these changes folk utopian consciousness remains heterogeneous and contradictory. The etatist ideals do not cancel out the old, market ideals of the people's sovereignty, local self-government and a minimal state which permeated this consciousness during the era of laissez-faire capitalism. The latter ideals either combine paradoxically with the former or are pushed to the periphery of this consciousness to reemerge and reclaim lost ground at a later stage, usually at a time of crisis. This cycle was illustrated in the late 1970s and early 1980s, when many Americans welcomed a new wave of conservative thinking, with its opposition to "big government in Washington" and "excessive" government regulation, and with

[1] V. L. Parrington, Jr., *op. cit.*, p. 195.

its advocacy of lower taxes and greater reliance on market mechanisms.

The American folk utopia branches out into several more or less autonomous and distinctive ethnic divisions. The traditional image of America as a melting pot which transforms all salient features of the different ethnic groups of immigrants is not true to life. Of course, "melting" does occur, but it is not comprehensive. The Black, Italian, Chinese and several other large communities have long existed in the United States. Their members have retained their cultural identity for generations, sharing sets of distinctive social ideals which can be viewed as ethnic versions of the American folk utopia.

The Black population of the United States holds a special place among the ethnic groups. The reason is not only the great number of Blacks or the size of their contribution to American civilization and culture but (in the context of the subject under discussion) the fact that Blacks—not Chinese or Italians—were forcibly brought to America and turned into slaves. Their situation was unique. This makes the so-called *Black utopia*[1] a unique feature of the American utopian tradition. The Black utopia arose out of the slaves' dreams of a different, better world; hence its status as an independent part of the folk utopia.

We can form a picture of the preemancipation Black utopia by examining Black folklore, especially folk songs, and particularly spirituals. "The rhythmic cry of the slave stands today not simply as the sole American music," W.E.B. DuBois wrote in 1903, "but as the most beautiful expression of human experience born this side of the seas."[2]

Folk utopias often assume religious forms, but this does not necessarily make them religious utopias. Strictly speaking, a religious utopia is a contradiction in terms because utopia is always oriented on the real world. According to the Soviet historian A. I. Klibanov, "the images generated by the idea of a perfect social order were prod-

[1] See, for example, William H. Pease and Jane Pease, *Black Utopia*, Madison, 1963; Preston N. Williams, "Black Perspectives on Utopia" in: *Utopia/Dystopia?*, Ed. by P. E. Richter, Schenkman Publishing Company, Cambr. Mass., 1975.

[2] W. E. B. DuBois, *The Souls of Black Folk*, Longmans, London, 1965, pp. 160-61.

ucts of the imagination reflecting actual relations in real life. But even the most fantastic of these images differed radically from the images of religious fantasy, even in cases when they donned religious garb. For they dealt not with heaven but with the best possible order of human relations, and when this order was referred to as 'paradise' or the 'Kingdom of God', these were paradise or Kingdom of God on Earth."[1]

Spirituals are chiefly religious songs, and this determines the structure of their images, their language, symbols and, consequently, the outward features of the utopian world encoded in these brilliant works of folk art. While it presents religious symbols and images, it is nevertheless an earthly world. And although these songs are sometimes stereotyped in content and monotonous in their vocabulary, they, as several U.S. researchers have demonstrated,[2] together with other works of folklore, make it possible to draw at least a general picture of the utopian ideals of the Black slave.

Justice is the foremost ideal of the Black utopia. Emancipation from slavery, equality with whites, a chance to find happiness—all this culminated in the Black man's yearning for a just society. "Through all the sorrows of the Sorrow Songs there breathes a hope—a faith in the ultimate justice of things.... Sometimes it is faith in life, sometimes a faith in death, sometimes assurance of boundless justice in some fair world beyond. But whichever it is, the meaning is always clear: that sometime, somewhere, men will judge men by their souls and not by their skins."[3]

The Black slave dreams of a world of *universal brotherhood* where human relations are based on *love*, a world *without exhausting toil*, a world of *joy and ease*.

Of course, the world imagined by the Black slave is devoid of government. It is not a state but rather a community without a clearly articulated political structure. It could not be any other way with the utopian world of people

[1] A. I. Klibanov, *The Folk Social Utopia in Russia*, Moscow, 1977, p. 4 (in Russian).

[2] See, for example, *The Book of American Negro Spirituals*, Ed. with an introduction by James Weldon Johnson, The Viking Press, New York, 1929.

[3] W. E. B. DuBois, *op. cit.*, p. 167.

who were barred from politics and, as a rule, lacked even an elementary education.

The Union's victory over the Confederacy of slaveholders finally brought freedom from slavery to Blacks. But the barrier which separated them from "civilized" society remained—both in actual fact and, not infrequently, on the books. No longer a slave but a U.S. citizen, the Black man was still Black, and this tied him to his former slave status with visible and invisible bonds.

This dual status bred a dual psychology described by W.E.B. DuBois early this century: "First, we must remember that living as the blacks do in close contact with a great modern nation, and sharing, although imperfectly, the soul-life of that nation, they must necessarily be affected more or less directly by all the religious and ethical forces that are today moving the United States. These questions and movements are, however, overshadowed and dwarfed by the (to them) all-important question of their civil, political, and economic status. They must perpetually discuss the 'Negro problem', must live, move, and have their being in it, and interpret all else in its light or darkness.... From the double life every American Negro must live, as a Negro and as an American, as swept on by the current of the nineteenth while yet struggling in the eddies of the fifteenth century, from this must arise a painful self-consciousness.... Such a double life, with double thoughts, double duties, and double social classes, must give rise to double words and double ideals, and tempt the mind to pretence or revolt, to hypocrisy or radicalism."[1]

Hence the dual nature of the Black utopia of the 19th and 20th centuries and the dual approach to its realization. As an American, as a member of a definite class, the Black man may share the ideals of this or that social utopia widespread among white Americans. At the same time his Black consciousness inevitably gravitates—especially at times of crisis—toward the ethnically restricted Black utopia which, having undergone a certain evolution by the beginning of the 20th century and having lost its former naiveté, still sees its ideal in a just, equal and free world. As an American, the Black man would like to build this just society on American soil. But as a Black man, constantly

[1] *Ibid.*, p. 129.

reminded of his place and facing countless obstacles to his integration in American society, he maintains that a utopian society can only be established outside America. Such were the motives behind the Black "utopia of escape" of Dr. Marcus Garvey, the Jamaican founder and leader of the Universal Negro Improvement Association. In the 1920s he launched the Back to Africa movement which advocated resettlement of Black Americans in Africa and the creation of a "great African empire". Garvey argued that Blacks were entitled to a place in the sun just like whites, that their striving for happiness, prosperity, social equality, democracy and progress was legitimate, but that they should (and could) establish a free state on their own, outside America. "The Negro will have to build his own government, industry, art, science, literature and culture, before the world will stop to consider him."[1]

Garvey did not invent the idea. Resettlement of Blacks in Africa had been debated for decades. Some saw it as a feasible way of solving America's Black problem, but no one before Garvey had attempted to implement it on such a large scale. His enterprise was a resounding failure, and he himself, a victim of a financial swindle, was put behind bars. But even if he had ended up differently, his project would hardly have been realized consistently or successfully. The important thing, however, was that the very idea of resettlement was welcomed broadly by the Black population of the United States, and thousands of families were ready to use every possible and impossible way of raising money in order to pay for the passage. To resettle millions of Blacks in Africa, to drive the white colonial rulers out and to establish an empire there was, putting it mildly, impractical. Still, the Back to Africa movement aroused the Black American masses. Garvey was supported by many Black leaders, including W.E.B. DuBois.

The fact that Garvey was discredited as a political figure dampened the movement abruptly. Nevertheless, subsequent decades proved that neither the idea of resettlement in Africa nor the folk utopian ideals rooted in the slave period disappeared from Black mentality. Even now that

[1] *Passport to Utopia. Great Panaceas in American History*, Ed. with an introduction by Arthur and Lila Weinberg, Quadrangle Books, Chicago, 1968, p. 221.

conditions have changed, that the degree of the Blacks' racial integration into American society, the level of their education and prosperity and their involvement in the working-class and the everall democratic movements have increased, the original folk utopian ideals remain the basis to which new ideals are merely added—the way it happened during the Black ghetto riots of the late 1960s.

2. The Utopia of a Farmers' America

During the 19th and the first half of the 20th centuries a stable utopian tradition emerged in American fiction and sociopolitical theory—in novels, treatises, manifestoes and the like. For all their diversity, these utopias can be grouped into several types which differ from one another more or less substantially and offer a picture of the major directions of American utopian thought, of the ideals and problems of Americans.

Many U.S. historians (specifically, V. L. Parrington, Jr.) note that the *theocratic* utopia was one of the first, if not the very first, to emerge during the Colonial period.

The idea of setting up a model theocratic state in the New World was born in Europe. The Puritans, who played a very important part in the shaping of American society, crossed the Atlantic in the hope of establishing piety—their ideal—as the ruling order of things and of building a sort of a model ecclesiastical state. Prominent religious public figures—John Cotton, John Winthrop and John Eliot who published his *Christian Commonwealth* in 1659—made a particularly great contribution to the development of the national theocratic utopia. In the list appended to Parrington's *American Dreams*, Eliot's treatise features as the first American utopia.

Eliot's utopia proceeded from the precept that the divine law was to be followed unquestioningly and proposed a government based on a system of magistrates. It was neither original nor profound, but it brought to a logical conclusion many ideals of 17th-century American theocrats who sincerely believed that the best possible society should embody the social ideals of the Old Testament and that democracy and free will were diametrically opposed to these ideals.

The theocratic utopia failed to develop further as an independent branch of the American utopian tradition. The only thing that established itself in the latter was the theocratic form, used occasionally by American utopians of different leanings.

Equally, the sway of theocrats in the New England of the late 17th and early 18th centuries could not prevent the emergence of democratic ideals in the thinking of some of the colonists in opposition to the ruling groups (Thomas Hooker, Roger Williams[1]). The future of these ideals, still not fully formed, was to be decided in the course of the political struggle which began after independence was proclaimed and which was linked directly with the debate over which road America should take. The road it finally did take blocked the realization of "agrarian democracy" ideals. One of the results was that these ideals were sublimated in a distinctive type of utopia, in what might be called the *utopias of a farmers' America.* Subsequent developments proved that this type of utopia was firmly embedded in national social thinking and, in one way or another, always made itself felt, especialy at times of crisis—first in the 1830s (during the first major economic crisis) and then from the 1870s to the 1890s, the decades of the Grangers', Greenbackers' and Populists' movement.

Petty-bourgeois in their social content, these utopias expressed above all the ideals and illusions of the masses of farmers, the age-old dreams of the petty landholder about a free farmer on free land. However, the utopias of a farmers' America were much broader in their social and political scope: they expressed the petty-bourgeois egalitarian thinking of the individualistic petty proprietor, typical not only of farmers but also of artisans and some industrial workers who, although not property owners, were striving to acquire it (which, incidentally, has always encouraged the centrifugal trends among the American proletariat). Mean-

---

[1] Roger Williams "was groping for a social order more generous than any theocracy—that should satisfy the aspirations of men for a catholic fellowship, greater than sect or church, village or nation, embracing all races and creeds, bringing together the sundered societies of men in a common spirit of good will.... He came transporting hither the new and disturbant doctrines of the Leveler, loosing wild foxes with firebrands to ravage the snug fields of the Presbyterian Utopia". (Vernon Louis Parrington, *Main Currents in American Thought*, p. 63).

while, the moral virtues connected with the domination of a system of petty property holders and clearly noticeable against the background of the contradictions generated by industrialization and urbanization made the ideals inherent in the utopias of a farmers' America attractive for social strata to which the desire of petty property was alien.

In theoretical and emotional terms, the utopias of a farmers' America were rooted in the ideas of the American Enlightenment of which many were imbued with the spirit of agrarian democracy. Moreover, the Enlighteners were the first to respond to the industrialization tendencies which appeared as early as the 1780s and to formulate ideals which formed the basis for the utopias of a farmers' America.

This applies, first and foremost, to Benjamin Franklin and Thomas Jefferson. While they did not produce any socioutopian works which could be called integral or all-embracing, they left certain sketches to be used, directly or indirectly, by later generations of utopians. In a letter to Benjamin Vaughan ("On Luxury, Idleness, and Industry"), Franklin wrote about his dreams of a world from which "want and misery would be banished", where "every man and woman would work for four hours each day on something useful", their labor "sufficient to procure all the necessaries and comforts of life", and where "the rest of the twenty-four hours might be leisure and pleasure".[1] In Franklin's opinion, the national economy should be based on agriculture, with the petty proprietor as the central figure, and industry playing a secondary and subordinate role: "While there is land enough in America for our people, there can never be manufactures to any amount of value."[2]

Thomas Jefferson produced what was perhaps the most consistent and complete expression of the utopia of a farmers' America (in its original form). The ways in which the rights proclaimed in the Declaration of Independence should be exercised were always a topical question for the Declaration's author. One utopian ideal inevitably pro-

[1] *The American Age of Reason*, Progress Publishers, Moscow, 1977, p. 95.

[2] *The Works of Benjamin Franklin (Containing Several Political and Historical Tracts)*, Vol. IV, Hilliard, Gray and Company, Boston, 1840, p. 19.

duced another. Jefferson realized that the Federalists' policies would obstruct the implementation of the Declaration's principles and that a different way toward this goal should be sought.

Jefferson saw this way in a self-governing commonwealth of free petty property owners securely tied to their land. He sketched such a society in his "Notes on the State of Virginia" (1782). To be sure, neither *Notes*, nor other works by Jefferson, nor, as a matter of fact, many other writings by American politicians that are going to be discussed in this book, can be, strictly speaking, termed as utopias. Yet it is an important feature of utopian consciousness that it may be present in this type of compositions as an organic element. The *Notes* is one confirmation of this: "We have an immensity of land courting the industry of the husbandman. Is it best then that all our citizens should be employed in its improvement, or that one half should be called off from that to exercise manufactures and handicraft arts for the other? Those who labor in the earth are the chosen people of God, if ever He had a chosen people, whose breasts He has made His peculiar deposit for substantial and genuine virtue.

"...Corruption of morals in the mass of cultivators is a phenomenon of which no age nor nation has furnished an example. It is the mark set on those, who, not looking up to heaven, to their own soil and industry, as does the husbandman, for their subsistence, depend for it on casualties and caprice of customers.

"Dependence begets subservience and venality, suffocates the germ of virtue, and prepares fit tools for the designs of ambition. This, the natural progress and consequence of the arts, has sometimes perhaps been retarded by accidental circumstances; but, generally speaking, the proportion which the aggregate of the other classes of citizens bears in any State to that of its husbandmen, is the proportion of its unsound to its healthy parts, and is a good enough barometer whereby to measure its degree of corruption. While we have land to labor then, let us never wish to see our citizens occupied at a workbench, or twirling a distaff. Carpenters, masons, smiths, are wanting in husbandry; but, for the general operations of manufacture, let our workshops remain in Europe. It is better to carry provisions and materials to workmen there, than bring them to the provisions and materials, and with them their manners and principles.... The mobs of great cities add just so much to the support of pure government, as sores do to the strength of the human body. It is the manners and spirit of a people which preserve a republic in vigor."[1]

In their analysis of Jefferson's social program (and specifically, of certain provisions of his *Notes*) spearheaded against the Federalists, the Soviet historians Grigori Sevostianov and Anatoli Utkin wrote: "An ideologist of the radical bourgeoisie in 1776, Jefferson saw that a system based on equality only before the law would not lead the nation to a better future. And so he turned to the social utopia.... Jefferson sought to consummate the revolutionary cause by establishing a kind of self-imposed isolationism—with friendly relations maintained vis-à-vis the more progressive European regimes—so as to guarantee the country's independence and security from wars and invasions; to complete the struggle by stabilizing society through reliance on American resources and not on European powers; he especially wanted woodland, frontier democracy where everyone was always ready to come to his neighbor's aid to become well-established. Jefferson's dream and utopia was not an America of smokestacks and overcrowded slums but an America of small land holdings sufficient for prosperity, an America of farmers, of people tilling their land. He connected every civic virtue to the patriarchal life of farmsteads and saw the only chance of improving the lot of the popular masses in constant and fruitful work in the woods and fields."[2]

Although subsequently Jefferson somewhat revised the principles proclaimed in his *Notes*—particularly, he softened his critical attitude to the work of craftsmen—his credo remained basically unchanged. He still advocated a society which, if not completely homogeneous in social terms, would at least display no clear-cut social contrasts, let alone polarization of classes—a society whose prosperity would be based on free self-employment of petty property owners and where there would be no place for either a proletariat or an oligarchy.

[1] *The American Age of Reason*, pp. 119-20.

[2] G. N. Sevostianov and A. I. Utkin, *Thomas Jefferson*, Moscow, 1976, p. 264 (in Russian).

The democracy which dominated Jefferson's utopia relied on *local self-government* as a principle naturally stemming from American conditions. In 1824, already an old man, he dreamed of legally establishing a system under which "each ward would thus be a small republic within itself, and every man in the State would thus become an acting member of the common government, transacting in person a great portion of its rights and duties, subordinate indeed, yet important, and entirely within his competence. The wit of man cannot devise a more solid basis for a free, durable and well-administered republic."[1]

Essentially, Jefferson did not reject the state as a legal and political institution. But he wanted it to be quite different from what it had long become in Europe and what it was threatening to become in America—centralized, despotic, expressing and upholding the interests of a minority. Jefferson's ideal was a state responsive to the will of the majority and striving to ensure universal prosperity. "A wise and frugal government, which shall restrain men from injuring one another, which shall leave them otherwise free to regulate their own pursuits of industry and improvement, and shall not take from the mouth of labor the bread it has earned.

"This is the sum of good government, and this is necessary to close the circle of our felicities."[2]

Jefferson did not reject the legal aspect of the state's activity either. But abstract justice, he held, was secondary to the will of the majority, and each new generation should be autonomous and independent of its predecessors in expressing its will. "The government that he desired," Parrington wrote, "would not rest on the legal fiction of an abstract justice above statutes and constitutions, whereof a group of judicial gentlemen were the repositories and guardians. It would be like Paine's, 'a plain thing, and fitted to the capacity of many heads', for 'where the law of the majority ceases to be acknowledged, there government ends; the law of the strongest takes its place'."[3] In other words, the state should be no more than an instrument in the practi-

[1] *Basic Writings of Thomas Jefferson*, Ed. by P. S. Foner, Willy Book Company, New York, 1944, p. 789.

[2] Quoted in: V. L. Parrington, *op. cit.*, Vol. 1, p. 355.

[3] *Ibid.*, p. 353.

cal realization of the natural rights of man originally proclaimed by Jefferson in his draft Declaration of Independence.

While not rejecting private property, Jefferson wanted America to steer clear of the contradictions arising from the logical development of private property relations and bourgeois individualism, ultimately leading to concentration of property, proletarianization of farmers and moral crisis, and eroding those popular democracy institutions which Jefferson had always upheld sincerely. In other words, he wanted to build, by following the classical logic of utopian thinking, a society which would make the best of the advantages of capitalism while protecting itself securely against the disadvantages.

This contradiction between a desire of property and the wish to avoid the negative consequences in the development of a system based on private property not only failed to destroy the utopia of a farmers' America from within but also, at first glance paradoxically, helped these ideals to survive. This is clear even from the fact that the latter have been reproduced in this or that form at virtually every decisive stage (accompanied by upsurges in mass movements) of America's transition from free competition capitalism to monopoly capitalism.

That happened in the 1830s, when the United States was feeling the impact of its first serious economic crisis. The only difference was that while Jefferson and his supporters had obviously tried to prevent or at least slow down America's advance along the industrial capitalist road, now that it was clear the nation had already chosen this path, the farmers' utopia acquired a new objective—to at least ease the consequences which affected the petty proprietor, to give him his chance.

That period produced neither great thinkers (like Jefferson) nor gifted authors advocating the ideals of the utopia of a farmers' America. At the new stage in the evolution of this utopia, however, when Grangers, Greenbackers and Populists (supporters of the People's Party) appeared on the political scene, the utopian ideals of a farmers' America were expressed by outstanding political figures of the times, such as Henry George and Ignatius Donnelly. Populism absorbed and applied to the new situation a number of traditional ideas of bourgeois democratic radicalism tracing their American genesis to Thomas Paine, Thomas Jefferson and the republican democratic clubs of the late 18th century.

Vastly popular was the utopia advanced y Henry George, the prolific author of books like *Progress and Poverty* and *Social Problems*; they became reference books for several bourgeois reformers. George sometimes called his project socialist, but he was never a socialist. According to Frederick Engels, "George is a genuine bourgeois and *his* plan of defraying all governmental expenditures out of ground rent is only a repetition of the plan of the Ricardo school and hence purely bourgeois."[1]

Still, George's bourgeois thinking and his utopianism both developed in the spirit of the ideals of a farmers' America. The reader of his books inevitably concludes that what Jefferson and his supporters feared, warned and fought against has come to pass. Unnatural injustice rules society: there is the "unnatural distribution of wealth which gives one man hundreds of millions and makes other men tramps",[2] there is "the unnatural distribution of population", because some suffer "in body, mind and soul from being crowded into too close contact" with their fellows while rural dwellers suffer equally "from being separated too far from them"; there is the separation of man from land and the unnatural severance of his ties with nature. Degradation threatens man and society, and this calls for immediate action in the spirit of the principles proclaimed in the Declaration of Independence and the Constitution of the United States. Natural justice must be restored—above all, a "natural distribution of population, which would give

[1] "Engels to A. Bebel in Leipzig", January 18, 1884 in: Marx, Engels, *Selected Correspondence*, Progress Publishers, Moscow, 1965, p. 367.

[2] Henry George, *Social Problems*, Kegan Paul, Trench & Co., London, 1884, p. 313. The Russian translation of this book had a foreword by Leo Tolstoy. The great Russian author was sympathetic to the American reformer: "Henry George's idea, which overturns the entire mode of nations' lives to the advantage of the oppressed and silent majority at the expense of the ruling minority, is expressed so incontrovertibly and convincingly and, more important, so simply that one cannot fail to grasp it. And, having grasped it, one cannot fail to try and implement it." (Foreword to the Russian edition of 1907, pp. IV, V.)

every one breathing space and neighborhood".[1] America needs neither to slow down "material progress" nor eliminate capitalism, for capital is not to blame for what has befallen the nation. He returns to this precept in virtually all his works. In *The Condition of Labor* he says that "oppression does not come from the nature of capital, but from the wrong that robs labor of capital by divorcing it from land, and that creates a fictitious capital that is really capitalized monopoly".[2]

"All we need do to secure a just distribution of wealth, is to do that which all theories agree to be the primary function of government—to secure to each the free use of his own powers, limited only by the equal freedom of all others, to secure to each the full enjoyment of his own earnings limited only by such contributions as he may be fairly called upon to make for purposes of common benefit."[3] The only thing necessary for it is to ensure "common right to the soil" (elsewhere he calls it "equal right to the soil") through tax reforms, specifically through the establishment of a "single tax on land" (a "tax on the value or profitability of land") combined with the repeal of all other taxes. In other words, this means *nationalization of land* through the transfer of rent to the bourgeois state or nationalization of land rent; in George's opinion, this would necessarily redistribute wealth while retaining the institution of private property.

Henry George was firmly convinced that he had found the cure-all utopians had always been searching for, that had his project been translated into practice, it would have immediately eradicated all social ills and ushered in an era of universal prosperity.

"With the resumption of common rights to the soil, the overcrowded population of the cities would spread, the scattered population of the country would grow denser.

"When no individual could profit by advance in the value of land, when no one need fear that his children could be jostled out of their natural rights, no one would want more land than he could profitably use. Instead of scraggy,

[1] Henry George, *Social Problems*, pp. 310, 313.

[2] Henry George, *The Condition of Labour*, Swan Sonnenschein & Co., London, 1891, pp. 90-91.

[3] Henri George, *Social Problems*, p. 112.

half-cultivated farms, separated by great tracts lying idle, homesteads would come close to each other.... The use of machinery would not be abandoned: where culture on a large scale secured economies it would still go on, but with the breaking up of monopolies, the rise in wages, and the better distribution of wealth, industry of this kind would assume the co-operative form ... labor would be far more productive ... rural life would tend to revert to the primitive type of the village surrounded by the cultivated fields, with its common pasturage and woodlands....

"That the masses now festering in the tenement houses of our cities, under conditions which breed disease and death, and vice and crime, should each family have its healthful home, set in its garden, that the working farmer should be able to make a living with a daily average of two or three hours' work, which more resembled healthy recreation than toil, that his home should be replete with all the conveniences yet esteemed luxuries, that it should be supplied with light and heat, and power if needed, and connected with those of his neighbors, by the telephone; that his family should be free to libraries, and lectures, and scientific apparatus, and instruction; that they should be able to visit the theater, or concert, or opera, as often as they cared to do so, and occasionally to make trips to other parts of the country or to Europe; that, in short, not merely the successful man, the one in a thousand, but the man of ordinary parts and ordinary foresight and prudence, should enjoy all that advancing civilization can bring to elevate and expand human life, seems, in the light of existing facts, as wild a dream as ever entered the brain of a hasheesh eater. Yet, the powers already within the grasp of man make it easily possible."[1]

This lenthy excerpt from Henry George is worth quoting if only because this used to be the dream of millions of American farmers, industrial workers, unemployed and lumpens of the late 19th century. One can, of course, smile condescendingly at the naive illusions with regard to the practicability of the ideals of a farmers' America (recognizing, in a modified form, the rapid growth of industry and the proletariat, the introduction of scientific and technological advances into everyday life, and the strength-

[1] Ibid., pp. 313-15.

ening of the state) combined with the retention of private property and the further advancement of capitalism, with concentration and centralization of capital as its inescapable concomitants. However, this paradox is what the entire utopia of a farmers' America stands on.

This utopia found its place in fiction during the last quarter of the 19th century. In 1890 Ignatius Donnelly, a popular leader of the People's Party, journalist and author, wrote *Caesar's Column*, a novel with a built-in utopia based on modified ideals of a farmers' America.

"The end of everything earthly," Donnelly writes, "is the good of man; and there is nothing sacred on earth but man, because he alone shares the Divine conscience."[1] To this end, inequality should be eradicated—at least in its more blatant forms. But as practical people well-versed in the subtleties of economics, Donnelly's protagonists propose that it should begin with the elimination of interest rates, of usury which, they believe, "is the cause of the first aristocracy, and out of this grow all the other aristocracies".[2] Donnelly also suggests the establishment of a "maximum" of possible wealth. "But just as I limited a man's possible wealth, so should I limit the amount of land he could own. I would fix a maximum of, say, 100 or 500 acres, or whatever amount might be deemed just and reasonable. I should abolish all corporations, or turn them back into individual partnerships,"[3] says one of the novel's protagonists. The government, which is "only a machine to insure justice and help the people",[4] could take care of much of what each used to take care of himeslf—water supply, postal sevice, education, law and order. It could also redistribute "surplus wealth" to the advantage of the poorer classes. This, Donnelly maintains, would lead to an order of things under which no one would be hungry or poor and people would cease robbing one another—in short, universal justice, and "universal justice means equal opportunities for all men and a repression by law of those gigantic

[1] Ignatius Donnelly, *Caesar's Column. A Story of the Twentieth Century*, Ed. by Walter B. Rideout, The Belknap Press of Harvard University Press, Cambridge, Mass., 1960, p. 106.

[2] *Ibid.*, p. 103.

[3] *Ibid.*, p. 105.

[4] *Ibid.*, p. 106.

abnormal selfishnesses which ruin millions for the benefit of thousands".[1]

One can easily see that, while striving to uphold the interests of the common folk, Donnelly—acting fully in the spirit of the times—made an important step toward recognizing such functions of the state (the central government) which would have been rejected out of hand by the utopian advocates of a farmers' America a mere three-quarters of a century before. A new trend was developing, combining the defense of the ideals of petty property, inalienable rights and equal opportunities with the recognition of a strong centralized state. The state, which the petty proprietor once used to regard as his foremost enemy, was now yielding its position to a still stronger and more ruthless enemy, the monopolies. And so, one was forced not only to accept the existence and consolidation of strong and centralized government but also to regard it as a force capable of curbing the monopolies.

The transition from free competition to monopoly capitalism shaped the further transformation of the utopia of a farmers' America. The further capitalism advanced and the less promising and stable the position of the petty proprietor (above all, the petty land holder) became, the more urgent it was to reconcile ideas like petty private property and individual enterprise on the one hand and, on the other, political freedom, democracy and local self-government within a single structure. History was offering new examples proving that, in order to uphold and implement some ideals, one had to sacrifice others, resorting to means which used to be considered contrary to the ends. To uphold the institution of private property and private enterprise, one had to sacrifice the ideal of local self-government and accept the authority of a strong state, for the latter was the only ally the petty proprietor could rely on in his life-or-death struggle with the monopolies. Naturally, the utopian dreamed of a state whose entire might would be spearheaded against big capital, which would be financed out of superprofits, and whose bureaucracy would not restrict the freedom of the petty proprietor.

The Great Depression of the 1930s strengthened the conviction of a large part of farmers, industrial workers and

[1] *Ibid.*, p. 100.

unemployed that the chief enemy of the petty proprietor was not the state but the monopoly which negated the principle of "equal opportunity". "If one may speak about some central idea of the agrarian radicalism of the 1930s," a Soviet historian says, "one should acknowledge that it was embodied most frequently in antimonopoly protest, in the overriding desire to throw off the yoke of finance and industrial capital which held petty and medium farmers in economic bondage, robbed them with the help of credit and price policies and rigid control over the agricultural market, and infringed painfully on the interests of the agricultural bourgeoisie too. In 1936 one of the sponsors of a conference of farmer organizations' leaders said: 'Our common ground is a belief that monopoly capitalism is evil and self-destructive, and that it is possible, while preserving private ownership, to build a true democracy in which men would be better off both morally and physically.'"[1]

Simultaneously, however, a directly opposite view, nurtured by the developments that had led up to this situation, was emerging: that, to uphold the institution of petty private property, it was no longer enough to simply accept the need for a strong centralized state which turned its repressive power against the monopolies; that protection of petty private property and private enterprise demanded not merely a better-equipped state but restrictions on democracy and the establishment of "strong government". These views, broadly supported at the grassroots level in the 1930s, were reflected in numerous utopian projects, the most popular of them put forward by Huey Long and Charles Coughlin.

Senator Huey Long, "dictator of Louisiana", presidential contender and "idol of shopkeepers, petty businessmen and moderately well-off white farmers",[2] was famous for his "redistribution of wealth" plan. He promised to make every American an uncrowned king (in the words of William Jennings Bryan, a Populist leader). Long's

[1] E. W. Hawley, *The New Deal and the Problem of Monopoly*, Princeton University Press, Princeton, N. J., 1966, p. 291 quoted in: V. L. Malkov, *The New Deal in the United States*, Moscow, 1973, p. 106 (in Russian).

[2] V. Z. Malkov, *op. cit.*, p. 148.

plan[1] was essentially to redistribute wealth—with the help of the state —in such a way which, without undermining the foundations of private enterprise, would make it possible to consolidate the prosperity and the position of the petty proprietor by somewhat restricting monopoly capital. While he insisted on the financing of his project out of taxes levied on big capital and through limitations on the power of banks, Huey Long connected its implementation with curbs on the "ineffective" system of democracy and with virtually dictatorial powers for the government. Thus the possibility of preserving petty property and protecting private individualism was presented as directly dependent on restrictions for democracy and a stronger central government.

Coughlin offered a similar plan. Like Long's project, it ignored objective trends in the development of American capitalism and expressed the illusions and expectations of the petty bourgeoisie oppressed by the monopolies. Proceeding from the traditional utopian precept of a farmers' America, the one maintaining that private property is the metaphysical basis of freedom and democracy, Coughlin interpreted it in a clearly anticommunist and antidemocratic light. "Private ownership," he said in one of the radio lectures he specialized in for years, "must be protected against corporate ownership. Small business must be safeguarded reasonably against monopolistic business. Were we to permit private ownership and small business gradually to be assimilated by corporate and monopolistic creations, then we are only preparing the way either for state capitalism or for communism."[2] Coughlin also suggested the introduction of a progressive income tax, nationalization of banks (Franklin Roosevelt's refusal to take this road resulted in his break with Coughlin who had previously supported the President vigorously), and sharp reductions in the bureaucracy which he saw as the epitome of the ills of democracy.

The plans of Long, Coughlin and several other petty-bourgeois reformers of the 1930s proved that the utopia of a farmers' America as the mass democratic utopia it had been almost throughout the 19th century was no longer

[1] *Passport to Utopia...*, p. 267.
[2] *Ibid.*, p. 280.

viable. Those essentially liberal ideals, like equal opportunities, private enterprise, petty private property, local self-government, the minimal government, etc., which had been the target of utopian effort, remained attractive to many Americans. However, having retained their critical function, in the new historical conditions they lost their formerly progressive role—both in their traditional composition and in combination with other, previously alien ideals, like those of a "strong state" or "strong government".

3. The Romantic Utopia

The utopia of a farmers' America emerged and developed as the petty proprietor's response to the advancement of capitalism which was pushing him to the periphery of economic, civic and political affairs. But simultaneously, capitalist contradictions gave rise to a different type of utopian response—the *romantic utopia*.

The birth of this type of utopian consciousness was closely connected with the rise of the American Romantic Movement as a literary and aesthetic trend. For this reason the romantic utopian ideal was expressed not so much in theoretical form as in the shape of fiction, and the romantic aesthetic credo often formed the basis of utopian projects. Beauty was frequently the romanticist's guide to action in his socioutopian experiments (the organization of the Brook Farm utopian community was a classic example). In this sense American Romanticism as a socioutopian tradition, an artistic and literary trend, an aesthetic doctrine and a model of social behavior embodied a single type of consciousness. Perhaps this explains why outstanding figures of American culture of the first half of the 19th century such as Henry David Thoreau or Nathaniel Hawthorne were, simultaneously, romantic authors, social utopian theorists and practical utopians (Thoreau's experiment reflected in his *Walden*, Hawthorne's participation in the Brook Farm community resulted in his *Blithedale Romance*).

Nevertheless, the romantic social utopia and romantic literature were not identical. They followed different laws, and this makes it possible to consider each independently of the other. Having appeared as a reaction to the social consequences of industrialization (the restructuring of the lifestyle, the collapse of the traditional patriarchal relations and the destruction of the old values), the American Romantic Movement was also a legitimate search—this was its salient sociohistorical feature—for ways to realize the promises of the American Revolution.

Critical of his contemporary sociopolitical order, the romanticist still remained an optimist. He pinned his hopes of more humane social relations not on the overthrow of capitalism but on the development of the traditions rooted in the principles proclaimed by the Founding Fathers. Specifically, this explains the fact that, in the words of Yuri Kovalev, a Soviet researcher, "the romantic protest against the new forms of economic, political and social affairs born of capitalist development was originally devoid of intransigence".[1]

The romantic utopia comprises a diversity of both aesthetic and social aspects. Its authors may hold different views of the specific forms of the utopian ideal and of the ways to attain it, but these differences do not erode their consensus as to the principles and major values of the utopian world; this makes it possible to classify the romantic utopia of the first half of the 19th century as an independent type. The consensus in question is largely explained by the unified nature of the philosophical basis of the American Romantic Movement, transcendentalism. Its central principle is the *natural* condition and its central value, the *free man*. The American romanticist is above all a *humanist* proclaiming "man's supremacy over the law, the state and the church".[2] It is man's position in society which is the measure of the existing system and the point of departure in the construction of a social utopia. The romantic ideal is a society in which the individual can follow his inner motivations, in which he is free from any external coercion or imposition by others, from the dictates of the state. "Man is not made for society, but society is made for man"[3]—this quotation from Margaret Fuller expresses,

[1] Yu. V. Kovalev, *Herman Melville and the American Romantic Movement*, Leningrad, 1972, p. 16 (in Russian).

[2] *Ibid.*, p. 25.

[3] Margaret Fuller, *American Romantic. A Selection from Her Writings and Correspondence*, Cornell University Press, Ithaca, New York, 1970, p. 64.

with sufficient clarity, the *individualistic credo* of the romantic utopian, particularly pronounced in the works of Thoreau. But romantic individualism is not the entrepreneurial individualism of the utopia of a farmers' America, based on the fetish of petty private property and the pursuit of wealth and social success. While the romantic utopian does not in principle reject private property, he does not make a fetish out of it either, seeing it merely as a condition for the normal existence of man and society. He is revolted by the mercenary spirit of greed and breathless pursuit of profit as something that denigrates man. The individualism of the romanticist is *ethical individualism*. There should be no place in society for a common moral code authorized by some higher authority. The romanticists countered the hypocritical morals of bourgeois society with the conscience of the individual, with the transcendentalist idea of an innate sense of justice which should be the highest criterion and law of human existence.

The *natural man* is the ideal of the romantic utopian. At first glance he appears as the "noble savage" like Melville's Typee, living on the fruits of the earth, free of the cares burdening the civilized man and of property which is virtually his *raison d'être*. But a closer scrutiny of the romantic works shows that the "natural man" is simply a man living a natural life, whether he is a savage or civilized. The only reason why Melville is looking for this man in the Marquesas and Thoreau and especially Emerson, in the Orient[1] and not in America is that they are convinced that this man does not and, given the then social conditions, simply cannot exist in America. To become a natural man, one had to *break with society*—organizationally (like Thoreau and the inhabitants of Brook Farm) or spiritually (like Emerson and Margaret Fuller) and to establish, or rather restore, *unity with nature* (in Emerson's[2] words, "harmony" of man and nature), a most important element of the romantic utopia.

[1] Naturally, the Orient to which American romanticists turned so often was not the geographical region with all its actual cultures and histories but a myth, the antithesis of Western dehumanization.

[2] Emerson's Nature—Origin, Growth, Meaning, Ed. by M. M. Sealts, Jr. and A. R. Ferguson, Dodd, Mead & Company, Inc., New York, Toronto, 1969, p. 8.

The romanticist sees nature as the only true source of moral purity, wisdom and power, and so in his utopia man's relations with nature are colored neither by "practical expediency" which places man *above* nature nor by "advances of civilization" which place him *outside* nature. Technology as such does not enslave man; it subjugates him only when it divorces him from nature. Reason as such is not a repressive force either as long as it does not make man blind to the life of nature, to its shapes and colors, and therefore, blind to his own life. And so the romantic utopia of the 19th century neither denounces nor extolls technology and reason: the railroad as such is not bad and could be a blessing—had it not been built on human bones. Reason could also benefit man had it served the cause of enlightenment and not petty everyday cares enslaving man and had it not turned into a tool for attaining mercenary goals. Consequently, the romantic utopia is not the kingdom of reason, the way it was with the Enlighteners. But neither is it the kingdom of "pure" nature; it is rather the realm of *universal harmony* everyone needs to make his happiness complete.

The romanticist rejects the real world of American bourgeois democracy, but this does not prevent him from seeing himself as a democrat and his utopia, as the world of true democracy. However, this is in no way the democracy of the politician or businessman. "When I ... speak of the democratic element," Emerson explains, "I do not mean that ill thing, vain and loud, which writes lying newspapers, spouts at caucuses, and sells its lies for gold; but that spirit of love, for the general good whose name this assumes. There is nothing of the true democratic element in what is called Democracy; it must fall, being wholly commercial." He adds that "the root and seed of democracy is the doctrine. Judge for yourself. Reverence thyself. It is the inevitable effect of the doctrine, where it has any effect (which is rare), to insulate the partisan, to make each man a state. At the same time it replaces the dead with a living check in a true, delicate reverence for superior, congenial minds."[1] Thus the ideal of the romantic utopian is *ethical democracy* having nothing in common with the democratic political process although undoubtedly having a

[1] Quoted in: V. L. Parrington, *op. cit.*, Vol. 2, p. 392.

profound social content.

It is natural that the romanticist treats the state with suspicion and mistrust. Although in principle he does not reject it as an institution, he would prefer a state which would govern to such a tiny degree and be so small in its institutions that it could hardly be noticed. Says Thoreau: "I heartily accept the motto,—'That government is best which governs least'; and I should like to see it acted up to more rapidly and systematically. Carried out, it finally amounts to this, which also I believe,—'That government is best which governs not at all'; and when men are prepared for it, that will be the kind of government which they will have."[1] The conclusion essentially echoes Emerson's: that government is best which enables everyone to be his own government. It follows that the ideal of the romantic utopian is a *nonpolitical (depoliticized) society* in which there is neither the state nor parties nor classes nor power struggle—a society ruled by custom, where one's own conscience is the highest authority.

The political problems which the utopian of a farmers' America or the socialist utopian seeks to solve do not exist for the romanticist; nor do economic puzzles. Tax reforms, interest rates, financing of public works, nationalization of land, rationalization of the economy and so on and so forth —everything Henry George, Edward Bellamy and scores of other utopians racked their brains to solve is solved by the romanticist as easily as Thoreau solved the tax problem: he refused to pay the tax. True, the romanticist discusses labor at length, and labor—free labor, of course—features prominently in his utopia. But to him, labor is not vigorous activity aimed at transforming the natural and social fabric but rather a mystery, a religious rite. "While our enterprise lay all in theory," says a protagonist of Hawthorne's *Blithedale Romance*, "we had pleased ourselves with delectable visions of the spiritualization of labor. It was to be our form of prayer and ceremonial of worship. Each stroke of the hoe was to uncover some aromatic root of wisdom."[2]

[1] Henry David Thoreau, *The Variorum Civil Disobedience*, Twayne Publishers, Inc., New York, 1967, p. 31.

[2] Nathaniel Hawthorne, *The Blithedale Romance*, Dell Publishing Company., Inc., New York, 1962, p. 92.

To us it is clear that the way suggested by the romanticist is no solution, that it is simply impossible to ignore economic problems. But the secret of utopia is that unlike the realist, the utopian does not at all have to answer all the questions, let alone answer them rationally. The meaning of a utopia may be to try and make unnecessary what is inevitable in real life, so as to imagine what life could be like if built to a "nonclassical" blueprint. In the context of American civilization, this task was tackled above all by romantic utopians.

The romantic utopian tradition which assumed its definite shape during the first half of the 19th century has always remained a living source of American culture and national social awareness. The 1960s highlighted the surprisingly topical nature of many of the ideas and ideals put forward by Thoreau (and consequently, the classic American Romantic Movement as a whole, for Thoreau's utopia is both the result and an encyclopedia of the romantic quest and discovery in the social field of human relations). But even prior to the 1960s the ideals of Cooper, Melville, Thoreau and Emerson had led a covert life in American utopian fiction and utopian practice. "Covert" we say meaning that these ideals underwent a transformation. First of all, romantic ideals underlay the principles which guided the life of many utopian communities of the latter half of the 19th and the early 20th centuries. Secondly, these ideals were echoed—true, often not only weakly but also unfaithfully— in adventure stories and new romantic utopias which appeared from time to time on the American literary scene, for example, James Hilton's *Lost Horizon* or Austin Wright's *Islandia*. Finally, utopian romantic ideals (at least some of them) exerted considerable pressure on the projects which developed throughout the 19th and the first half of the 20th centuries, within the mainstreams of other utopian traditions, including the socialist tradition.

After the Civil War the romantic utopian tradition never rose to its erstwhile heights. That was partly because the social processes that occurred in America in the latter half of the 19th and the first half of the 20th centuries developed in direct contradiction to the romantic ideals but did not yet (at that time) go as far as to provoke, as a reaction, a powerful and vigorously creative utopian upsurge (signs of this upsurge were clearly in evidence in the 1950s).

And part of the reason was that the social ideals of romantic utopia of the first half of the 19th century were so highly transcendental and so far from the actual social reality that to this day they remain unrealized and inexhaustible (hence the topicality of Thoreau's ideas). At best, they could be reproduced, but not surpassed.

4. The Socialist Utopia

The *socialist utopia* had a different fate in America. "Utopian novels were produced at intervals throughout the century," V. L. Parrington, Jr. writes about the 19th century, "but it was not till the 80s that utopianism became the vogue. New ideas were in the air; men began to think and write and talk socialism."[1] Indeed, utopian socialist novels became fashionable only in the last quarter of the 19th century. However, Americans had begun to "think, write and talk socialism" much earlier. This should be emphasized specially because many American historians maintain that socialist thought in the United States is devoid of national roots, that it was introduced into the country by immigrants and propagandists from Europe. This view obviously underrates (1) the independent search for a socialist ideal by Americans themselves; (2) the transformations the European socialist theories underwent on American soil; and (3) the practical communitarian experiments which America staged on a scale far surpassing anything attempted in Europe and many of which were a practical expression of the socialist quest. Upton Sinclair was quite right when he said that "even in the midst of our pioneer individualism there were Americans who dreamed of an ordered society based upon justice. We had our Brook Farm and a score of other colonies nearly a hundred years ago. We had our native Socialist movement, with leaders such as Albert Brisbane and Horace Greeley and Phillips Wendell and Frances Willard and Edward Bellamy—and so on down to Gene Debs and Jack London. All these were native Americans, who spoke our language, and the only reason they are not understood is that their words so sel-

[1] V. L. Parrington, Jr., *op. cit.*, p. 57.

dom reach the people."[1]

One must obviously keep from going to the other extreme and underrating the great work done by European utopian socialists, above all Robert Owen, Etienne Cabet with his followers and the supporters of Fourier and Saint-Simon, to disseminate and put into practice socialist (communist) ideas in America, especially in the first half of the 19th century. Utopian socialist ideas were especially widespread in America from the 1820s to the 1840s, when the contradictions of U.S. capitalism became obvious for the first time but the political machinery which was to shape the ways in which American society would function for years to come was as yet far from complete. This produced a peculiar situation which affected the destiny of socialism in the New World. Many Americans regarded socialism not as a theoretical and practical negation of capitalism but as one of the ways—and perfectly legitimate at that—of realizing the ideas and promises of the American Revolution and correcting the deviations from the "ordained" path, committed by inept politicians and greedy businessmen. Socialism was interpreted as consonant with the very spirit of the ideas expounded by the Founding Fathers, with the Declaration of Independence, the Constitution, the Bill of Rights and, consequently, with the very "idea of America". European utopian socialists, specifically Robert Owen, did much to promote that interpretation. As a result, Americans approached socialism from the point of view of its effectiveness in ensuring the implementation of the ideals advanced by the American Enlighteners.

Initially, the socialist utopia and its creators who visited the United States were not simply welcomed by the Americans; the officialdom also clearly displayed interest in it and its founders. Suffice it to recall that Robert Owen addressed Congress twice and met with prominent public figures such as Jefferson, Madison, John Adams, Andrew Jackson and Monroe. The speeches he delivered at the joint House and Senate sessions attended by Cabinet and Supreme Court members were published in the press.[2] Howev-

[1] *Upton Sinclair Anthology*, Murray and Gee, Culver City, 1947, p. 280.

[2] See R. Owen, "A Discourse on a New System of Society", in: *Robert Owen in the United States*, Ed. by O. Johnson, New York, 1970.

er, having inquired into the plans of the European socialist, American politicians were in no hurry to respond to Owen's pleas for financial assistance. Fully in the spirit of the free market, they left it to him to win the hearts, minds and purses of Americans.

One should note that Americans approached different European socialist utopias differently. According to Morris Hillquit, "the system of the great French utopian, Charles Saint-Simon, that had for its principal aim the organization of national and international industry on a scientific basis, and was a universal social philosophy which did not admit of experiments on a miniature scale, found no echo in the United States. The philosophy of Robert Owen, in which communities are not an essential factor, but play an important part as preparatory schools for the communistic *regime* and as object lessons in the communistic mode of life, gained a considerable foothold in the United States, although it did not attain the same degree of strength or exercise the same measure of influence on social thought as it did in the country of its birth, England. On the other hand, the system of the French utopian, Charles Fourier, which was based principally upon social organizations on a small scale, developed more strength in this country than it did in France."[1] Americans were indeed sensitive to the practical effectiveness of socialist doctrines and as the fate of Owen and his comrades bears out, quickly lost interest in those which, although initially welcomed enthusiastically, could not "make it".

Still, there was another reason why Americans found doctrines like Fourier's attractive, at least as long as their true worth remained unclear. Fourier not only opposed crude egalitarianism but, unlike Owen and other utopian socialists, did not advocate abolition of private property. In spite of this circumstance (which gave rise to arguments among students of Fourier's socialism), Marx and Engels had a high opinion of Fourier and held that scientific socialism "rests on the shoulders of Saint-Simon".[2] Appa-

[1] Morris Hillquit, *History of Socialism in the United States*, Funk & Wagnalls Co., New York and London, 1903, p. 21.

[2] Frederick Engels, "Supplement to the Preface to the Peasant War in Germany" in: Marx, Engels, *Selected Works*, Vol. 2, Progress Publishers, Moscow, 1969, p. 169.

rently, to them the actually humanistic content of Fourier's principal ideas was more important than his formal acceptance of private property.

From the economic viewpoint, Fourier's phalanstery was a sort of joint-stock company which valued individual success and offered additional rewards for it but in which there was neither competition (in the forms in which it existed outside) nor the threat of bankruptcy. In other words, Fourier's utopia combined the ideal of economic individualism (embodied in the utopia of a farmers' America), which many Americans found attractive, with an ideal typical of all socialist utopias and, generally, also traditionally favored by many 19th-century Americans. The word "community" would be the best expression of this ideal's essence—"community", or "fraternal unity", or "commonwealth of free men", or "community of equal citizens". It was precisely the *community* ideal and not the ideal of socialized production or of "equality in property" that attracted, as a feature of socialism, Americans in the 1820s, 30s and 40s. As to relations concerning property, most American adherents of socialism preferred *even distribution of property* to its socialization.

That, for example, was the approach of Thomas Skidmore, a prominent American utopian socialist of the early 19th century. The very title of the book he published in 1829 was significant; it sounded like a manifesto: *The Rights of Man to Property: Being a Proposition to Make It Equal Among the Adults of the Present Generation; and to Provide for its Equal Transmission to Every Individual of Each Succeeding Generation, on Arriving at the Age of Maturity.* "Skidmore," Foner writes, "proposed that every young man, twenty-one years of age, and every unmarried woman should receive a free grant of one hundred and sixty acres of land, to be held in perpetuity so long as the settler tilled his soil. But the right to sell or rent land was to be abolished forever."[1]

Of course, voices were raised in defense of socialized property at that time too. However, it took several dramatic decades of economic and political crises and bitter

[1] See Philip S. Foner, *History of the Labor Movement in the United States*, Vol. I, International Publishers, New York, 1978, pp. 130, 131.

clashes between classes for the ideal of public property in the means of production to become attractive to American working people.

This happened during the last quarter of the 19th century, when a new stage began in the development of the socialist utopia in the United States.

The rapid progress of U.S. capitalism which exacerbated social contradictions and clearly displayed its inconsistency with the ideals proclaimed by the American Revolution, as well as the growth of the farmers' and industrial workers' movement contributed to the emergence of a series of properly American socialist utopias. The most successful among them was Edward Bellamy's utopian novel *Looking Backward* (1888).

Like the American utopian socialists who were active in the 1820s, 30s and 40s, Bellamy proclaims a society based on "the idea of the solidarity of humanity, the brotherhood of all men" as his ideal. He stresses the need to ensure "equality of condition" which presupposes "equal wealth and equal opportunities of culture".[1] However, unlike his precursors, Bellamy is convinced that this cannot be achieved by even distribution of property alone. Human nature is immutable; therefore more radical measures which could change human motives equally radically are what is needed. This refers to a change in the system of property resulting in "one capitalist in the place of all other capitalists, the sole employer, the final monopoly in which all previous and lesser monopolies" would be absorbed, "a monopoly in the profits and economies of which all citizens shared,"[2] with the people becoming the sole master of all riches. *Socialized property* is regarded as the only effective basis of the "community". Bellamy tries to blend the two ideals previously separated in the thinking of American utopian socialists.

But, having accepted socialization of property, Bellamy has to remove from his "society of solidarity" all those elements of anarchy which the institution of private property entails. As a result, his free society becomes almost as strictly regulated as the utopian societies imagined by More, Campanella or Fourier. And, while Bellamy himself in-

[1] Edward Bellamy, *Looking Backward, 2000-1887*, The Modern Library, New York, 1942, p. 125.

[2] *Ibid.*, p. 41.

sists that in the Boston of the year 2000, the scene of his novel, personal freedom is restricted much less than before and relations represent a logical consequence of natural human activities under rational conditions, the life of the society he describes appears strikingly poor and dull in political, cultural and social terms; and thus the freedom that is proclaimed proves on the whole to be formal freedom.

Bellamy was America's first socialist-oriented utopian who, having attempted to combine the "community" ideal with that of public property, drew up a model of a strictly regimented society. However, he failed to blend the two ideals and to show how a society based on public property in the means of production could ensure not lesser but greater freedom for the individual than that obtaining in a society based on the operation of the market.

Nevertheless, Bellamy's utopia became extremely popular both in the United States and abroad, specifically in Russia. Moreover, it stimulated the movement of the so-called nationalists who tried to put Bellamy's ideas into practice. That was understandable. *Looking Backward* aptly expressed the discontent of those groups of Americans who traced all their troubles to the sway of uncontrollable market forces and were looking for alternative structures to regulate social developments. These alternatives were to ensure equality of opportunity and guarantee increasing prosperity—even at the expense of restricted personal freedom and a stronger authority of the state. "The crux of the problem," V. L. Parrington says about the America of the 1880s and 1890s, "seemed to reside in an extention of the powers of the political state, converting to social ends powers that hitherto had been serving private gain."[1] This means that Bellamy's novel reflected not only the state of mass consciousness but also a new trend in the development of American society—toward restriction of the free market mechanism and a gradual strengthening of the role of the state in social developments, with all the social, political and cultural consequences that entailed.

Looking Backward was truly a landmark, both in literary and in sociopolitical terms. "Along with certain repercussion abroad—notably William Morris' *News from No-*

[1] V. L. Parrington, *Main Current in American Thought*, Vol. 3, Harcourt, Brace and Company, New York, 1930, p. 301.

where (1890)–*Looking Backward* initiated in the United States a vogue of Utopian debate that lasted until after the turn of the century. The book became all but universally known, and its immense popularity overshadowed and determined Bellamy's later work. With the formation of numerous Bellamy clubs, with the rise of the amorphous Nationalist 'party', Bellamy felt it his duty and opportunity to lead in the reform movements directed toward the realization of his own dreams."[1] In 1897, Bellamy published *Equality*, an attempt at a theoretical substantiation of the social relations described in *Looking Backward*. But the sequel was only a poor relation of the first utopian novel. Bellamy went down in popular history as the author of *Looking Backward* only.

Looking Backward produced conflicting reactions in the United States. On the one hand, it gave rise to a series of utopian parodies and refutations (*The Republic of the Future* by Anna B. Dodd, 1891; *Looking Inward* by J. W. Roberts, 1893; *Caesar's Column* by Ignatius Donnelly, 1890). But it also prompted a stream of imitations (*The Co-opolitan* by Zebine Forbush, 1889, *Letters from New America* by C. E. Persinger, 1900; *The Legal Revolution of 1902* by Bert J. Wellman and others). Supporting the ideals of public property in the means of production, of universal labor and eradication of class antagonism, these utopias, nevertheless, firmly rejected any revolutionary transformation of American society and, like Bellamy's novel, advocated a nonviolent, "legitimate" and evolutionary path toward socialism. The ways which the authors of socialist utopias believed capable of establishing a "just society" in America included a carefully designed system of education, a government policy of gradually ousting private business from the national economy, organization of production and consumer cooperatives, winning a majority in local or Federal government, redemption of industrial enterprises from their owners and the like. (Significantly, most authors of such works, including Bellamy himself, preferred to call themselves "radicals", "champions of justice", etc., but not socialists.) Another salient feature of the American socialist utopia was that "justice" was often interpreted in the spirit of "equality of opportunity" which cate-

[1] *Literary History of the United States*, p. 991.

gorically rejected crude egalitarianism, a concept always repulsive to most Americans. For example, Charles Persinger explained that in the new society, "a man's progress depends upon himself, and not upon an accident of his birth or the circumstances of his life", but added that this society would not try to "make men equal when Nature failed in that endeavor".[1]

William Dean Howells was perhaps the best known and most gifted of Bellamy's followers. In 1894 he produced his first socialist utopian ("Altrurian") novel. Entitled *A Traveler from Altruria*, this was, in the words of the literary critic Howard Mumford Jones, "a book about the American dream published during an American nightmare.... The nightmare was the great depression that hung over the country from 1893 to 1898.... To many it seemed that the bloody prophecy in Ignatius Donnelly's *Caesar's Column* (1891), that grim melodramatic masterpiece, was coming true."[2] Jones notes quite rightly that, in Howells' opinion, "Altruria is what America would be if it really took to heart the principles of the Declaration.... Altruria is what a country could be if everyone really loved his neighbor as himself."[3] But in constructing his utopian image of America, Howells, whether consciously or unwittingly, was working within the framework of the American socialist utopian tradition.

The plot of the novel is simple. A Mr. Homos, citizen of Altruria, an island nation which the rest of the world has lost sight of, arrives in the United States of the 1990s. After examining the life of American society, Homos concludes that it is extremely unreasonable. There is no social equality. ("I don't know," one of the Americans says, "how the notion of our social equality originated, but I think it has been fostered mainly by the expectation of foreigners, who argued it from our political equality. As a matter of fact, it never existed, except in our poorest and most primitive communities, in the pioneer days of the West, and among the gold-hunters of California.") There is

---

[1] Charles Edward Persinger, *Letters from New America*, quoted in: V. L. Parrington, Jr., *op. cit.*, p. 122.

[2] William Dean Howells, *A Traveler from Altruria*, Introduction by H. M. Jones, Sagamore Press, New York, 1957, p. V.

[3] *Ibid.*, p. VIII.

no respect for the man of labor, care for one's neighbor, no spirit of fraternal cooperation ("There is ... as little love in this country as in any country on the globe."). It turns out that "the American ideal is not to change the conditions for all, but for each to rise above the rest if he can."[1]

Finally Homos concludes that America needs the type of radical transformations that were once carried out in Altruria. "We," the Altrurian says, "are still far from thinking our civilization perfect; but we are sure that our civic ideals are perfect. What we have already accomplished is to have given a whole continent perpetual peace; to have founded an economy in which there is no possibility of want; to have killed our political and social ambition; to have disused money and eliminated chance; to have realized the brotherhood of the race, and to have outlived the fear of death."[2] All this has become possible because a basically new system of social relations has been established in Altruria. Private property does not exist: "No man owned anything, but every man had the right to anything that he could use; when he could not use it, his right lapsed." Chance as a source of social inequality has been banished from economic and social relations: "We have totally eliminated chance from our economic life. There is still a chance that a man will be tall or short, in Altruria, that he will be strong or weak, well or ill, gay or grave, happy or unhappy in love, but none that he will be rich or poor, busy or idle, live splendidly or meanly." And all men are brothers: in the "great political brotherhood, the commonwealth of Altruria" people live not "*upon* each other", the way they did before, under a plutocratic oligarchy in the times of the "Accumulation", but "*for* each other".[3] In Altruria aesthetic laws have become universal in all creative effort; life is easy and unhurried; cities have been replaced by small village-type communities. Economic equality has abolished political struggle, and administrative work has lost its erstwhile prestige.

In full conformity with the American socialist utopian tradition, Howells emphasizes that all radical change in Altruria has been carried out without any bloodshed,

[1] *Ibid.*, pp. 41, 42.

[2] *Ibid.*, p. 206.

[3] *Ibid.*, pp. 202, 203-04, 181.

via an evolutionary, "parliamentary" way: the strictly law-abiding proletariat has won a majority in the parliament. Nonviolence is the underlying idea of many of Howells' books. The old socialist David Hughes, a character of his *World of Chance* (1893), says that "society is not saved by self-outlawry.... The way to have the golden age is to elect it by the Australian ballot."[1]

Through the Eye of the Needle, Howells' second utopian novel, appeared in 1907. A detailed description of Altruria, it contributed nothing essentially new to the socialist utopia of his *Traveler*.

Unlike Bellamy who, in a typically American way, plunged into politics to realize the principles he suggested for restructuring American society, Howells remained merely an observer and commentator, although he was one of the few who openly called themselves socialists. He wrote to Henry James in 1888: "After fifty years of optimistic content with 'civilization' and its ability to come out all right in the end, I now abhor it, and feel that it is coming out all wrong in the end, unless it bases itself anew on a real equality. Meantime, I wear a furlined overcoat, and live in all the luxury my money can buy."[2] In the words of the Soviet researcher Boris Gilenson, Howells was a link of sorts which kept the socialist tradition whole across the turn of the century. In the early 1900s socialism was no longer only a subject for theoretical debate; it emerged as a practical slogan in class action by working people.[3]

This action assumed particularly great proportions in the late 1910s and early 1920s, largely encouraged by World War I and the October 1917 Revolution in Russia. In those years, the American Left were engaged not so much in the theoretical development of new social projects as in a search for means to involve American working people in the world revolution and in political struggle to establish a revolutionary organization for them. A new stage in the development of socialist utopian thought in the United States started in the 1930s, when advocates of socialism joined the common effort to lead the country out of the crisis and transform

---

[1] *Literary History of the United States*, p. 896.

[2] *Ibid.*

[3] B. A. Gilenson, *The Socialist Tradition in U. S. Literature*, Moscow, 1975, p. 64 (in Russian).

American society. At that time the EPIC Plan became widely known. It was worked out by Upton Sinclair, who also tried to implement it.

Sinclair was a prominent figure on the American literary and public scene. As early as World War I Lenin noted his "anti-war manifesto". His evaluation of Sinclair as a socialist went to the heart of his utopianism and highlighted what was typical of many other American socialist-oriented utopians. "Sinclair is a socialist of the emotions, without any theoretical training," Lenin wrote. "He states the issue in 'simple' fashion; incensed by the approach of war, he seeks salvation from it in socialism." Lenin referred to the following statement by Sinclair: "We are told ... that the socialist movement is yet too weak so that we must wait for its evolution. But evolution is working in the hearts of men; we are its instruments, and if we do not struggle, there is no evolution.... A thousand men aglow with faith and determination are stronger than a million grown cautious and respectable; and there is no danger to the socialist movement so great as the danger of becoming an established institution."

This was a typically utopian (and very American) approach: to act proceeding from a sense of justice and ignoring actual circumstances, so as to create the necessary conditions and attain the desired goal. Analyzing the above statement, Lenin wrote: "Sinclair is naïve in his appeal, although fundamentally it is a very correct one; he is naïve because he ignores the development of mass socialism over the last fifty years and the struggle of trends within socialism; he ignores the conditions for the growth of revolutionary action when an objectively revolutionary situation and a revolutionary organization exist. The 'emotional' approach cannot make up for that."[1]

In 1933 and 1934 Sinclair put forward the EPIC (End Poverty in California) Plan of sociopolitical change. Sinclair's political program featured many aspects of Bellamy's and the Nationalists' utopian project. Like Bellamy, Sinclair maintained that workers and industrialists, bank tellers and financiers, landowners and farmhands could be easily converted to his faith by mere persuasion. He also sub-

[1] V. I. Lenin, "British Pacifism and the British Dislike of Theory", in: *Collected Works*, Vol. 21, Moscow, 1980, pp. 263, 264, 265.

scribed to the theory asserting that the opposite social poles suffered equally from the inadequacy of economic relations and should be thus mutually attracted. Sinclair's naive belief was that democracy could be easily saved, the unemployed given jobs and a violent revolution avoided if only all classes set to work in concert.

Sinclair set forth the essence of the plan in the Twelve Principles of EPIC which deserve to be quoted here in full.

"1. God created the natural wealth of the earth for the use of all men, not of a few.

"2. God created men to seek their own welfare, not that of masters.

"3. Private ownership of tools, a basis of freedom when tools are simple, becomes a basis of enslavement when tools are complex.

"3. Autocracy in industry cannot exist alongside democracy in government.

"5. When some men live without working, other men are working without living.

"6. The existence of luxury in the presence of poverty and destitution is contrary to good morals and sound public policy.

"7. The present depression is one of abundace, not of scarcity.

"8. The cause of the trouble is that a small class has the wealth, while the rest have the debts.

"9. It is contrary to common sense that men should starve because they have raised too much food.

"10. The destruction of food or other wealth, or the limitation of production, is economic insanity.

"11. The remedy is to give the workers access to the means of production, and let them produce for themselves, not for others.

"12. This change can be brought about by action of a majority of the people, and that is the American way."[1]

Sinclair pinned great hopes on the establishment of cooperatives to assist in the implementation of the plan, which was also his election platform (he was running for Governor). He maintained that cooperatives could help—first within one state and then throughout the nation—end unemployment, direct production at meeting the require-

[1] *Upton Sinclair Anthology*, p. 339.

ments of working people and, in the final analysis, establish, within the capitalist economic framework, an autonomous cooperative sector—the material basis for a new society. Quite seriously, Sinclair expected the Democratic Party to help him realize the EPIC Plan. It was clear that he remained a "socialist of the emotions" in the 1930s too.

Naturally, the EPIC Plan fell through. But it marked an important stage in the development of the American socialist utopian tradition. It was a concentrated reflection of many major features and principles which had established themselves over the more than a century of utopian socialism in the United States: *optimism*, faith in the possibility of attaining the proclaimed objectives and restructuring society according to socialist principles despite all obstacles; *orientation on the moral impulse* (emotion) as the motive force or at least the original impetus of the socialist process; preference of *common sense* over theory; reliance on *personal practical verification* of the projects proposed; *respect for the law and legal forms of struggle*; advocacy of a *nonviolent*, i.e., essentially *reformist* introduction of socialism; the intention to use the existing "democratic machinery" on condition that it be "made pure"; and the conviction that the struggle for socialism should rely not on the working class but on "a majority of the people".

These aspects, which had featured more or less prominently in every American socialist utopia of any importance in the 19th and the first half of the 20th centuries, reflected distinctive characteristics in the development of the United States and the American working-class and mass democratic movements. In turn, they influenced both these movements and American socialist thought.

Sinclair was the last great utopian socialist in the prewar United States. In the late 1930s and early 1940s utopian socialist ideas lost their former popularity with Americans, to remain on the periphery of the utopian tradition for nearly a quarter of a century.

5. The Technocratic Utopia

A new social utopia type began to take shape in the United States in the 1930s. This was the so-called *techno-*

cratic utopia, which subsequently played an important part in American culture and political thought.

It reflected those changes in America's social consciousness and interpretation of social ideals which had affected first and foremost, part of the industrial bourgeoisie and experts in science and technology and had been caused, on the one hand, by rapid advances in science and technology and the social change they produced and, on the other, by the crisis of laissez-faire liberalism, the transition from free competition capitalism to monopoly capitalism, and the development of the working-class movement.

Aimed at a radical transformation of the bourgeois-democratic institutions of government, which it saw as the only way to save and consolidate capitalism, the technocratic utopia broke with the ideals (and even with the rhetoric) of democratic self-government and proclaimed the ideal of a centralized society built according to the principles of rationality and efficiency. In that world, all life of society, all institutions, relations and values are determined by positivistically interpreted *laws of science* (natural science) and *technology*. The principles which operate in the limited sphere of human activity are extended—fully in the spirit of scientific and technological fetishism—to all spheres of activity, ousting and replacing social laws and thus appearing universal. Man is subordinate to machine; he loses his identity and becomes an easily replaceable cog in a giant bureaucracy which is built with the help of modern science and technology and according to their principles.

The second salient feature of the technocratic utopia—and a logical consequence of the approach described above—is that society is ruled by the masters of technology and by scientists (this is what makes it possible to call this type of utopia "technocratic"). The result is a latter-day version of a utopian society headed by a wise ruler; the only difference is that he is a technocrat, not a humanitarian philosopher.

Despite its break with the democratic tradition of the American utopia and social consciousness, the technocratic utopia attracted many Americans by its promises. In the words of Robert Walker, "technocracy ... appealed to a broad stripe in the national character by arguing that the country should become more—rather than less—productive and at the same time more efficient."[1] V. L. Parrington, Jr. agrees but adds that the technocratic utopia attracted Americans not only by promises of abundance but also by images of a technological world so dear to the American's heart. "This willingness to accept the promise of plenty," he notes, "this faith in the fruits of the machine, is typical of the American dream. For a hundred years and more we have beguiled ourselves with visions of a utopia which was a sort of mechanical heaven where the goods coming off the conveyor belts were always bigger and better and more functional. The Technocrats capitalized on this faith with their romantic and frequently exaggerated promises."[2]

The technocratic utopian projects most popular in the United States of the 1930s were those developed by a group of engineers, economists and architects led by Howard Scott. In late 1931 and early 1932 a group of experts under Howard Scott studied the relationship between technological development and the economy. In April 1932 the Energy Survey of North America was created on the basis of that group. Members of the Survey were soon called "technocrats".[3] Subsequently, the term "technocracy" acquired a broader, more general meaning and was no longer associated directly with Scott's group.

As could be expected, the technocrats disclaimed both the utopian nature of their projects and their involvement in the utopian tradition. Berating "utopians and socialists" for basing their constructs on "*a priori* objectives", "eventual desired human goals", "value orientations" and the like, they did point to the actual substantive features of utopianism. This, however, did not prevent the technocrats themselves from claiming to have found the perfect solution to the problems which had defied authors of projects based on "moral or philosophical constructs", and from advancing a typically utopian model of a "rationally harmonized society". "Between 1933 and 1936 the Scottians, who defined technocracy as a form of social organization, drafted an idealized social system based on their assump-

[1] *The Reform Spirit in America*, p. 216.

[2] V. L. Parrington, Jr., *op. cit.*, p. 203.

[3] Henry Elsner, Jr., *The Technocrats, Prophets of Automation*, Syracuse University Press, 1967, pp. 1-2.

tions about the nature of modern science and society. They could not imagine anyone choosing the austerity of a nonindustrial world; and, they reasoned, having elected to partake of the material benefits of a high-energy civilization, man would have to organize himself around its immutable laws and principles in a way that would maximize efficiency and harmony. Following this reasoning, their thinking led them to construct mentally the most rigorously mechanical society Yankee ingenuity had yet devised."[1]

The technocratic utopia is shot through with the spirit of criticism of American society—its politics, economy and culture. But this criticism is very unlike that offered by romantic or socialist utopians. For all the distinctions that separated them, those utopians criticized society for restrictions on freedom and democracy, suppression of individuality, and absence of the true equality of opportunity. Making references to the Declaration of Independence and the Constitution, they suggested blueprints for a more humane, free, egalitarian and democratic society because, they held, democracy and freedom were indispensable for abundance, prosperity, personal security and meaningful recreation.

The utopian technocrats abandon that type of critical tradition; in their opinion, the root of all evil is not a lack or shortage of democracy but the lack of harmony born of the disbalance between the logic of efficiency and the logic of social relations in conditions of bourgeois democracy. To prevent social chaos and save the nation, it is indispensable to establish harmony between the social structure and the imperatives of science and technology, or, to be more precise, to subordinate the former to the latter. But democracy, the technocrat maintains, is essentially incapable of coping with the task. Decisions have always been and will always be taken by a minority; this is perfectly reasonable, and the important thing is for this minority to be competent and not to engage in pointless games of politics while taking decisions on important matters, not to stage the usual cheap

[1] William E. Akin, *Technocracy and the American Dream. The Technocrat Movement, 1900-1941*, University of California Press, Berkeley, 1977, p. 131.

political shows.

Like the romantic utopian, the technocrat would like to take power out of the hands of politicians and to build a *depoliticized society*. However, unlike the romanticist who sees the meaning of depoliticization in investing each individual with power and thus eliminating centralized government, the technocrat would like to replace political institutions with organizations of scientific and technological experts and hand power over to a *technocratic elite*.

The Scottian technocrats pictured a powerful social hierarchy which Scott defined as the "technate", a single continent-wide corporate structure (Scott held that it should include, aside from the United States, Canada, Mexico and Central America) in which social and production divisions coincided. These "functional divisions" were to comprise industry, services, education, health care, etc. They would also include "certain social and quasi-political sequences to handle research, foreign relations, armed forces and 'social control'."[1]

In Scott's view, the technate was to be a pyramid, with functional divisions at its base, each represented by a director and all directors making up a Continental Control Board which would be responsible for all important decisions bearing on the functioning of the social mechanism as a whole; at the top of the pyramid there would be a Continental Director elected by the members of the Board and responsible for the normal operation of the technate. As a result, instead of an ineffective democracy with its three branches of power and its mechanisms of control and regulation, America would be blessed with an efficient Director relying on a narrow group of top experts.

The technocrats did not deny that their system was not only undemocratic but also inhumane in the sense in which humanism and humanitarianism had been interpreted heretofor. But they held that humanism, freedom and democracy were worthless in a technological civilization since they were not directly indispensable for rationality and efficiency. Why should man, merely a human animal composed of atoms, they argued, need freedom and democracy? Man is "an engine taking potential energy ... and con-

[1] *Ibid.*, p. 138.

verting [it] into heat, work, and body tissue",[1] while freedom and democracy introduce anarchy and arbitrariness into a rational system. They claimed that while the technate, ruled by engineers and scientists, would mean a dictatorship, it would be a dictatorship not of an individual but of science; people could expect only good from it, for this dictatorship would be totally objective and free of any preferences or mistakes.

The technocrats proposed that the technate include a special division dealing with social control to ensure that "human relations be subordinated to efficiency". The institutions regulating human relations on the basis of a subjective approach and "passion", like the "judgment by the twelve good men" were to be abolished; the matters they dealt with were to be decided *by the most impersonal and scientific methods available*.[2]

The technocrats also intended to radically restructure the economy in order to abolish pursuit of profit as the goal of production and change the system of pricing and distribution of material goods. "The cost of any particular commodity," Howard Scott wrote, "would be determined entirely by the energy consumed in the process of its production and delivery to the point of consumption."[3] The plan was to abolish money, replacing it with "energy certificates" each state-employed worker under the "energy contract" would receive. "Such a period of service should not exceed four hours per day, four consecutive days at a shift, and 165 days per year. For a period of about twenty years, from the age of twenty-five to forty-five, this period of service would cover the fulfillment of the energy contract."[4] The technocrats promised to involve all able-bodied people in useful work and thus eliminate unemployment; to ensure equal profits for all, including the technocracy which, Scott assured, would not enjoy any material privileges; and to balance the ratio of production, thus creating a stable and crisis-free economy.

[1] *Technocracy Study Course*, N. Y. Technocracy, Inc., 1934, pp. 105, 117. Quoted in: W. E. Akin, *Technocracy and the American Dream*, p. 134.

[2] Ibid., p. 141.

[3] *Passport to Utopia...*, p. 235.

[4] *Ibid.*, pp. 234-35.

Essentially, *economic and social stability*, a new ideal for the American Utopia, was the prime objective of the technocratic utopians. Besides, they were becoming increasingly convinced that the level of socioeconomic stability was inversely proportionate to the level of political activity and directly dependent on the degree of centralization of government. It was not surprising that the technocrats regarded the army as the most efficient and rational organization and, with the advent of World War II, they called for a nationwide labor conscription.

The concrete forms of the technocratic utopia which it assumed originally in the 1930s proved to be short-lived, but as a distinct type, this utopia took firm root in the mainstream of the American socioutopian tradition.

Ideologically and theoretically, Scott and his colleagues in "Technocracy, Inc." did not invent the technocratic utopia. Its formation was to a high extent influenced by Thorstein Veblen's ideas about rational organization as the substantive basis of social forms capable of ensuring effective functioning of capitalist society against the background of growing social tensions on the global, regional or local scale. Curbing the unruly market and social elements, generally regulating social processes to make them rational and effective, nominating "engineers" to rule society—all these ideas had been formulated, in one form or another, in Veblen's book *The Engineers and the Price System.* Scott's plan was merely an ambitious attempt to project Veblen's ideas onto a specific social situation and on this foundation to build an alternative (given the utopian pluralism of the 1930s) utopia. This utopia was crude, simplistic and theoretically artless (the fate of almost all initial forms of new utopian types). But as a type, it was a sign of the times. The technocratic utopia reflected not only the crisis of the traditional political and economic forms brought on by the changes in the structure and functions of the state and the market which became clear in the mid-1930s. It also reflected the disintegration of the traditional constructs of consciousness which was manifested in the crisis of the liberal ideology and the consequent rift among liberals.

The idea of a direct correlation between bourgeois democracy and the efficiency of the institutions it generated and sanctified, including economic institutions, that matured in the thinking of the third estate and forced its way into the political science and political practice of the 17th-19th-century bourgeois revolutions, that idea emerged as one of the fundamental ideological precepts of 19th-century liberalism. The sociopolitical practice of "mass" society, that is, bourgeois society at the time of imperialism, showed that in the new conditions traditional democracy was no longer capable of ensuring the former efficiency of social institutions.

One of the most important lessons of the technocratic utopia was perhaps the fact that it demonstrated not only the volatile and unstable nature of the links between democracy and efficiency, but also the readiness of many Americans to sacrifice, in certain conditions, the traditional democratic values to the promises of "abundance", "rationality", "efficiency" and "order". On this scale, this was a new development in social consciousness; and it prompted critical remarks from some in the Left to the effect a fascist-type dictatorship could be established in the United States.

From the mid-1930s to the mid-1960s the technocratic utopia consolidated its positions in American culture; naturally, this influenced the status and functions of this utopia in the national perceptions. But, having consolidated its positions, this utopia was never to absorb, let alone eliminate, other types of utopia. On the contrary, the 1960s proved that each new stage in the development of technocratic consciousness triggered a "democratic", romantic or socialist reaction (and this was reflected in the sphere of utopia), simultaneously generating social despair and pessimism expressed in negative utopia and antiutopia.

Chapter III

THE EVOLUTION OF U.S. CAPITALISM
AND THE MODERN AMERICAN UTOPIA

1. The Contradictions of American Society and the Utopian Tradition in the United States

Three factors shaped America's postwar utopian consciousness and utopian tradition.

First and foremost it was the state of U.S. capitalism, its problems and contradictions which made themselves felt amid changes in the roles played by the state and the market as instruments for regulating social affairs. The stronger role of the bourgeois state appropriating, step by step, the functions which used to belong to the free market transformed not only the reproduction mechanism of social consciousness, including utopian consciousness. It also contributed to the change in the attitude to the state (the government) and the market on the part of all social strata and groups. It destroyed the old concepts relating to the limits of the individual's freedom, to his rights and duties and his relations with the state. All this eventually affected concepts of the social ideal and of the ways to attain it. The emergence of the liberal "welfare state" was a phenomenon deserving special mention. Its social policy, aimed at maintaining the necessary social stability by providing the masses with some of the benefits which had been the subject of utopian dreams only recently, inevitably influenced both the content of utopian ideals and the understanding of the ways to achieve them and their limits.

The second factor in the evolution of utopian consciousness in postwar America was the scientific and technological revolution and its social, political and cultural consequences.

It appeared that the advances of science and technology in the late 19th and early 20th centuries gave one every reason to question the future viability of the utopian tradition—at least in scientifically and technologically advanced countries. Technocratic illusions, widespread even beyond the academic and technical communities, gave rise to the belief that, in time, science would make it possible to "cleanse" both theoretical and mass consciousness of all sorts of "metaphysics", including utopian deposits, and to impart to it the clarity of mathematical equations. However, subsequent developments demonstrated that scientific and technological progress not only failed to end the utopian tradition and to prevent the formation of utopian consciousness but also gave them a new creative impetus.

First, advances in science and technology contributed to an inflated evaluation of the powers of modern man and of his ability to restructure the world according to arbitrarily set goals.

Second, the scientific and technological revolution broadened the synchronization gap between the rhythm and dynamics of different sociotemporal flows. Generally, scientific and technological changes often move faster than socioeconomic changes. Today, the gap between these two flows has increased greatly in industrialized capitalist nations—naturally, including the United States. This contributes to the disintegration of the relatively stable and traditional links which took shape at earlier sociohistorical stages and connect individuals, institutions or groups. As a result, social consciousnesss develops the illusory opinion that there are gaps in the sociotemporal continuum and that the subject of a historical process can free himself from the "tyranny" of time and history; this is fertile ground for utopian consciousness and utopian experiments.

And finally, the third and very important factor in the evolution of utopian consciousness was the change in the sociopolitical structure of the world, in the place the United States held in the international community. The emergence of the world socialist system which consolidated its international positions considerably over the postwar decades; the rise of developing nations, many of them militarily and politically nonaligned; the internationalization of social developments and the growing interdependence of nations—all this changed not only the overall objective image of the world but also the picture the Americans had of themselves as a nation, of other nations and of America's future. The notion of "American exceptionalism", deeply ingrained in the nation's political mentality, was undermined. "Today," Daniel Bell wrote in 1975, "the belief in American exceptionalism has vanished with the end of empire, the weakening of power, the loss of faith in the nation's future."[1] Old concepts were to be replaced by new ones; the search for them stimulated the sociological imagination and also utopian consciousness.

American scholars and politicians worked vigorously on models of an alternative world order, an effort sponsored by the Club of Rome in the 1970s. Designed by the organizers and leaders of the club to prevent global conflicts and solve global problems,[2] these models often comprised utopian qualities and could—in the opinion of Ian Clark, for example—be viewed as a new wave of global utopias. Clark maintains that these projects are utopian not because they are impracticable but because of the way in which their reforms are substantiated. He singles out "four interrelated distinguishing marks of utopianism" more or less typical of new world order projects. These are "belief in progress"; a "nondeterministic view of the world", i.e., the faith that man can "push" the historical process in the desired direction; a pervasive rationalism, i.e., the conviction that as soon as decision-makers realize the irrationality of this or that phenomenon, they, guided by the demands of reason, will put an end to them; and "the assumption of a natural harmony of interests" of various nations.[3] While some of Clark's points appear debatable—for example, his interpretation of a "belief in progress" as exclusively utopian—generally, he has correctly grasped the main utopian aspects of the social projects in question.

All the three factors—the state of U.S. capitalism and the exacerbation of its contradictions, the scientific and technological revolution and its social consequences, and the new alignment of world forces and the change in the international position of the United States—were not only

[1] Daniel Bell, "The End of American Exceptionalism" in: *The Public Interest*, No. 41, Fall 1975, p. 197.

[2] See: Aurelio Peccei, *The Human Quality*, Pergamon Press, Oxford, 1977.

[3] Ian Clark, "World Order Reforms and Utopian Thought: A Contemporary Watershed?" in: *The Review of Politics*, Vol. 41, No. 1, January 1979, pp. 98-100.

a powerful impetus to the development of utopian consciousness in the postwar United States. They contributed to a realignment of spheres in which utopian consciousness is formed and to a change in their priorities. They also induced changes in the structure, content and forms of utopian ideals.

In the United States, as in other countries, fiction and social theory, along with art and architecture, long remained the major spheres in which utopian consciousness took shape and socioutopian projects were constructed; authors and thinkers trained in the humanities were particularly active as creators of social utopias. And finally, a distinctly American feature, social utopias were also shaped in the sphere of practical politics and social endeavor. As to science ("science" meaning the natural sciences and technology), for a long time it laid no claim to such a role, just as the natural scientists to the role of creator of social utopias. Of course, scientists could and did author utopias, but they did that as writers, philosophers or politicians. However, as the status of science in the system of knowledge and social production changed, its claims to the construction of a utopian ideal became a well-established trend especially pronounced in the postwar period. This factor considerably changed the composition and the order of priority of the spheres in which utopian consciousness took shape both in the United States and in some other developed capitalist countries.

Suffice it to turn to the utopian novels and short stories current in the United States (many of them are also part of science fiction) to see what prominence their authors accord to science and technology in their utopian constructs and how many of these authors are scientists, engineers or writers with a scientific or technical background. But that is not the most important aspect. The period after World War II highlighted, with much greater clarity than before, the close relationship the utopian approach bore to certain modes of scientific thinking and research. According to Robert Boguslaw, an American sociologist and author of *The New Utopians*, his study of "problems in the analysis and design of contemporary large-scale computer-based command and control systems" has led him to conclude that "modern system designers" are treading well-worn utopian paths. "There is a new breed of utopians afoot, threatening to rush down all the exciting pathways and blind alleys frequented by utopians since the days of Plato. These are the people who are known by such titles as system engineer, computer manufacturer, operations researcher, computer programmer, data processing specialist, or, more simply, system designer."[1]

What brings the "new utopians" close to their forerunners is, first and foremost, the very approach to the solution of their tasks, and also their principal objective. "Utopians are builders," Boguslaw explains, "who reject their contemporary status quos and reach out for new forms within which to shape their wished-for worlds". They are striving to intellectually overcome the limits of the real world and design a perfect system functioning according to a given program. On this both the traditional utopian trained in the humanities and the systems analyst agree. And if so, why cannot the analyst try and assume the role of a social engineer? Why not try and restructure society according to the methods which guide him in the design of "perfect systems"? Such is the logic which today leads many scientists and engineers into the field of the socioutopian quest and underlies the sociomessianic claims of science and technology. Such is the objective basis enabling today's science to function as a major sphere in which social consciousness takes shape and utopian ideals are constructed.

One must, however, note an important difference between the traditional and the new utopians. With regard to building a society free from the flaws and suffering caused by man's imperfection, "the classical utopians tried to achieve this end by populating their social systems with perfect human beings, perfect social structures, perfect situations, or perfect principles". But the new utopians proceed from a different principle. They attempt to perfect their systems not by introducing an improved subject into them but by radically removing this subject (as essentially incapable of attaining the level of perfection necessary for utopia) from the system. "The theoretical and practical solutions they seek," Boguslaw says, "call increasingly for decreases in the number and in the scope of responsibility of human beings within the operating structures of their new

[1] Robert Boguslaw, *The New Utopians. A Study of System Design and Social Change*, Englewood Cliffs, New York, 1965, pp. V, 1.

machined systems."[1]

Since "machined systems" are the object, this approach appears perfectly justified; it does not give rise to any fears with regard to the social consequences which can result from the use of this type of the designing effort. But the social engineering sphere is a different matter. After all, the rationale of the "new utopianism" inevitably arrives at its logical but paradoxical conclusion that there would be no place for man in the world of utopia. It is this paradox, even though not always fully perceived or clearly articulated, which underlies (more about this later) some versions of the contemporary American technocratic utopia. This same paradox, even though perceived at the level of aesthetic intuition, motivates the creation of antiutopias (negative utopias).

Another important change affecting the spheres in which utopian consciousness takes shape and utopian ideals are constructed is the increasing prominence of futurology. As a distinct sphere of activity and of knowledge it lays claim to, futurology differs from utopia above all in the definite nature of the object it seeks to develop and in the way it is developed. The very word "futurology" means that it is oriented on constructing the image of the future, while social utopia aims at producing the image of a desired world the utopian considers to be perfect, a world which can be projected not only into the future but also into the past or into the present, the way it was in More's utopia.

However, the actual status of futurology in the system of spiritual production far from coincides with the status it formally claims. Many futurological forecasts display the typically utopian norm- and value-oriented approach: the projected image is not of the world as it should most probably appear in the future but of a world the futurologist would like to see. This is acknowledged by some of America's foremost futurologists. "Unfortunately," Herman Kahn and B. Bruce-Briggs say in their *Things to Come*, "the field of future studies is thick with normative forecasting masquerading as descriptive. Many prognostications of many distinguished American thinkers are statements of what the author wants to happen, not necessarily what he thinks will happen, and frequently they are a bald pitch for

[1] *Ibid.*, p. 2.

some express policy or program. If done openly and honestly this is a perfectly valid method of political advocacy, with many honorable precedents (such as Bellamy's *Looking Backward*), but it tells us very little about what the future *will* be, except insofar as it is influenced by the ideas and desires of important men today."[1]

In this case futurology not only acts as an external stimulus to the development of utopian consciousness but also becomes the field in which it actually takes shape, while the futurological scenario turns into something like an authorized form of social utopia.

Naturally, the prominence of futurology and science as spheres in which utopian consciousness takes shape does not mean that fiction is losing its traditional role. Many works of fiction published in the United States after the war (including books by brilliant authors such as Kurt Vonnegut, J. D. Salinger, Ray Bradbury, Saul Bellow or John Gardner) have been either wholly utopian or contained built-in utopian fragments and expressed more or less clearly articulated utopian ideals. Nevertheless, one cannot disagree with those experts who maintain that on the whole, modern American—and not only American—fiction plays a secondary role to science, futurology or social theory in the formation of the utopian ideal. Perhaps there is a connection here with the fact that science and futurology have taken over some of the functions which used to be performed by fiction when it introduced the reader to an imagined world, imparting a wealth of data to him in the process.

Things are different with social theory, a traditional sphere for the formation of utopian consciousness. In 1959 Ralf Dahrendorf, a West German sociologist, published his article "Out of Utopia: Toward a Reorientation of Sociological Analysis" in the *American Journal of Sociology*. In it, citing specific examples, he showed that a type of consciousness characteristic of the classical social utopia (for example, of Plato's *Republic*) became widespread in postwar American sociology. "If the immobility of utopia, its isolation in time and space, the absence of conflict and disruptive processes, is a product of poetic imagination divorced from the commonplaces of reality," was Dahren-

[1] Herman Kahn, B. Bruce-Briggs, *Things to Come. Thinking About the Seventies and Eighties*, Macmillan, New York, 1972, p. 246.

dorf's rhetorical question, "how is it that so much of recent sociological theory has been based on exactly these assumptions and has, in fact, consistently operated with a utopian model of society."[1]

The peculiarity of sociological theory Dahrendorf classified as social utopia was that it did not construct any new social ideals which would lead beyond the existing society because the latter was itself described as the limit. This was what enabled Dahrendorf to charge Talcott Parsons and his structural functionalist followers with utopianism.

Indeed, when a living, evolving and therefore conflicting society is described as free of contradictions or conflicts, as based on a universal consensus with regard to the fundamental values of life and culture, as the epitome of sociopolitical harmony and the preordained development goal attained, it essentially turns into a realized utopian ideal and sociological theory, into a sphere in which such ideals are constructed.

The subsequent development of American sociology proved that the phenomenon described by Dahrendorf was not something accidental. Dahrendorf recorded the trend (which later proved to be quite enduring) toward increased integration of value-oriented elements into sociological theory and toward a greater role of sociology and political science in the shaping of the socioutopian ideal.

This does not at all mean that all modern American sociological theories can be invariably classified as utopias in the strict sense of the world. As a rule, such theories present a variety of dimensions—both in terms of the way the existing society is described and in terms of how the social ideal is posited. They can be compared to a layer cake, each layer expressing a different approach, a different attitude of the author to social reality, each serving the solution of different tasks. On the one hand, these theories record certain actual phenomena and trends in the evolution of American society. But on the other, their authors very often introduce into them, whether consciously or not, arbitrary constructs (running counter to the objective trends of social development) and arbitrarily posited utopian ideals.

[1] *Utopia*, Ed. by George Kateb, Atherton Press, New York, 1971, p. 108.

As a result, some theories combine the scientific approach with the utopian, the two "layers" are so closely intertwined as to make it difficult to tell them apart.

Finally, there is one more sphere in which, as before, utopian consciousness takes form and utopian ideals are constructed, and that sphere is everyday life and sociopolitcal practice.

The average American[1] is not as simple a figure as he might appear at first glance, especially to an outside observer. The man in the street cannot be pictured as a "one-dimensional", rational individual guided exclusively by considerations of practical gain and devoid of romantic impulses or utopian yearnings. For all their practicality, Americans have always tended to entertain exaggerated expectations and to lay exaggerated claims which contribute to the emergence of a utopian world view. Postwar developments only enhanced these qualities. The increasing complexity of the social fabric, the covert and therefore largely mysterious nature of the new social relations, the deliberate efforts of the ruling class to arrange mass consciousness in a certain way with the help of the ramified mass media network, the comparatively favorable economic situation which existed in the United States at least up to the mid-1970s—all this was fertile soil for the spread of utopian consciousness on a mass scale. One might add that the comparatively rapid rise in the prosperity of a large part of "white America" in the 1950s and 1960s, the relative leveling-out of the structure of requirements, the consumption and the value orientations of many middle-class Americans led the masses to the illusion that the ideals of democracy, freedom, equality, abundance and the like, sanctified by the official utopia, were actually attainable.

Discussing the typically American utopian notions, the sociologist Irving Kristol traces them, among other things, to the generous promises politicians and ideologists freely offer to the public—promises which this very public realizes to be demagogic but which have become part of the

___

[1] The terms "average American" and "man in the street" do not denote here a type of individual or social group but one of the many social roles virtually every member of society involuntarily plays in everyday life.

sociopolitical decorum the average man considers indispensable for "normal" politics.

Here one should note, however, that utopian illusions which capture the imagination of the masses are like a delayed-action fuse. American history has proved repeatedly that they can stimulate mass movements, whether secular or religious, social or political, "white" or "Black". This was what happened in the 1960s and 1970s, when mass movements in which the New Left played an important part swept the country. In turn, these movements gave a powerful impetus to the development of the utopian imagination and generated numerous utopian notions.

The postwar changes in the American utopian tradition were by no means confined to the composition and order of priority of the spheres in which utopian consciousness germinated. They also affected the content of utopian ideals and the types of utopia the latter encouraged. But a direct analysis of these types should be preceded by a few words about certain features which all these types shared and which recorded the new situation postwar American society found itself in.

Today, few American authors would be prepared to offer a utopia aimed at a radical transformation of the existing society and setting radically new goals and tasks for it. Of course, this does not mean that the utopian ideal is now deduced from the actual trends of historical development. But, remaining in an arbitrary position vis-à-vis these trends, it is becoming more down-to-earth and moderate. Several Western sociologists have noted this. "Utopia," Daniel Bell wrote in *The Coming of the Post-Industrial Society*, "has always been conceived as a design of harmony and perfection in the relations between men. In the wisdom of the ancients, Utopia was a fruitful impossibility, a conception of the desirable which man should always strive to attain but which, in the nature of things, could not be achieved. And yet, by its very idea, Utopia would serve as a standard of judgement on men, an ideal by which to measure the real. The modern *hubris* has sought to cross that gap and embody the ideal in the real; and in the effort the perspective of the ideal has become diminished and the idea of Utopia has become tarnished."[1]

[1] Daniel Bell, *The Coming of the Post-Industrial Society. A Venture in Social Forecasting*, Heinemann, London, 1974, pp. 488-89.

Returning to this question in his book *The Cultural Contradictions of Capitalism*, Bell seeks to establish a connection between, on the one hand, utopia's loss of its transcendental nature and, on the other, the weakening in the positions of religion and the positivist approach to social reality. "Modern societies have substituted utopia for religion—utopia not as a transcendental ideal, but one to be realized through history (progress, rationality, science) with the nutrients of technology and the midwifery of revolution."[1]

The trend toward a more *down-to-earth (no longer absolute)* utopian ideal has been caused by several factors simultaneously. These include the influence of positivist philosophy and the fear that orientation on transcendental values poses a real threat of a "tyranny of the idea", i.e., an overriding passion to implement a utopian idea with the logic of a computer and the dedication of a grand inquisitor, no matter what obstacles objective conditions place in the path of the effort. But to my mind, the prime cause behind the trend making the ideal of the modern American utopia no longer absolute is that its creators lack a maximum ideal. In most utopias it has been replaced by what might be called a preference ideal, since it is aimed at the best of what is possible within the framework of existing civilization. This sort of utopia posits the parameters of the imagined society in accordance with the utopian's views of the problems contemporary capitalism is to solve to ensure its improvement and survival. And, contrary to what Bell asserts, most modern American utopians reject social revolution as a means of practical realization of the proclaimed utopian ideal.

Another feature many modern utopias share is that they are open to alternative. Past utopias were usually dominated by principles which completely ruled out any alternative solutions. A utopian project used to describe literally every single aspect of life in a perfect society, subject, as a rule, to constant petty regulation. Suffice it to recall Charles Fourier who considered it his duty to envisage, pedantically describe and, if possible, also substantiate metaphysically all aspects of life in a utopian community. Viewed against

[1] D. Bell, *The Cultural Contradictions of Capitalism*, Basic Books, New York, 1976, p. 28.

this background, many modern utopias—naturally, not all—appear as some sort of fragmentary essays since they present merely a general outline and general principles of human activity and contain no detailed regulation, rigid order or gradation. In other words, modern utopia provides its citizens with a greater degree of free will and greater opportunities for their personal initiative.

It is interesting to note that H. G. Wells stressed the need for such utopias as far back as the early 1900s. "The Modern Utopia," he wrote in 1905, "must be not static but kinetic, must shape not as a permanent state but as a hopeful stage, leading to a long ascent of stages.... We build now not citadels but ships of state."[1]

However, it took some time for utopians to begin switching from citadels to ships. And this step, like the trend to deprive the utopian ideal of its absolute nature, was not so much a consequence of pure speculation as a practical reaction—whether conscious or unconscious—to the lessons of 20th-century social history.

Clearly, historical experience is not the only factor shaping the distinct image of modern utopia. If one traces the evolution of utopian thought over several centuries, it becomes obvious that utopia has always responded to developments in the sphere of scientific knowledge. Influenced, directly or indirectly, by the more advanced or fashionable sciences of its time, utopia reflected that influence in the structure of its own values, images, language—in short, in the content of the social ideal and in the views of how it should be attained. Several students of the problem (in particular, Fred Manuel) have noted that while utopian consciousness in the 18th and early 19th centuries was influenced by the then rapidly advancing physical sciences, and the Newtonian view of the world was a model for Saint-Simon and Fourier, with the advent of the Darwinian theory, the 20th-century progress of psychology and especially the emergence of Freudianism, utopia underwent a more or less thorough restructuring. As a result, modern utopia lays a much greater emphasis than its forerunners on man's inner world and psychology because it maintains that a society in which people feel happy and not one in which there are

[1] H. G. Wells, *A Modern Utopia*, Charles Scribner's Sons, New York, 1907, p. 5.

objective conditions for happiness is the desired (and perfect) society.

Besides, the interest modern utopia displays in man's inner world and socially determined feelings is subjectively linked to those complex processes which occurred in American culture over the postwar decades—from the intellectuals' penchant for oversimplified interpretations of existentialism to the emergence of a counterculture in the 1960s.

Obviously, the American utopia's new features which reflected the spirit of the times and the changes in human needs, could not fail to alter the systems and major parameters of its types. But they were also unable to destroy its age-old traditional aspects. All the types of utopia described above either continue to exist in modern American society, albeit in modified form, or, having lost their independent status, become an important integral part of other types.

2. The Technocratic Utopia

The *technocratic utopia* consolidated its positions considerably and moved to the foreground in the postwar years. Retaining the principles, ideals and orientations formulated by Veblen, Scott and their followers half a century ago, modern technocratic utopians have adjusted and complemented them, added subtle theoretical touches, and geared them to the interests, orientations and expectations of those rather large groups which connect the survival of bourgeois civilization with scientific and technological progress, with the use of its advances to stabilize the existing social relations and with stronger positions of the social stratum of professionals often described as the technostructure.

Utopian elements are visible in the sociological theories Daniel Bell, Zbigniew Brzezinski and John Kenneth Galbraith formulated in the 1960s and 1970s ("industrial society", "post-industrial state", "technetronic society"). A utopian spirit is present in the works of Stuart Chase, the dean of American technocracy and author of *The Tragedy of Waste* (1925) and *The Most Probable World* (1968), a number of prominent futurologists such as Herman Kahn, Norbert Wiener, B. Bruce-Briggs and several outstanding scientists such as Burrhus Skinner.

It goes without saying the technocratic utopians' concepts of the social ideal or of the ways to establish the utopian society differ more or less substantially, depending on the authors' political stand, the range of their intellectual grasp, the extent of their personal experience and on their specialization in this or that science. Still, these concepts share a number of common features, and this makes it possible to classify them as a single trend in modern utopia.

Stability is central to the hierarchy of values making up the composite ideal of the modern technocratic utopia. This was expressed with the utmost clarity in a small but exhaustive article entitled "A Modest Utopia" and published by Stuart Chase in 1975. Noting that modern American (and not only American) society faces difficult problems such as the arms race, the energy crisis, unemployment, pollution, dwindling natural resources, etc., Chase concludes that, given all this, mankind can find salvation only in utopia viewed as a planetwide system established by purposeful action based on rationality and efficiency.[1] He quotes John Platt: "The world is now too dangerous for anything less than Utopia."[2] "The logic of the situation, whatever the politics," Chase writes, "runs increasingly in the direction of a single civilization where a steady-state condition is dominant.... The idea of a world state has been discussed for centuries, but the steady-state society is a relatively new concept,"[3] yet its outlines, Chase holds, can already be imagined.

First and foremost, a steady-state society stabilizes population growth, its rate gradually diminishing to zero; this, the author of the project asserts, invoking Aldous Huxley's ideas, is the key to the solution of all other problems. "A steady-state society, thus stabilized, can and should assure adequate living for every human being—food, shelter, education, health protection (though not a car and a color TV). This should go a long way toward stabilizing the human family. It should go a long way toward providing useful work for all. With slums abolished and meaningful occupation developed, the crime rate should drop, and juvenile delinquency all but disappear. One good working def-

[1] *The Futurist*, Vol. IX, No. 5, October 1975, pp. 249-50.
[2] *Ibid.*, p. 252.
[3] *Ibid.*, p. 250.

inition of Utopia might be a place where everyone feels he has an important role. The steady-state society should make considerable progress in that direction.

"It would demand, of course, the conservation of the ecosphere and the biosphere; the balance of nature respected and held firmly at par.

"War would have to be disallowed, perhaps with a planetary guard in command of all nuclear, chemical, biological, and conventional weapons." Energy and material resources would be regulated, transport problems solved and so on and so forth—and all this given strong centralized government. "The planet will be administered, one might guess, by a consortium of functional Planning Authorities in charge of vital material resources; of the oceans with their riches and fragile food chains; of international pollution abatement; of satellites and global communication, trade routes, and international finance. Gold will be strictly for dentists and jewellers. Nations will continue to control local affairs insofar as they are not in conflict with steady-state priorities."[1]

Essentially, there is nothing novel in Chase's project, but it deserves to be mentioned because it lays such great emphasis on the ideal of stability—a typical (although not always clearly articulated) feature of the modern technocratic utopia.

True, classical utopian projects, too, often presented society as stable. But that was the stability of harmony, of the absolute, of a society which had reached the uppermost limits of perfection. The modern technocratic utopia is another matter. Here, the yearning for stability is dictated not only by the realization that Earth's resources are finite but also by the desire to preserve a certain state of society, albeit quite far—and some utopians admit that—from perfection. This is the stability of a system threatened by disintegration, stability as a means of survival. John Kenneth Galbraith has once remarked that "for any organization, as for any organism, the goal or objective that has a natural assumption of preeminence is the organization's own survival."[2] However, the meaning of self-preserva-

[1] *Ibid.*, p. 252.

[2] John Kenneth Galbraith, *The New Industrial State*, Houghton Mifflin Co., Boston, 1969, p. 167.

tion to a system (and its realization by the latter) is different at different stages. Most frequently, self-preservation becomes a utopian ideal at the stage of disintegration, when survival becomes the system's highest goal—a rule demonstrated by Plato and confirmed by many politicians, sociologists and natural scientists today.

The technocratic utopia does not rule out certain social changes. Moreover, it insists on them (and here it cannot be accused of being static) since it is by partial changes from within that the desired stability is deemed to be made possible. But, unlike Plato, whose stability was based on "justice", today's utopian technocrat connects stability with organization based on rationality and efficiency. As to "justice", its specific expression is the principle of meritocracy— each man remunerated according to his "merit".[1]

Meritocracy does provide all citizens with a certain minimum of benefits which, the technocrat holds, will be high enough for his utopian society to be called a "welfare state". True, the Club of Rome reports, especially *Limits to Growth*, the response they generated and, most importantly, the economic difficulties the United States encountered in the 1970s and 1980s, did dampen the technocrat's optimism somewhat. Nevertheless, the "welfare state" ideal is firmly established as part of the technocratic utopia which promises a guaranteed minimum of profit, a certain measure of personal security, a considerable easing of human labor, as well as recreation.

However, operating beyond the universal guaranteed minimum is the principle that the evaluation of the individual and the remuneration society accords him differ depending on his merit and his intellect determined by special tests.

In the classical utopia, the principle of justice underlay the authority of the philosopher-prince as legitimate; similarly, the modern technocratic utopia uses the principle of meritocracy to justify the claims to power made by the scientist and the engineer. Bell maintains that in a "post-industrial society" they should occupy the same place the businessman, and the industrial manager held in "industrial society".

[1] For principles of meritocracy, see Daniel Bell, *The Coming of Post-Industrial Society*.

Today's utopian technocrat does not aim directly at eliminating the existing institutions of power. But he would like to transfer control over them from professional politicians and businessmen to experts who would restructure these institutions to meet the needs of science and technology, possibly making them more rigid and centralized.

In a "scientifically managed" utopia, where organization dominates man, determining all the major parameters of his activity, the limits to individual freedom are set strictly functionally. Freedom is not an end, not a condition for the development and existence of a harmonious personality but only a means of maintaining society's rational and effective functioning and stability. In this respect, the utopian technocrats follow in the footsteps of Howard Scott; the only difference is that they are less cynical and promise more material benefits in exchange for freedom.

Kahn and Bruce-Briggs claim that in a "post-industrial society" all men will live at about the level enjoyed by the high-income groups, like "the managers and professionals" in the 1970s. "They have very large homes filled with gadgets, and often have two homes, one just for vacations. They have day servants, once or twice a week, but we do not need them in our post-industrial society—there have long been dreams of household robots or trained simians, and why not? ... They travel frequently both on business and pleasure, penetrating all parts of the globe. When not dieting they eat well, whether the cosmopolitan food of the East or the grade A beefstakes of the West. They have two or more cars, a Cadillac or a Mercedes-Benz, a station wagon, and a sports car for the kids. Many of them have planes or boats. Their children go to graduate school and do not start work until they damn well like it, and the parents do not seem to mind. Of course, they may have the mild alcoholism of too many martinis, neurotic wives popping pills, junior who is wild and undisciplined, and little Sally who is sleeping around."[1]

This cozy picture, drawn with good-natured irony, offers little explanation of the way a utopian society based on technocratic principles may function. But it is possible to visit such a society—through the good offices of B. F. Skinner, prominent American psychologist, sociologist

[1] Herman Kahn, B. Bruce-Briggs, *op. cit.*, pp. 229-30.

and Harvard professor. His utopian novel *Walden Two*, published back in 1948, has long earned the status of a classic and his views are regarded as a classical expression of modern technocratic ideology in its behaviorist version.

"*Walden Two* is, of course, science fiction," Skinner wrote many years later. "I was not saying, 'This is the way it should be.' I was simply describing one possible culture designed on behavioral principles. The book does not seem to me to have been too bad a guess. It was written nearly thirty years ago and seems to me more relevant than ever."[1]

The novel is about an imagined utopian community of some one thousand members. One thousand healthy, cheerful, happy and content people living—the author stresses this—not on a desert island and not in the 21st century but in postwar America with all its problems and contradictions.

This is especially important to Skinner who, in the late 1940s, arrived at the conclusion proclaimed (though for entirely different reasons) by the left radicals many years later: utopia has ceased to exist; what used to be considered utopian is perfectly possible today. "The Good Life is waiting for us—here and now," exclaimes Frazier, the community's founder. "I almost fancied I heard a Salvation Army drum throbbing in the distance.... At this very moment we have the necessary techniques, both material and psychological, to create a full and satisfying life for everyone."[2]

Later we heard similar assertions from "critical" philosophers and sociologists who immediately added, however, that while the necessary technical prerequisites were already available, the political conditions for realizing the utopia were not yet ready. But Skinner does not recognize these obstacles. The traditional opinion that people can build a perfect society through political transformation is a fallacy, asserts Skinner's Frazier. "Political action was of no use in building a better world, and men of good will had better turn to other measures as soon as possible".[3] These measures are science, specifically psychology, or, to be more

---

[1] *The American Political Science Review,* Vol. LXIX, March 1975, p. 228.

[2] B. F. Skinner, *Walden Two*, Macmillan, Toronto, 1970, p. 193.

[3] *Ibid.*, p. 14.

precise, behaviorism. A "technology of behavior" based on behavioral principles, Skinner maintains, can achieve that which politics cannot ensure.

Frazier (Skinner) goes on to explain that the behavioral principle of "positive reinforcement" makes it possible easily to solve problems which have plagued utopians for centuries. "The things that can happen to us fall into three classes. To some things we are indifferent. Other things we like—we want them to happen, and we take steps to make them happen again. Still other things we don't like—we don't want them to happen and we take steps to get rid of them or keep them from happening again.... If it's in our power to create any of the situations which a person likes or to remove any situation he doesn't like, we can control his behavior. When he behaves as we want him to behave, we simply create a situation he likes, or remove one he doesn't like. As a result, the probability that he will behave that way again goes up, which is what we want. Technically it's called 'positive reinforcement'."[1]

This "positive reinforcement" is what shapes life in Walden Two. There is no external coercion in the community— neither an army nor a police nor courts nor prisons nor overseers. There is a code of conduct drawn up on the basis of "positive reinforcement" and gladly observed by all members of the community. But the code exists mostly for newcomers. Those born in the community are handled by psychologists from the moment of their birth; these experts bring them up fully in accordance with "behavioral engineering" principles, taking care that now and later the children *not only do what they like but also like only what should be liked.* Here, the last word belongs to "behavioral engineers" making up a Board of Planners. "Our only government is a Board of Planners," Frazier explains. "The name goes back to the days when Walden Two existed only on paper. There are six Planners, usually three men and three women.... The Planners are charged with the success of the community. They make policies, review the work of the Managers, keep an eye on the state of the nation in general. They also have certain judicial functions."[2] Aside from the Planners and Managers who are

[1] *Ibid.*, pp. 259-60.
[2] *Ibid.*, p. 54.

responsible for the operation of functional divisions and services, the community also includes scientists who conduct experimental research and issue recommendations to "behavioral engineers".

Neither rank-and-file community members nor even scientists, Frazier adds, have any say in determining the composition of the Boards of Planners and Managers, but that does not bother them at all—the important thing is that they are happy. When Frazier's opponents charge that there is neither freedom nor democracy in his utopian community, he calmly agrees.

More than 20 years after *Walden Two* Skinner published a book that scandalized the academic (and not only the academic) community. The book, entitled *Beyond the Freedom and Dignity*, claimed that the concepts of freedom and human dignity were obsolete and fictitious. But this view, expressed by Skinner directly and openly in 1971, had long been expounded by Frazier, his alter ego, in virtually the same language.

No, there is no democracy in Frazier's community—because it is not needed. Democracy "isn't, and can't be, the best form of government, because it's based on a scientifically invalid conception of man".[1] No, there is no freedom—because it is not needed either. "Dictatorship and freedom—predestination and free will.... What are these but pseudoquestions of linguistic origin?"[2] Frazier proudly declares that "we can achieve a sort of control under which the controlled, though they are following a code much more scrupulously than was ever the case under the old system, nevertheless *fell free*. They are doing what they want to do, not what they are forced to do.... By a careful cultural design, we control not the final behavior, but the *inclination* to behave—the motives, the desires, the wishes. The curious thing is that in that case the *question of freedom never arises*."[3] It does not because "we see to it that they will want to do precisely the things which are best for themselves and the community".[4]

Soon after it appeared, *Walden Two* was attacked by pub-

[1] *Ibid.*, p. 273.
[2] *Ibid.*, p. 297.
[3] *Ibid.*, p. 262.
[4] *Ibid.*, p. 297.

lic figures, authors and scientists, some calling Skinner a fascist. In all probability, Skinner expected such accusations: in his novel, Frazier's opponents call him a fascist, to which he replies that he is neither a fascist nor a democrat. The attacks came not only from the left but also from the right wing, from the opponents of scientism who accused the author of *Walden Two* of unwarranted denigration of American democracy.

It is indeed obvious that Skinner's criticism of democracy, freedom and other "obsolete" values sometimes closely resembles the curses the Nazis used to heap on them. Skinner, of course, is no fascist. He is one of those gifted but socially narrow-minded professionals of the positivistic type who see science, especially their own discipline, as a cure-all and man as an aggregate of "scientifically" verifiable processes and phenomena. They naively believe that in a society ruled by the laws of physics, biology and other natural sciences, politics would be useless, social conflicts would be eliminated at one stroke and complete harmony would be established. They either ignore or dismiss as "metaphysics" the fact that society cannot be governed by the laws operating in this or that sphere of nature, that man cannot be reduced to the level of an animal or a machine.

A closer look at Skinner's community shows that its citizens are not really people but rather beings resembling robots. The all-round personality, the dream of thinkers of the past, has no place in his utopia. The Procrustean logic of "behavioral engineering" cannot accommodate a harmonious and free individual. A model member of Skinner's community is not only depersonalized but also dehumanized. Man is human only as long as he retains (and realizes through his activity) a connection with culture as a concentrated expression of the experience of the preceding generations, with objects representing their creative efforts, with history. This connection colors man's reaction to various stimuli. Man does not simply respond automatically to external orders, his reaction is adjusted by culture (in this or that form), specifically by ethics and the knowledge of the past—his own and his own nation's. Incidentally, fascism took this into account and declared war on culture, trying to produce a depersonalized man ignorant of his own history and acting like an automaton.

Essentially, Skinner suggests the same thing, the only difference being that the individual would receive his orders not from a drill sergeant but from the "psychologist"—that is, a well-balanced program of behavior—inside him. No wonder that *Walden Two* distrusts history which may, all of a sudden, disrupt the path from "stimulus" to "reaction". It is perfectly possible that, could Skinner realize his project on a large scale, the result would be an updated and improved version of Huxley's *Brave New World*. And should the Planners (who are supposed to operate virtually uncontrolled) include people not only dictatorially but also fascistically minded, the "happy" utopia would turn into a concentration camp. In 1967 a group of young people established the Twin Oaks community which, as originally conceived, was to be based on the principles described in *Walden Two*. However, life forced Twin Oaks to alter these principles so drastically that this experiment can be regarded as a practical refutation of Skinner's project.[1]

And yet, the community built to Skinner's blueprint has one quality that the utopian technocrat finds valuable—it guarantees the survival of the whole. At any rate, he has stated repeatedly that "survival of Western civilization" is his prime objective. This is an important admission in that it records the change in the priority of ideals typical of many modern Western utopians. Their goal is not a perfect society but preservation of the existing society (even though in a somewhat modified form).

Thus the modern technocratic utopia opens no new humanitarian vistas and promises essentially nothing beyond what the "welfare state" promises and, apparently, can provide. At the same time it demonstrates that the "non-political" dictatorship of science (and scientists)—should it, by some miracle, be established—would be no more humanitarian and, ironically, no more efficient than the currently existing dictatorship of the monopoly bourgeoisie which uses technocrats but gives them only limited leeway. As for the efficiency of social system (from a small group to society as a whole), it depends not only on rational organization but also on the degree to which the acting individuals realize their personal potential.

[1] See: Kathleen Kinkade, *A Walden Two Experiment; The First Five Years of Twin Oaks Community*, Morrow, New York, 1973.

3. The Utopia of a "Traditional" America

Antipodal to the technocratic utopia are projects which can be described either as utopias of a "traditional" America (since their authors very often refer to the libertarian tradition) or as "anarchic capitalist" utopias (since they are oriented on the corresponding social ideal).

The works of practically all prominent theoreticians of American conservative thought, particularly such as Ludwig von Mises or Richard Weaver, feature aspects of the social ideal posited in the anarchic capitalist utopia. But the most consistent, clear and up-to-date exposition of this type of utopia can be found in *Anarchy, State and Utopia*, a book by Robert Nozick, professor of philosophy at Harvard University.[1]

"With reluctance," writes Nozick, "I found myself becoming convinced of (as they are now often called) libertarian views, due to various consideration and arguments."[2] Taking a libertarian position, Nozick assails modern bourgeois society for its interference not only in the economy but also in virtually all other spheres of activity. He advocates a "free" and "just" community of self-sufficient individuals. It is a community in which social relations would be regulated by free market mechanisms but which would be cleansed of structures that demolish an actual market society and in which there would be no independent sphere of political activity and, consequently, no organized political forces capable of destroying that society from within.

And so, while the anarchic capitalist utopia appeals to the past and orients its ideal on a definite historical system of social relations, it proves to be as artificial as any other utopia. Moreover, a closer look shows that it shares certain features with the very technocratic utopia it rejects.

Indeed, despite their distinctions in terms of many parameters, to say nothing of the differences in the social status and political potential of the forces behind each of the two types, both the technocratic and the libertarian utopias are based on one and the same paradox: both ideal-

[1] Robert Nozick, *Anarchy, State, and Utopia*, Basic Books, New York, 1974.

[2] *Ibid.*, p. IX.

ize a society which, while remaining capitalist, would become increasingly depoliticized—that is, where political mechanisms for regulating social processes would be replaced with nonpolitical ones and from where politics as an independent sphere of activity would be eliminated. The only difference is that in the technocratic utopia, political institutions and relations are replaced by scientific and technological, while in the libertarian—by economic ones.

The ideal society imagined by the advocate of anarchic capitalism is based on private property in the means of production. However, unlike other American utopias where it is also present as an institution, in the anarchic capitalist utopia it plays a special role, functioning, the way it once did in the utopias of a farmers' America, as the metaphysical basis of freedom. An individual's private property is his alter ego, the only real basis of existence. And what is meant here is not big corporate property but petty property whose links with the individual are not mediated by any bureaucratic institutions.

By proclaiming a community of petty producers as its social ideal, the anarchic capitalist utopia appears to continue certain traditional aspects of the utopia of a farmers' America. At the same time, there is a substantial difference between the two. The utopia of a farmers' America, especially in its Jeffersonian version, does not consider private property as a natural right, while the anarchic utopian places it alongside inalienable "natural" rights such as life and freedom.

The anarchic capitalist utopia is the petty proprietor's spontaneous response to the growing role and functions of the capitalist state and its bureaucracy, to the encroachment of the monopolies and the rise of their power, and to the increasing political activity of working people which the petty bourgeoisie sees as a latent threat to the very institution of private property. This reaction determines the attitude of the advocate of anarchic capitalism to the state and the market as universal antagonistic mechanisms of social regulation.

In the libertarian's utopia, the state plays a "minimal" role; it is only a "minimal state". Robert Nozick holds that only "a minimal state, limited to the narrow functions of protection against force, theft, fraud, enforcement of contracts and so on, is justified."[1] Any state which assumes additional functions, for example, of coercing some citizens (through the use of more or less complex mechanisms) to assist others, or of forcing them to desist from certain actions for the sake of their own welfare, the anarchic capitalist maintains, encroaches on the individual's right to take autonomous decisions with regard to his own behavior and should therefore be considered a morally unjustified political dictatorship. Nozick emphasizes that man cannot be subjected to violence by the state; the state's only duty is to ensure the greatest possible freedom for the individual. The state should respect the right of each to shape his life as he pleases and to enter into free cooperation with others who enjoy the same rights.[2]

The "minimal state" resembles Jefferson's limited state only superficially but differs from it in essence. Jefferson determined the extent and functions of the state proceeding from the state's objective—realizing the will and ensuring the welfare of the "productive majority". He believed that it is this will and this welfare that were to shape the state's parameters in the final count. The anarchic capitalist approaches this question from a totally different angle, maintaining that a "minimal state" can and should realize this will and ensure this welfare in any conditions, especially today. But this is an arbitrary presumption, born of the anarchic utopian's critical attitude toward the "welfare state" which he correctly sees as a "mass" state. While taking care of the individual to a certain degree, it limits his freedom and his right to organize his life as he sees fit.

The utopian "minimal state" is not a projection of the Jeffersonian state into today's world; it is a result of the contradictions current in American society as seen by the petty proprietor, oppressed by the state and the monopolies. Essentially it is a fictitious "antiwelfare" state, an artificial construct, a utopia, and quite unlike the Jeffersonian state which was a natural product of the historical conditions obtaining in the late 18th and early 19th centuries.

The anarchic utopian appeals to the free market, picturing it as the ideal mechanism for social regulation. He holds that market relations are capable of discharging the

[1] *Ibid.*
[2] *Ibid.*, p. 334.

function the state is trying to usurp—ensuring equality of opportunity for each and giving everyone his due. Like the technocrat (here one utopia is again drawing close to another), he would like to stabilize the social structure because stability is a substantive feature of his social ideal. Unlike the technocrat, however, the anarchic utopian connects social stability with the preservation of individual freedom (he proclaims it as a major value)—inasmuch as the self-regulating market can ensure it. His ideal is the individual who is not subject to tutelage and, consequently, to uniformity (for any mass tutelage calls for uniformity and standardization as its preconditions) and who is naturally exercising his self-determination within the "minimal state". Let each man live as he wants, the anarchic utopian says; the state must not force anyone to accept any uniform pattern. "Wittgenstein, Elizabeth Taylor, Bertrand Russell, Thomas Merton, Yogi Berra, Allen Ginsburg, Harry Wolfson, Thoreau, Casey Stengel, The Lubavitcher Rebbe, Picasso, Moses, Einstein, Hugh Heffner, Socrates, Henry Ford, Lenny Bruce, Baba Ram Dass, Gandhi, Sir Edmund Hillary, Raymond Lubitz, Buddha, Frank Sinatra, Columbus, Freud, Norman Mailer, Ayn Rand, Baron Rothschild, Ted Williams, Thomas Edison, H. L. Mencken, Thomas Jefferson, Ralph Ellison, Bobby Fischer, Emma Goldman, Peter Kropotkin, you, and your parents. Is there really *one* kind of life which is best for each of these people? Imagine all of them living in any utopia you've ever seen described in detail. Try to describe the society which would be best for all of these persons to live in. Would it be agricultural or urban? Of great material luxury or of austerity with basic needs satisfied? What would relations between the sexes be like? Would there be any institution similar to marriage?... Would there be private property?... Would there be one, many, any religion?"[1]

After asking a dozen more similar questions, Nozick concludes that there can be no single answer, just as there can be no single best society in which not only the people listed in the quotation but also any other combination of individuals could be happy. Therefore, the anarchic capitalist believes, it is not only pointless but even harmful to strive for the establishment of any uniform community,

[1] Robert Nozick, *op. cit.*, pp. 310-11.

the age-old dream of utopians.

One must admit that Nozick deals a heavy blow to the traditional utopian opinion that there can be an absolute and "best" type of utopian society equally acceptable to all, that a uniform and "best" way of life in a utopia can be discovered. These are truly illusory notions repeatedly rejected by the founders of scientific socialism who resolutely opposed any attempts to "bless" humanity with all sorts of universal projects. Nozick himself claims that there is a way out, but that it lies outside the traditional mainstream of the utopian quest. "Utopia will consist of utopias, of many different and divergent communities in which people lead different kinds of lives under different institutions.... Utopia is a framework for utopias, a place where people are at liberty to join together voluntarily to pursue and attempt to realize their own vision of the good life in the ideal community but where no one can *impose* his own utopian vision upon others.... Utopia is a meta-utopia: the environment in which utopian experiments may be tried out; the environment in which people are free to do their own thing; the environment which must, to a great extent, be realized first if more particular utopian visions are to be realized stably."[1]

In Nozick's view, let people live in communities, let these communities be many, let them be based on diverse material and spiritual principles, including socialist ones; let people choose a community after their own heart, let them switch from community to community if they want; let those who cannot find anything they like create communities of their own, geared to their own conceptions of the best possible world; but let no one be in anyone's way. And let life itself—or rather, not life but "meta-utopia", the "environment", the "framework" equivalent, Nozick emphasizes, to the "minimal state"—determine which community is to survive and develop and which is to perish. In the final analysis, the "minimal state" itself, a market of utopias, an auction of utopias, is the true utopia.

"Though the framework is libertarian and laissez-faire, individual communities within it need not be, and perhaps no community within it will choose to be so. Thus, the characteristics of the framework need not pervade the indi-

[1] Robert Nozick, *op. cit.*, p. 312.

vidual communities. In this laissez-faire system it could turn out that though they are permitted, there are no actually functioning 'capitalist' institutions."[1] Nozick ignores the fact that the laws operating in subsystems cannot be contrary to those operating within the system ("framework") of which they are a part. Otherwise the system itself would disintegrate, together with its constituent elements.

As many of Nozick's critics point out, and with good reason, his assertion that stable coexistence of different types of utopia (including socialist utopias) is possible within the bourgeois society is no more than a logical proposition incapable of standing the test of practice: contrary to all claims by Professor Nozick, communities which do not follow the imperatives of the market and the bourgeois state will cease to exist sooner or later. Here, even hypotheses are redundant: suffice it to simply recall the fate of 19th-century utopian communities in America.

Still, while dismissing Nozick's project as illusory, one must admit that there is reason behind his vision of an alternate world: it reflects the interests, illusions and social psychology of certain groups in American society. Pushed around by the state and the monopolies, these groups—which exist now and will, in all probability, continue to exist—feel more secure and free within an imagined laissez-faire society than in the United States as it exists in actual fact. It would be logical to assume that anarchic capitalist utopias will retain their role of a conservative social alternative in the near future. However, even taking into account the growing trend toward a stronger state, the consequent criticism of the state and the nostalgia after free market relations, anarchic capitalist utopias will hardly attract as many followers as technocratic utopias; most probably, their long life will be confined to the utopian periphery.

4. The Romantic Utopia

The *romantic utopia* has now become a natural ally of the anarchic capitalist utopia in its struggle against the bourgeois welfare state and technocratic civilization. How-

[1] *Ibid.*, pp. 320-21.

ever, the romantic utopia is developing within the mainstream of a well-established American historical tradition, with many of its ideals and principles in opposition to those of the anarchic capitalist utopia.

While the American romantic utopia of the first half of the 19th century was a kind of cultural reaction to capitalist industrialization in expanding free market conditions, today's romantic utopia should be considered in close connection with the scientific and technological revolution and its social consequences and with the new stage in the development of state-monopoly capitalism. At this stage, the role and functions of the bourgeois state are growing stronger (with all this entails in the humanitarian sphere), science is gradually turning into a direct productive force, technology is advancing rapidly and its impact is being felt increasingly not only in production but in everyday life too.

Tradition has played an important part in the emergence of the modern romantic utopia: the transcendentalist spirit and the ideas of Emerson, Melville and Thoreau experienced a revival and acquired a new popularity among the nonconformist intellectuals in the 1960s. But in the new conditions, the ideas of 19th-century romanticists were often colored by the concepts of Marcuse, Brown, Goodman and some other sociologists and psychologists who advocated what was known as radical Freudianism. This was all the more natural because these sociologists and psychologists, as Richard King notes in his *Party of Eros*, "worked within an intellectual tradition some 150 years old. In the context of American intellectual history ... one might classify these three thinkers as the theorists of a second transcendentalist revolt."[1]

As in the past, the romantic utopia is a spontaneous reaction, on the one hand, to the complexity and, on the other, to the ordinariness of the real world, to the changing boundaries of individual freedom. No wonder that in the eyes of the romanticist, naturalness remains the central principle of utopian society and the ideal of the free man, its foremost value. Hence the pronounced naturalism and anthropocentrism of the romantic utopia. Hence also the

[1] Richard King, *The Party of Eros. Radical Social Thought and the Realm of Freedom*, the University of North Carolina Press, Chapel Hill, 1972, pp. 173-74.

obscurity or peripheral nature of justice, democracy, efficiency and other issues which are almost central to other types of utopia.

The first thing that catches the eye of an observer in a romantic utopian world is its *simplicity* (if not primitivism) which contrasts sharply with the complexity and conflict of the real world. But it is the simplicity of an inherently integral world, not the result of a purposeful organizing effort by the state or the market. It is a natural and therefore the most stable and coherent wholeness possible—the wholeness of a free society.

The romantic utopia values *freedom* above all else. Outwardly, it is expressed in the lack of social rigidity, of clearly delineated structures of institutions, organizations and groups and lines separating them; this offers virtually unlimited opportunities for spontaneous self-assertion by the individual. With approval, Norman Brown quoted Henry Miller's *Sunday After the War*: "The cultural era is past. The new civilization, which may take centuries or a few thousand years to usher in, will not be another civilization—it will be the open stretch of realization which all the past civilizations have pointed to. The city, which was the birthplace of civilization, such as we know it to be, will exist no more. There will be nuclei, of course, but they will be mobile and fluid. The peoples of the earth will no longer be shut off from one another within states but will flow freely over the surface of the earth and intermingle. There will be no fixed constellations of human aggregates. Governments will give way to management, using the word in a broad sense. The politician will become as superannuated as the dodo bird. The machine will never be dominated, as some imagine; it will be scrapped, eventually, but not before men have understood the nature of the mystery which binds them to their creation. The worship, investigation and subjugation of the machine will give way to the lure of all that is truly occult. This problem is bound up with the larger one of power—and of possession. Man will be forced to realize that power must be kept open, fluid and free. His aim will be not to possess power but to radiate it."[1]

[1] Norman O. Brown, *Life Against Death. The Psychoanalytical Meaning of History*, Wesleyan University Press, Middletown, Conn., 1959, p. 305.

"Utopian speculations, such as these of Henry Miller," Norman Brown wrote in 1959, "must come back into fashion. They are a way of affirming faith in the possibility of solving problems that seem at the moment insoluble. Today even the survival of humanity is a utopian hope."[1] In all probability, Brown never anticipated that this last phrase expressed the essence of the quest many American utopians would undertake in the two decades that followed.

The picture drawn by Miller presents not only the outward but also some of the inner features of freedom in the romantic utopia—a society freed from diktat and oppression on the part of the state, the market, the masses and culture with its codified norms.

The romantic utopian can be described as an advocate of the "minimal state" because, like Emerson and Thoreau, he believes that the less the state governs (and generally, the lesser it is), the better. At any rate, he sees today's "corporate state" as one of the mortal evils of American society. And so the romanticist would be ready to embrace Robert Nozick's project of a commonwealth of autonomous utopian communities had it not been for the sales talk about the market "meta-utopia" he abhors; individualistic enterprise is where the romanticist parts ways with the anarchic capitalist.

An opponent of the "corporate state", the romanticist dreams of a society without a bureaucracy. But to him, debureaucratization does not mean simply restricting the functions of the state (and of the political machine as a whole) severely, narrowing down its field of activity and destroying relations based on rationality and efficiency. It is a transition from the *Gesellschaft* with its artificial and impersonal human relations to the *Gemeinschaft* which ensure new interpersonal relations of organic collectivism, transgressing both traditional individualism and artificial collectivism. This is why many romantic utopians see the ideal form of social organization in a small, relatively autonomous community of free working people sharing a common philosophy—something resembling perhaps a classical Greek polis, or a utopian commune, or an idealized pioneer settlement.

[1] *Ibid.*

With 19th-century romanticists, man gave himself to nature which absorbed him as its integral part. This trend has survived to this day. But today, a different trend has appeared alongside it: although he worships nature, man sees it rather as an equal partner in his life and work than as an object of blind adoration.

Ernest Callenbach's *Ecotopia* (first published in 1975), a clearly romantic novel, describes what can only be termed as idyllic relations between man and nature. The novel is set in 1999, in the independent nation of Ecotopia comprising the former states of California, Washington and Oregon which ceded from the United States in 1980. While the rest of America is sinking deeper in the quagmire of rampant violence and pollution, Ecotopia is thriving thanks to its rational environmental policies. The Ecotopians treat land, animals and plants with affection, they have returned to the natural life, and nature repays their love with interest. They have an abundance of vegetables, grain and meat. Animals grazing peacefully on lush pastures delight the eye. The cowboy is again a respected occupation. The country is covered with forests, a source of health, happiness—and timber, too, which has replaced aluminum and plastics. Harmony in Ecotopia is not confined to man's relations with nature; it reigns in his relations with everything that surrounds him, with all his environment. The Ecotopians' emotions are akin to the way the Indians feel, that "the horse and the teepee and the bow and arrow all sprang, like the human being, from the womb of nature, organically". When they build a wooden house, they seem "almost to be collaborating with the wood, rather than forcing it into the shape of a building",[1] and so the barrier separating the tree from the man disappears.

Ecotopia's harmony of man, nature and the world of objects is accompanied by a change in the attitude to technology and in technology itself. The automobile has vanished completely, and household appliances are noiseless: man's life should be filled with natural sounds only, such as the rustle of the wind, footfalls, or the crying of a baby.

Life in Ecotopia as pictured by Callenbach offers a

[1] Ernest Callenbach, *Ecotopia. The Notebooks and Reports of William Weston*, New York, Bantam Books, 1977, p. 173.

sufficiently accurate reflection of the way the modern romantic utopian views the world: in his opinion, fundamental change in relations between man and nature depends on either eliminating or radically changing the functions of the factors that stand between them. This applies above all to science and technology; in his eyes, they are obstacles to the understanding of the hidden meaning of nature and to the process which brings man closer to his fellow man and frees him from various forms of tyranny caused by the worship of technology and scientistic thinking.

The romantic utopia of the first half of the 19th century did not revile or reject science and technology because by that time they had not yet displayed their contradictions to a degree at which the critical consciousness of bourgeois society would have regarded them as an obstacle to man's "natural" development. The modern American romanticist is generally critical of science and technology and their mandarins, the technocrats. Hence his criticism of "reason", rationality and efficiency; hence his idealization of the direct sensory experience which sometimes appears as an apologia of mysticism. This is the basis underlying all relations in the romantic utopia where there is neither any technocracy as a system of domination nor any caste of technocrats, and where science (with its methods) is no longer regarded as a cure-all, even if it does retain some rights.

The romantic utopia is a tangible embodiment of anti-technocratic culture which blends together nostalgia after the past, whether real or imagined, and the refusal (or inability) to accept the new world which is becoming increasingly complex and increasingly inaccessible (in its entirety) to direct perception. And so, if any utopia is an attempted escape into a simpler and more comprehensible world, none express this desire more forcefully and clearly than the romantic utopia.

The romantic mode of thinking is based on a reappraisal of the nature and meaning of all human activity, first and foremost in the form of labor. In the romantic utopia, labor is not simply exploitation-free activity but a process akin to play, even when labor is not identified with play directly. This approach to labor is rooted in the European folk utopia. And although, as Marx demonstrates, the idea of turning labor into play has no chance of being realized, different types of utopia, especially the romantic one, have been reproducing it with increasing intensity. It is almost an eternal utopian idea, connected with the fact that the hired worker inevitably views labor as a curse, and this opinion is confirmed by certain trends in the development of the production and the lifestyle of modern capitalist society. "Smith is right," Marx wrote, "in that in historical forms of labor, such as slavery, corvee and wage work, labor is always seen as something repulsive, it is always *labor by external coercion*, and, conversely, non-labor is seen as 'freedom and happiness'."[1]

The further disappearance of elements of play from everyday life and from production, the "management revolution" and the scientific and technological revolution in developed capitalist nations have changed the personal psychological orientation of most people. They now have to display new qualities, such as subordinating their own activity and interests to collectivist purposes, discipline and conformism, which enhance the view of labor as something external, alien and devoid of any elements of play. Add to that the standardization of everyday life and recreation, the impact of "mass culture" which shapes the thinking of scores of millions of readers, listeners and viewers— and the conclusion becomes inescapable that for the overwhelming majority of Americans not only labor but also recreation becomes largely regimented and imposed from without. In these conditions, "programmed" existence is rejected from the standpoint of play—play not as entertainment but as liberation from rigid limits imposed from without, as a spontaneous expression of man's essence, with its purpose lying within and not outside man.

Some romanticists, those relying on psychoanalysis, connect the transformation of labor into play with the reestablishment of Eros as the life instinct. Norman Brown is one advocate of this approach. "The life instinct, or sexual instinct," he wrote in the late 1950s, "demands activity of a kind that, in contrast to our current mode of activity, can only be called play."[2] That is why the romantic utopian considers the attainment of inner and external

[1] Karl Marx, *Grundrisse Der Kritik Der Politischen Okonomie*, Verlag Für Fremdsprachige Literature, Moskau, 1939, p. 505.

[2] Norman O. Brown, *op. cit.*, p. 307.

freedom, the transformation of labor, if not life itself, into play, and the elimination of psychological oppression as interconnected and interdependent goals.

In his discussions of a free society, mention of relations of property is only cursory. Usually the romanticist does not reject the institution of private property as such; his criticism is spearheaded largely against the monopolies—to him, the economic basis of all forms of coercion. On the whole, the modern romanticist is as little concerned about economic problems as were his predecessors. The United States, he maintains, has reached a level of material development at which the emphasis may be freely shifted to the nonmaterial values and factors of development, which he regards as more important.

Hence the anthropocentric nature of the romantic utopia which accords the highest status to man—"free", endowed with a "new sensuality", living a "natural life" and generally little resembling, no matter how different the various alternative profiles, the inhabitants of the "industrial wasteland" of the latter half of the 20th century. "The Ecotopians," Callenbach writes in his novel, "are almost Dickensian: often strange enough, but not crazy-looking or sordid, as the hippies of the sixties were. Fanciful hats and hair-dos, jackets, vests, leggings, tights.... People seem to be very loose and playful with each other, as if they had endless time on their hands to explore whatever possibilities might come up. There's none of the implicit threat of open criminal violence that pervades our public places, but there's an awful lot of strong emotion, willfully expressed."[1]

Modern romantic utopians attach particular importance to the psychological freedom of the personality in the new society and interpret this freedom as a spontaneous expression of primal passions. This interpretation, developed by Marcuse, Brown and Goodman, is based on the postulate that psychic repression is behind all forms of oppression and exploitation which underlie a civilization oriented on productivity and efficiency and not on personality development.

True, there is no unanimity among the proponents of this view as to which primal passions should be "rehabili-

[1] Ernest Callenbach, *op. cit.*, pp. 12-13.

tated" and "liberated" and to what degree—whether this should be Eros alone, the life instinct (in the opinion of Marcuse) or both Eros and Thanatos, the death instinct (a point on which Brown insisted), whether they should be liberated completely or partially. But this does nothing to alter the essence of the problem: the passions should be rehabilitated and liberated in such a way as to eliminate the antagonism between body and soul, reason and emotion, work and play, individual and society and, eventually, return man (and, consequently, society, too) to a "natural" state. But this is a natural state different from that embodied in many 19th-century romantic (Rousseauist) utopias. The utopian romanticists of the past were searching for a model free man and a happy society mostly in faraway, "wild" lands (somewhere in the Marquesas)— essentially, in an archaic, precapitalist state of society which, associated sometimes with certain "third world" regions, attracts the utopian romanticist to this day. But now he is far more concerned with finding this model in "archaic" and "pre-repressive" states of the human psyche, both in phylogeny and in ontogeny. In other words, he is looking for his ideal not in the sociohistorical but in the psychological childhood of man and mankind taken both literally and figuratively: childhood is associated with a state of the psyche, of the world view and perception in which the primal passions are not yet suppressed, time is perceived in a leisurely manner, and activity is play.

The modern American romanticist has no clear idea of how a free society should be built. The only thing he can offer as a general prerequisite is the echo of his predecessors' appeal urging a break with the existing society, an escape into a utopian commune or into one's own Walden. Apparently, the only difference is that today's romanticist interprets this escape (in the spirit of certain Oriental doctrines, specifically, Zen Buddhism which was popular in the United States in the 1960s) not simply as a physical break with the real world but as an escape into man's inner world. Man, it is maintained, should strive not to rebuild the real world or to find some enclave in it, but to rebuild his inner world; this would enable him to impart a new meaning to his existence and to feel a free man. This means that the romantic utopia upholds the distinctly American tradition of an individual quest for happiness. This path rejects both entrepreneurial individualism and corporate collectivism.

The technocratic, the libertarian and the romantic utopias all share a common feature: they reject or belittle the role of politics as an independent sphere of the effort to transform life and want to solve the problems facing America by nonpolitical means. Among the contributing factors are certain distinct aspects of the emergence of American society, the strong undercurrent of distrust of the state which has always been present in the United States, and, finally, the skeptical attitude to politics widespread among Americans.

However, the mainstream of the American utopia has always contained a firmly established tradition which links the solution to the nation's problems and the creation of an ideal society with the use of political mechanisms and the implementation of political transformations. Today this tradition is reflected in two types of utopia—the socialist and what might be termed the democratic.

5. The Democratic Utopia

The democratic utopia appeals to the ideas and ideals of the American Enlightenment, to the legal norms formalized in constitutional instruments, to the spirit of the mass democratic movements which existed in the late 19th and the first half of the 20th centuries. It reproduces and develops in an updated version some aspects of the utopia of a farmers' America.

The basis of the democratic utopia, the product of the search for alternative ways in which modern American capitalism could develop, is the notion of a society where political power is in the hands of the people, each citizen being directly involved both in the taking and implementation of the decisions affecting his interests (participatory democracy) and in "projecting" his own future (anticipatory democracy).

The relative weakness of the central authority (the state) which opened broad opportunities for local initiative, the power of communal tradition, and the protracted colonization of the American West helped to establish the participatory democracy idea as part of the national awareness and as an important element of the political culture of the opposition. Most American utopian communities have practiced the principle of participatory democracy in this or that form. This practice often gave rise to debate. This is how a member of the Ruskin Colony which existed in Tennessee in the 1890s, explained a principle the world of today could define as participatory democracy. In a representative democracy, the entire organic community yields its rights and functions to a small number of people who are only a part of it; but these people represent only a tiny portion of the intellect and the will of the community as a whole; in the final analysis, the inner workings of a representative legislature lead to a situation in which one person holds all power. But if all members of the community take part in government and if there is no representative legislature to impede this, it is possible to offer a role in the common task of government to the most capable people who would direct the will of the community. Naturally, here the ambitious and the power-hungry will also have a say, but this is no more than just in conditions of universal equality; besides, the opinion of the wise will not be suppressed by criminal moves of representatives.[1]

And so the search for a democratic alternative has often prompted Americans to look up to this principle, which some saw almost as a panacea for ridding the social fabric of domination by the bureaucracy and the state and for handing power back to the people. That happened in the latter half of the 1960s and the early 1970s too, when protest movements temporarily adopted this idea as one of their slogans.

This was the direction in which the S.D.S. (Students for a Democratic Society) activists moved in the 1960s—witness the well-known Port Huron Statement. Some former activists of the New Left, grouped around the *Working Papers for a New Society* periodical, are working along these lines to this day.

But it was perhaps Alvin Toffler who, in his *Third Wave*, undertook the most interesting attempt to present a model of a new society where the principle of participatory

[1] Quoted in: V. F. Totomints and V. M. Ustinov, *Utopias: A Social Paradise on Earth*, Moscow, 1917, p. 47 (in Russian).

democracy would be embodied concretely.

Toffler proceeds from a fundamental precept shared by many modern American sociologists and political scientists of different hues—namely, that the political institutions existing in the United States and other industrial countries are overburdened, hopelessly out-of-date and no longer functioning. Therefore, in the course of the transition from "industrial society", or Second Wave civilization as he also calls it, to the new, Third Wave, society, the political structure is to undergo fundamental change. In the new society, Toffler holds, political activity should be based on three key principles.

The first is minority power. Majority rule, the key legitimizing principle of the Second Wave, is increasingly obsolete. The leading role belongs not to the majority as a single and indivisible whole but to the minorities that make it up. The political system should reflect this.[1] Toffler links this change to the "de-massification" of modern society; with this, he believes, both the legitimacy of majority rule and a possibility to "mobilize a majority or even a governing coalition" lose any meaning.[2] "In place of a highly stratified society, in which a few major blocs ally themselves to form a majority, we have a configurative society—one in which thousands of minorities, many of them temporary, swirl and form highly novel, transient patterns, seldom coalescing into a 51 percent consensus on major issues."[3]

But how can one actually ensure the participation of minorities in the decision-making process? How can it be made truly democratic? Here Toffler offers a variety of answers: "We may even eventually have to elect at least some of our officials in the oldest way of all: by drawing lots."[4] But, he adds, other, more modern ways can be found—for example, to retain the existing representative institutions while changing their terms of reference and decision-making procedures; they would be left with 50 percent of the decision-making vote, the other 50 percent going

---

[1] Alvin Toffler, *The Third Wave*, William Morrow and Co., New York, 1980, p. 435.

[2] *Ibid.*, p. 436.

[3] *Ibid.*

[4] *Ibid.*, p. 441.

to the "random" representatives of the nation. "Such a system," Toffler believes, "would not merely provide a more representative process than 'representative' government ever did, but would strike a devastating blow at the special interest groups and lobbies who infest the corridors of most parliaments. Such groups would have to lobby the people—not just a few elected officials.

"Going even further, one might conceive of voters in a district electing not a single individual as their 'representative' but, in fact, a random sample of the population. This random sample could 'serve in Congress' directly— as though it were a person—its opinions statistically tallied into votes. Or it could choose a single individual, in turn, to 'represent' *it*, instructing him or her how to vote."[1]

The so-called semi-direct democracy is the second key principle of the future political system—when the will of the people is expressed both through their representatives and through their direct participation in the decision-making process at the legislative and executive levels. "Using advanced computers, satellites, telephones, cable, polling techniques, and other tools, an educated citizenry can, for the first time in history, begin making many of its own political decisions.

"The issue is not either/or. It is not a question of direct democracy *versus* indirect, representation by self *versus* representation by others.

"For both systems have advantages, and there are highly creative, as yet underutilized, ways to combine direct citizen participation with 'representation' into a new system of semi-direct democracy."[2] This system, Toffler holds, could be realized through the use of various technical procedures. For example, to the votes of the legislators voting on this or that draft legislation, could be added the votes of its opponents and supporters beyond the legislature, the end result expressing the will of the people.

And finally, the third key principle underlying the new political system is that of "decision division", which neutralizes, to a certain extent, the current overload. The essence of this principle is simple: government should be decentralized and decisions should be taken at different levels

[1] *Ibid.*, p. 442.
[2] *Ibid.*, p. 446.

(decisions affecting local affairs—at the local level, and those concerning nationwide matters—at the national level). Some questions would probably have to be resolved at all levels simultaneously. It is also very important, Toffler emphasizes, to set up a system of transnational institutions, for today, the national state can no longer cope with many problems, such as monetary or environmental issues.

Such are the outlines of the political system which, in Toffler's opinion, could lead to true democracy in America if political change is complemented by changes in the organization of production, the dissemination of information, in education and the like. The corporations would have to operate within more rigid limits, so that the good of all society become a major motive with them. Industry should be decentralized and its output demassified. Demassification should also apply to other aspects of the social fabric, such as the so-called infosphere—that is, the sphere in which information is produced and disseminated: the mass media should serve the minorities because each minority has its own special interests and needs special information. Education should be geared to the modern level of knowledge and should shape the new social character of the individual of the future. This individual deserves to be described here at least in general terms.

Toffler would like the people of the 21st century to grow up sooner and to "show responsibility at an earlier age". He sees them as evincing greater individuality and therefore "more likely than their parents to question authority". They will want money but will not work for money alone, they will be less consumer-minded and less hedonistic than the present generations. They will know how to achieve a balance "between work and play, between production and prosumption, between headwork and handwork, between the abstract and the concrete, between objectivity and subjectivity". They will not be, Toffler explains, "a superhuman race of Goethes and Aristotles (or Genghis Khans or Hitlers)", but simply humane and happy people deriving pleasure from their work, from contact with one another and from being close to nature; people freely shaping their inner and outer world.[1]

[1] *Ibid.*, p. 407.

It is interesting that Toffler, who advocated the creation of social utopias in his *Future Shock*, defines his project as a "practopia" and not utopia. "What we see here," he says in *The Third Wave*, "are the outlines ... of a wholly new way of life.... The new civilization sketched here can hardly be termed a utopia.... We glimpse here instead the emergence of what might be called a 'practopia'—neither the best nor the worst of all possible worlds, but one that is both practical and preferable to the one we had.... In short, a practopia offers a positive, even a revolutionary alternative, yet lies within 'the range of the realistically attainable'."[1] Indeed, Toffler does not describe the best of all possible worlds, but the way in which it is constructed can be easily called utopian.

Toffler does not make the establishment of democratic society in the United States dependent on a radical transformation of property relations, on social revolution. He advocates change through reform, the latter carried out with direct participation and guidance by the people. Naturally, he does not present his project as an anticapitalist alternative. Nevertheless, the model he offers is incompatible, whether he is aware of it or not, either with the logic of modern capitalist evolution or with the objectives the corporations and the bourgeois state consciously strive to attain. And, while Toffler's utopia (like other projects within the mainstream of the democratic utopia) fails to map out practicable ways out of the crisis, it does outline the ideas and ideals of the left wing of the American bourgeoisie.

6. The Socialist Tradition in Modern Utopia

Over recent decades, America's socialist consciousness has been shaped within different sociopolitical movements and taking different shapes. Within the organized communist movement it exists in the form of revolutionary socialist consciousness (scientific socialism). But at the same time, this type of consciousness also matures within the bourgeois-democratic movements and processes rooted in the liberal tradition. Here it appears as what Marx and

[1] *Ibid.*, pp. 374-75.

Engels used to call "bourgeois socialism". And finally, socialist consciousness is produced by the mass democratic protest movements of a nonproletarian nature, which uphold the intellectual and political tradition of left-wing radicalism.

The utopian nature of the socialist ideal shaped on a non-Marxist basis is more or less clearly pronounced. And so, although the postwar United States has failed to produce either utopian novels comparable to the works of Bellamy or Howells or fundamental socialist utopian doctrines, the socialist utopian tradition lives on in America.

Among the branches of the utopian tradition, the social-ist utopia displays what is perhaps the greatest gap separat-ing the past from the present. In the 19th and early 20th centuries it was a kind of speculative fantasy, a distinct reaction to the contradictions of capitalism, often interpret-ing socialism as anticapitalism or, to be more precise, as capitalism turned upside down. Today's socialist-oriented utopian reacts not only to the ills of capitalism but also to the flaws (whether real or imagined) in the building of the existing socialist society. For this reason, his utopia is often critical both of capitalism as a system of social relations and of specific forms and methods used to tran-slate the socialist ideal into reality—those that he regards as essentially incompatible with the ideal. And while in some cases this utopia claims to belong to the Marxist tradition and in others disavows it openly, it invariably develops outside Marxism, although sometimes borrowing Marxist-sounding terminology.

These qualities are inherent in the modern American socialist utopia; but it also displays distinctive features rooted in the nature of American politics, above all in the absence of a mass socialist movement and mass socialist organizations.

One of the earliest forms of postwar utopian socialism in America was Erich Fromm's so-called communitarian socialism. Brought up in the critical theoretical spirit of the Frankfurt School, Fromm was never active in the socialist movement (although he did join the American Socialist Party in the 1950s) and always rejected socialist revolution. He saw methods of "social therapy" and "com-munitarian socialism" as its concrete form as the only ef-fective way of making social relations more human and attaining Marx's ideal of the all-round man, a concept he found attractive. "The humanization of technological society," he wrote in one of his last works, "can find full expression only in a *movement* which is not bureaucratic, not connected with the political machines, and which is the result of active and imaginative efforts by those who share the same aims. Such a movement itself, in its organization and method, would be expressive of the aim to which it is devoted: to educate its members for the new kind of society in the process of striving for it".[1]

Fromm's project in its first version formulated in the 1950s is connected with the socialist tradition only inasmuch as it is conceived as a way to eliminate the forms of alienation produced by capitalist social relations. In some other respects, it is closer to the romantic and democratic rather than to the socialist utopia.

Fromm sets four groups of tasks designed, he believes, to "humanize technological society": "(1) Planning which includes the system Man and which is based on norms which follow from the examination of the optimal functioning of the human being. (2) Activation of the individual by methods of grass-roots activity and responsibility, by changing the present methods of alienated bureaucracy into one of humanistic management. (3) Changing of the consumption pattern in the direction of consumption that contributes to activation and discourages 'passivation'. (4) The emergence of new forms of psychospiritual orientation and devotion, which are equivalents of the religious systems of the past."[2]

In *The Revolution of Hope* Fromm sketched a specific plan to achieve these goals. He claimed it was necessary to organize the Movement to mobilize people of goodwill for the effort to humanize America. The Movement was to be guided by national and local Councils composed of competent people united by their common striving to humanize technological society and capable of influencing the public. The Councils would direct the work of the Clubs ("cultural, social, and personalistic centers"), each comprising 100 to 300 members, engaging in political education

[1] Erich Fromm, *The Revolution of Hope. Toward a Humanized Technology*, Harper & Row, New York, 1968, p. 151.

[2] Erich Fromm, *The Revolution of Hope* ..., pp. 94-95.

and doing their best to influence various social forces so as to humanize the political process. Finally, the Groups, each with a membership of up to 25 people, would be the most numerous and active elements. It is in the Groups, Fromm maintains, that everyday transformation of Americans and the shaping of the new type of social relations could be carried out in the most vigorous way. "Their members would share a new philosophy, a philosophy of the love of life, its manifestations in human relations, politics, art, social organization.... None of these areas of human activities is isolated from each other, but each aspect gets its meaning by being related to all others."[1]

In 1976 Erich Fromm produced his last book, *To Have or to Be?*, where he developed in detail his opinion of "communitarian socialism" as a new type of society in which the "mode of existence" would be oriented not on "having", the way it is in modern industrialized society, but on the "being" of the individual, on the very process of his existence. As the first step toward such society, Fromm recommends that production be subordinated to "healthy consumption", whose forms would be chosen by the consumers themselves and not imposed on them by the corporations or the state. Fromm is convinced that it is the change in the structure of demand that would aid in the creation of "a new form of economic system, one that is as different from present-day capitalism as it is from the Soviet centralized state capitalism and from the Swedish total welfare bureaucracy".[2] As to the socialization of the means of production, Fromm asserts that such a "general goal" without a concrete plan to humanize social relations cannot be a reliable guarantee of progress toward genuine socialism.

Practical realization of the principles of "industrial and political participatory democracy" is the second important condition of the building of the new society. This, Fromm explains, means that each member of a production or any other organization would play an active role in its life both at the level of the individual productive effort and at the highest level, when overall decisions are being taken that

[1] *Ibid.*, pp. 157, 158.

[2] Erich Fromm, *To Have or to Be?*, Harper & Row, New York, 1976, p. 179.

affect the entire organization. This would also mean that the individual would be equally interested in the solution of problems affecting both the community and himself. "A true political democracy can be defined as one in which life is just that, interesting."[1] Naturally, Fromm adds, "active participation in political life requires maximum decentralization throughout industry and politics",[2] because a humane society can be only decentralized and debureaucratized, with people never even contemplating things they are forced to do in a bureaucratic society where behavioral patterns are imposed on them from without.

In his last book the American sociologist returns to the old utopian idea (he expounded it in *The Sane Society*) of "guaranteed yearly income": "All persons, regardless of whether they work or not, shall have the unconditional right not to starve and not to be without shelter. They shall receive not more than is basically required to sustain themselves—but neither shall they receive less."[3] Fromm stresses that this requirement is all the more important since "it is unacceptable to any system based on exploitation and control" and is therefore radically liberation-oriented.

Fromm's project is a typical armchair utopia, a product of petty-bourgeois consciousness. Having acquired its general shape in the 1940s and 1950s (what came later were mostly additional details), it could not, either at that time or subsequently, serve as a feasible program for transforming American (or any other) society. Its humanism is abstract and devoid of any political, economic or organizational "logistical support". Nevertheless, the utopia of "communitarian socialism" provided a sufficiently clear picture of the crisis non-Marxist socialist consciousness experienced in the United States from the 1940s to the 1960s, of the aberrant and illusory "critical thinking" which blamed dehumanization above all on technology, and on the manner of production and social organization incompatible with human needs in their abstract interpretation.

[1] *Ibid.*, p. 182.
[2] *Ibid.*, p. 184.
[3] *Ibid.*, p. 190.

In the 1960s and early 1970s, when democratic movements were on the rise in the United States, the search for a socialist alternative broadened. Although these movements generally developed outside the mainstream of socialism, some of the social projects advanced by the New Left displayed more or less noticeable traces of socialism. But it was "surrealistic socialism" (as Marcuse called it later), −couched in fine-sounding language but ignoring the actual trends in the development of modern American society and embodying the imperatives of abstract humanism.

The New Left envisaged a society with its typical features including "(1) the elimination of ... labor which is enforced and determined by the private needs of monopoly capital ... and ultimately the creation of a truly post-scarcity society in which work would be converted into play and the market abolished by complete automation of the labor process...; (2) the creation of a non-repressive culture, governed by the conversion of need into desire, by the transformation of sexuality into Eros−that is, the passage from genital sexuality to an eroticizing of the whole human personality and the total social milieu−and by the freeing of the human body from repressive de-sublimated sex; (3) the creation of decentralized and fully libertarian communities of authentic selves−shored on a liberating technological and ecological base−where the fulfillment of the common good would be a necessary condition for the personal self-realization of all...; (4) the abolition of cultural ethnocentrism and the creation of a world-cultural community, free of economic avarice and political domination, and nourished by love and mutual self-understanding; (5) the abolition of private property, the collective ownership of the means of production, and the utilization of economic resources for the pacification and harmonization of all the peoples of the earth; and (6) the structuring of new, experimental social life paradigms−extended family structures, communes, etc."[1]

It is easy to see that the striving for a break with "corporate capitalism" which permeated this program determined the nature of its free society ideals and its concepts of

[1] Introduction to *"All We Are Saying..." The Philosophy of the New Left*, Ed. by Arthur Lothstein, G. P. Patnam's Sons, New York, 1970, p. 21.

socialism. It is also easy to see that the New Left wanted a break with established socialism (as they saw it), to them the epitome of "bureaucracy" and "etatism". As a result, the image of socialist society presented by the theoreticians of the radical Left was a challenge to all, a slap in the face of all "bureaucrats", "etatists" and "antihumanists"—the labels they often pinned on all who disagreed with them.

The search for a socialist alternative continued after the radical Left movements of the 1960s and 1970s began to lose momentum.

This search, conducted amid a reappraisal of values, was reflected, *inter alia*, in the "revolutionary socialism" concept formulated by Michael Lerner who interpreted socialism as "the ownership and control of the means of production, and, through that, the control of all areas of life, by the majority of people who work. So socialism is another way of saying 'power to the people'.... Socialism is radical democracy, democracy extended to every area of our collective lives."[1]

This ownership and control by the people, Lerner underlines, open the way to self-determination and self-realization, and, consequently, to a life of "beauty", pleasure", "love" and "wisdom".

Lerner sets great store by the revolutionary potential of youth (above all students), national minorities (especially Blacks) and women; he stresses that a majority revolution in which scores of millions of people would be involved and which, he believes, is the only type of revolution practicable in America, is impossible without vigorous participation by the working class (in his view, comprising most hired labor). Here, he notes, it is important to prepare the masses in advance for directing sociopolitical processes. Lerner proposes the establishment of mass organizations of the "people's councils" type which, operating at industrial enterprises, in offices, colleges and universities, and in residential areas, could aid in the elaboration of alternative decisions on a broad range of issues and, in the final analysis, in the rallying of the masses to the struggle against the existing institutions. As a result, the "councils" could take political power into their own hands, and this would

[1] Michael P. Lerner, *The New Socialist Revolution. An Introduction to its Theory and Strategy*, Delta Books, New York, 1973, p. 287.

be the beginning of a protracted process of socialist transformation.

The "revolutionary socialist" is a dedicated opponent
of violence. He would like the revolution to be completely
nonviolent, and in this he echoes most 19th-century utopian
socialists who opposed revolution. Realizing, however, that
the American bourgeoisie will not give up power without
a fight, Lerner reluctantly acknowledges the revolutionary's
right to resort to necessary violence, at the same time ex-
horting him to exercise extreme caution.

No doubt, Lerner's project is a step forward compared
to the plans of the New Left, let alone of Erich Fromm.
But he fails to take into account either the actual conditions in which the American working class exists, or the
level of its political awareness, or the actual alignment
of forces within the nation, or the nature of the social
revolution—to say nothing of the fact that he offers a
narrow and primitive interpretation of what socialism is
all about.

A discussion of the socialist ideal formed on a utopian
basis would be incomplete without mention of the so-
called democratic socialism represented by Michael Harrington and other members of the Democratic Socialist
Organizing Committee he chairs. Harrington maintains that
the capitalist era is drawing to a close, since our time is
the twilight of the era that has lasted four centuries.[1]
He postulates that the self-destructiveness of capitalism—
a feature inherent in it—is gaining momentum, and the
United States is no exception. This "self-destructiveness"
is supposed to stem from collectivization—that is, from
the use of "political mechanisms to allocate economic
resources rather than relying on the market".[2] Given
certain conditions this trend may open the way to socialist transformations.

Although Harrington leaves open many issues of strategy
and tactics involved in these transformations and refrains
from drawing a specific picture of a socialist America,
he does formulate certain principles which highlight his
vision of socialism. He is convinced that the question of

[1] M. Harrington, "The Socialist Case" in: *The Center Magazine*,
Vol. IX, No. 4, July-August 1976, p. 60.

[2] *Ibid.*, p. 60.

property in and control of the means of production is a central issue of direct relevance to social transformations. But since he believes that the self-destructiveness of capitalism works in favor of socialism, the foremost task is to channel this process along democratic lines, that is, to work toward a consistent and all-round realization of democratic principles. "Where the men and women of 1776 fought to make democracy the principle of our political life, we strive to make it the principle of our economic and social life as well."[1]

Harrington rejects the social, economic and political structures which exist in the socialist countries, just as he does the strategy and tactics of socialist change typical of these nations. He advocates "democratic" socialization and collectivization via the use of legal mechanisms and institutions of power—specifically, the use of the Democratic Party which, in his opinion, could be transformed, should the circumstances be favorable, into a mass party of the Left.

Harrington's program follows socialist lines since it envisages a radical transformation of property relations and the elimination of capitalist exploitation. But it is utopian because, like many others, it fails to take into account actual trends in the development of capitalist America.

One can approach the socialist utopian projects arising in the United States today from different angles. From the political viewpoint, all theoretical constructs discussed here (and others in the same bracket) merely lead away from the practicable path of transforming capitalist society, the path mapped out by scientific socialism. The prescriptions compiled by Fromm, Lerner or Harrington are incapable of curing the ills of capitalism—whether in the United States or anywhere else—to say nothing of offering any new productive ideas concerning further development of the communist social formation. In this sense one can, with justification, say that modern American utopian socialism is barren, even that it displays clear signs of deterioration compared to what it used to be in the 19th century.

But there is another, educational aspect to the problem.

[1] *Ibid.*, p. 61.

It is entirely possible that for some critics of capitalism—especially those who come from the middle strata and who, for this or that reason, are not yet ready to accept scientific socialism—utopian socialist projects may prove to be a preparatory stage they will leave behind when they grasp the truth. In the words of A.L. Morton, "utopianism may be compared to a bridge, which, when one is on the far side of a river, is a means of crossing it, but which, when once crossed, leads only *backwards.*"[1]

7. The Official and the Folk Utopias in Today's America

The changes which have occurred in the world after the Second World War have left their imprint on all levels of utopian consciousness, including that of the official utopia.

A new stage in its development was connected above all with the presidency of John F. Kennedy. His team formulated the New Frontier concept, designed to sketch the outlines of a social ideal capable of revitalizing American society, making the American model of capitalism attractive to millions of people outside the United States, and offsetting the growing influence of socialism on the international scene. "What we need now in this nation," President Kennedy said, "more than atomic power, or air-power, or financial, industrial, or even manpower, is brain power."[2]

The very term "New Frontier" Kennedy chose to describe his official course had a profound political and psychological meaning. The President was actually telling his countrymen that there was room for further expansion, that the Frontier which had been closed in the last quarter of the 19th century, when the nation had completed its westward drive by reaching the Pacific, was "open" again—although this was now a different, global frontier.

A world power, a model to be emulated, a great nation which, having recaptured the bold spirit of the pioneers,

---

[1] A. L. Morton, *The Matter of Britain. Essays in a Living Culture*, Lawrence & Wishart, London, 1966, p. 67.

[2] John F. Kennedy, *The Strategy of Peace*, Ed. by A. Nevins, Hamish Hamilton, London, 1960, p. 164.

is exploring outer space, unraveling the mysteries of science and creating the most advanced technology, a nation which has put an end to poverty and disease at home and is assisting "free men and free governments in casting off the chains of poverty",[1] a just but stern guardian of world peace which protects its friends and is capable of dealing with any foe—such was the picture of the new society President Kennedy promised to build with the help of his fellow Americans. "Now the trumpet summons us again—not as a call to bear arms, though arms we need; not as a call to battle, though embattled we are; but a call to bear the burden of a long twilight struggle, ... a struggle against the common enemies of man: tyranny, poverty, disease, and war itself."[2]

Like all the previous versions of the official credo, the New Frontier was not the result of a dispassionate analysis of the objective trends in the development of the United States and the world as a whole. Providing a peculiar reflection of the new processes and phenomena in the life of the nation and of the international community, the new version of the official utopia generally reproduced not so much America's real prospects derived from an objective analysis of world developments (these showed that the United States was gradually losing its former status in international affairs) as the outlines of an ideal society constructed arbitrarily and serving propaganda purposes.

The New Frontier left its imprint on the nation's consciousness. Although most expectations the Americans connected with John Kennedy's program remained unfulfilled, the very fact that such expectations appeared, the revival of hope and faith in a better future was a force which accelerated the development of the United States over several years.

To a certain extent, another contributing factor was Lyndon Johnson's Great Society program. A logical continuation and specification of the New Frontier (as most historians believe), it differed from it in emphasis. In fact, Kennedy, too, was speaking of transforming America into

[1] *Inaugural Addresses of the Presidents of the United States from George Washington 1789 to John F. Kennedy 1961*, U.S. Government Printing Office, Washington, D.C., 1961, p. 268.

[2] *Ibid.*, p. 269.

a great society. But, unlike Kennedy, whose credo had a high-sounding ring to it and stressed above all the interests of the nation as a whole, Johnson accentuated problems of more immediate, everyday concern to Americans. He also tried to link the goals proclaimed in the official program with the American Dream, ·emphasizing the eternal value of private enterprise and personal initiative. "We," Johnson said, "have never lost sight of our goal: an America in which every citizen shares all the opportunities of his society, in which every man has a chance to advance his welfare to the limit of his capabilities." Johnson stressed that America's development would provide the "opportunity for almost every American to hope that through work and talent he could create a better life for himself and his family".[1]

Johnson pictured a "great society" based on freedom for all, in which each young man would be able to receive an education and inherit the entire wealth of human thought, all would live in new, rebuilt cities without slums (Johnson reckoned that this objective would be attained within 40 years), racial equality would reign and—this was virtually the central element of the new program—poverty would be banished forever ("our objective: total victory").

Essentially, this was an official program of a welfare state, with the welfare of each citizen and the elimination of poverty through a certain redistribution of wealth proclaimed the condition of the nation's prosperity. "Our history has proved that each time we broaden the base of abundance, giving more people the chance to produce and consume, we create new industry, higher production, increased earnings and better income for all."[2]

The critics of Johnson's program pointed, with good reason, to its impracticability and to its elements of propaganda rhetoric. Indeed, one could proclaim the goal of an end to poverty (poverty as understood by Americans) only if one totally ignored the fact that growth of the national wealth as such was not enough for attaining that objective and that a redistribution of wealth which could really solve the problem was blocked by the existing structure of social relations. One would be hard put to believe

[1] Quoted in: *The Reform Spirit in America*, p. 261.
[2] *Ibid.*, p. 263.

that Johnson failed to understand that, just as it would probably be wrong to dismiss the whole program as pure demagoguery, although no American official utopia is free of it.

More than any other postwar U.S. President, Johnson reflected in his program the utopian ideals of many Americans. (This refers only to the domestic aspects of the program with which the unpopular foreign policy of the Johnson Administration was at variance.) And that was, in all probability, deliberate. For the Great Society program was drawn up under direct pressure from the public which neither Johnson nor the U.S. ruling class he represented could ignore, especially with mass democratic movements on the rise in the 1960s.

Today, both the New Frontier and the Great Society are things of the past, although the ideals proclaimed by Kennedy and Johnson have never been officially disavowed or declared achieved. The 1970s introduced corrections both into the life of American society and into the official utopia—which, incidentally, reflects changes in the situation much more promptly and precisely than theoretical, let alone literary utopias.

Jimmy Carter moved into the White House during a difficult period: in his own words, "the tragedies of Cambodia and Viet Nam—the shock, embarrassment and shame of Watergate—the doubt and confusion surrounding the economic woes of our nation have created unprecedented doubt and soul searching among our people."[1] Against this background, the President's task (as he and those who brought him to power saw it) was apparently not to advance a fundamentally new credo but to reaffirm his commitment to earlier principles and to emphasize those especially important at the moment. As some of his predecessors used to do, Carter stressed moral values and proclaimed moral society as the social ideal. He wrote in his policy book *Why Not the Best?*: "As the philosopher Soren Kierkegaard said, 'Every man is an exception'. We Americans are proud of such individuality and diversity. But we still share common dreams. Neither Viet Nam, nor Watergate, nor the hardships of a mismanaged eco-

[1] Jimmy Carter, *Why Not the Best?*, Bantam Books, New York, 1976, p. 3.

nomy can change that.

"Some of our shared dreams are easy to state, if not always so easy to achieve. They include the beliefs that all Americans should stand equal before the law, that our country should, among the community of nations, set an example of courage, compassion, honor and dedication to basic human rights and freedoms, and that government should be controlled by our citizens."[1]

In his day, John Kennedy made it clear that he saw America as a "just" world policeman, or rather as a latter-day world pioneer and squatter. Fifteen years later the situation called for a new utopian picture of America, for the image of a "just moral arbiter" honestly observing the law at home and jealously guarding against any illegal attempts on the international scene.

Of course—and an analysis of the actual domestic and foreign policy pursued by the Carter Administration proves this easily—the United States did not, and could not, even if the President had really wanted it, have acted as the world's moral arbiter, and America itself did not develop in the direction of a moral society. But the official utopia sets a rigid set of rules by which the President must play and which, one might repeat, are an inalienable element of American political culture.

It was easy to forecast that the new problems and contradictions American society would face in the 1980s would force the ruling class to adjust the official credo and to reformulate the social ideal. That was what happened when power passed to Ronald Reagan, a conservative Republican.

Unlike Kennedy or Johnson, the new President did not offer any integral or comprehensive program of the New Frontier or Great Society type. But Reagan's numerous speeches, addresses and interviews make it clear that he and the group of the ruling class behind him have a social ideal of their own which they offer to America as an official utopia.

In his *Post-Conservative America*, the well-known American sociologist and journalist Kevin Phillips speaks about the mood of nostalgia the new President has brought to the White House. "No sooner was Ronald Reagan inaugurated as president in 1981 than the era of F. Scott Fitzge-

[1] *Ibid.*, p. 4

rald became fashionable again, invoked by White House aides paying great tribute to Andrew Mellon's economics or applauding Calvin Coolidge's refusal to tolerate strikes by public employees. The Gatsby years were a decade when politicians and preachers extolled the lost virtues of the kerosene lamp as they confronted the revolution produced by radio, transatlantic flights and the vote for women. The nostalgia of the 1980s is even bolder."[1]

Naturally, Reagan and his supporters are nostalgic not after the kerosene lamp or other accounterments of the past but after the times which, in the nation's awareness, evoke memories of economic success, social stability, a firm dollar and a firm faith of the majority in traditional institutions, values and America's "great mission". "Ronald Reagan and his supporters, on coming to power," Phillips develops his idea, "were not really trying to maintain the status quo. On the contrary, in some important ways they sought to restore the *status quo ante* of fifteen, twenty-five or even sixty years earlier."[2]

Today it is already clear what kind of "restoration" they are after. Above all Reagan would like to restore the Pax Americana—a term frequently used in the West to denote the first postwar decades, when the United States, economically and technologically stronger than other nations, used this strength openly, imposing its goods, views, tastes and, naturally, an economic and political course favorable to U.S. capital, on its friends in Europe and elsewhere.

But Reagan and his team also dream of mass revival of the social and moral values inherent in the "utopia of a traditional America". They see a country whose citizens would recapture the spirit of diligence and industry the Protestant ethics has maintained for over two centuries, revive the spirit of individualism and enterprise, rely more on themselves and on luck than on the government, and look for the roots of "perfectly natural" social injustice in their own mistakes and not in the social system. It is a country where the "traditional family" would again become a central social virtue, where the spirit of religious

[1] Kevin P. Phillips, *Post-Conservative America*, Random House, New York, 1982, p. 3.

[2] *Ibid.*, p. 13.

165

brotherhood and class collaboration would be strong, and where the people would trust firmly in the institutions of government.

No doubt, Reagan's official utopia may appeal to a certain part of American society—above all to those who, like the President, yearn for a return of the times when America was Number One, when it felt militarily invulnerable and economically and technologically superior, when problems were fewer and simpler.

But even this part of the public cannot fail to realize that the current social utopia looks not to the future but to the past, that it leads American society into a historical *cul-de-sac*, opening no new vistas and deaf to the problems awaiting the United States and other countries beyond the turn of the century. Like the Gatsby years, the Pax Americana is long past, and the fact that the official utopia extolls these virtues reflects not only its conservative nature but also its state of crisis.

Another fact which bears this out is that the current official ideals run counter to the social and political orientations and values widespread in the United States at the mass consciousness level and reflected in the folk utopia.

But is the folk utopian tradition still alive in today's America? Can it be that the development of the mass media, better education and culture and increasing population mobility have made the folk utopia extinct in the United States and other highly industrialized capitalist countries?

Yet folklore, an independent form of the folk creative effort, lives on in America; spontaneous mass movements (nationwide and local, left-wing and right-wing) continue to spring up and to produce utopian slogans and programs. This means that the folk utopia, a branch of the national utopian tradition, is alive.

It goes without saying that this utopia has undergone considerable change both in form and in content over recent decades. It has lost its erstwhile originality and independence. If one turns to folklore, to Gallup, Harris or Yankelovich polls, to the interviews collected in the books of Studs Terkel, a sociologist and journalist from Chicago, one will see that for all the diversity of popular concepts of the "best possible" society, they essentially coincide with the current theoretical or literary utopias.

Take the social ideal proclaimed in the Port Huron Statement, the utopian declaration of many thousands of American students. It is a society where man is the highest value, a society without violence or wars, where the abundant material benefits are distributed equally among all and where power belongs to the people. "We would replace power rooted in possession, privilege, or circumstance by power and uniqueness rooted in love, reflectiveness, reason and creativity. As a social system we seek the establishment of a democracy of individual participation, governed by two central aims: that the individual share in those social decisions determining the quality and direction of his life; that society be organized to encourage independence in men and provide the media for their common participation."[1] These social ideals are obviously close to the modern democratic and socialist utopias.

The interviews collected by Studs Terkel give an indication of the desired world as seen by the "man in the street" who does not even have a university degree. It is a world of plenty where the worker does not have to work himself ragged, where everything is fair and each can do the job he likes, where there is no oppression or violence; a world which, unlike the real world, is not commercialized or permeated with greed, a world of brotherhood and love. The imagination of the interviewees offers nothing new compared to the utopias listed above—not surprisingly, since the latter influence, whether directly or indirectly, mass consciousness and mass culture.

True, the utopian images formed by an individual or a group of people do not always conform strictly to this or that type of sociotheoretical or literary utopia. They are usually a blend of ideals taken from different utopias.

Nevertheless, I do not think that the folk utopia is gradually disappearing as an independent form of the national utopian tradition. The spontaneous creative effort of the people is inexhaustible, and this alone is sufficient guarantee that the folk utopia will remain stable in modern society—and especially in the United States, with its large,

[1] *The New Left: A Documentary History*, Ed. by Massimo Teodori, Bobbs-Merrill, Co., Indianapolis, New York, 1969, p. 167.

distinct and more or less ethnically autonomous groups. This applies above all to the Black population.

The Black utopia exists as an integral element of American culture to this day. In his famous speech he delivered at a rally in Washington on August 28, 1963, Martin Luther King stressed the unity between the dream of the Black Americans and the American Dream. "I say to you today, my friends, that in spite of the difficulties and frustrations of the moment I still have a dream. It is a dream deeply rooted in the American dream." This is his dream: "I have a dream that one day this nation will rise up and live out the true meaning of its creed: 'We hold these truths to be self-evident; that all men are created equal.' I have a dream that one day on the red hills of Georgia the sons of former slaves and the sons of former slaveowners will be able to sit down together at the table of brotherhood.

"I have a dream that one day even the state of Mississippi, a desert state sweltering with the heat of injustice and oppression, will be transformed into an oasis of freedom and justice.

"I have a dream that my four little children will one day live in a nation where they will not be judged by the color of their skin but by the content of their character."[1]

It is clear from King's speeches that the ideals central to the "white" folk utopia, the American Dream, were not alien to him. He saw a prosperous America of equal opportunity, a nation enabling each citizen to realize his potential. Still, in his policy speech King singled out the ideals central to the Black utopia—the ideal of racial equality in the economic, political and social context, the ideal of freedom as freedom of the Black man in white America.

King advocated nonviolent action and the integration of the Black population into American society. He did not share the ideas of Black separatism several extremist groups preached in the 1960s. However, the social ideal he proclaimed was closer to the traditional Black utopia than to the American Dream. Besides, no matter how widespread, popular or respected his views, King was not the only figure expressing the social ideal of America's Black minority.

[1] *The Day They Marched*, Ed. by Doris E. Saunders, Johnson Publishing Co., Chicago, 1969, pp. 83-84.

"Black Power", the slogan proclaimed by Stokeley Carmichael in the summer of 1966, upheld by a number of extremist groups and generally welcomed by a large part of the Black Americans not affiliated with them, proved that many Blacks had a view of America different from King's. The separatist trends of the 1960s ensured a degree of revival for the old idea of an independent Black state within the United States and even for Marcus Garvey's old resettlement-in-Africa scheme. These revivalist attempts were, of course, no more than a curious twist of developments, for no one seriously contemplated these projects; but here the important thing was not so much the project as such as the idea itself, the very expression of protest and the recourse to a radical—and essentially utopian—alternative.

Apparently, as long as the position of Blacks in the United States differs from that of the white majority socially, economically and politically, as long as there is racial inequality, the Black utopia will exist as an independent branch of the American folk utopia.

Chapter IV

━━━━━━◆━━━━━━

FROM UTOPIA TO ANTIUTOPIA

1. The Negative Utopia from Donnelly to Lewis

At every stage of its development the inherently contra-dictory tradition of utopian thought has encountered more or less active resistance. It has not been merely a clash of different temperaments, a debate between optimists and pessimists. It has also been a clash of different political forces and different social ideals. "The concept *utopia*," the American scholar Frank E. Manuel writes, "has from the beginning been used in both a positive and a pejorative sense; it has connoted at the same time an ideal longed-for and a crackpot scheme. The negation of the great dream has always constituted a parallel stream, from the very inception of utopian thought. The antiutopia was not the invention of Aldous Huxley and Zamiatin: after all, *The Parliament of Women* by Aristophanes was contempora-neous with Plato's *Republic*; More's *Utopia* produced a gal-axy of mocking parodies."[1]

One could agree with this statement but for an element which, at first glance, appears purely semantic but proves to be quite important. Today's experts use—often indiscri-minately—a variety of terms: "antiutopia", "negative uto-pia", "dystopia" and "cacotopia". Meanwhile, the history of utopia proves that these terms denote two different phe-nomena, and to confuse them means to distort the picture.

There are books which, unlike utopias with their image of a desired world, picture an undesirable world whose emergence must be prevented. It is very important that such works may accept the utopian quest, utopian ideals

[1] Frank E. Manuel, "Toward a Psychological History of Utopias" in: *Studies in Social Movements. A Social Psychological Perspec-tive*, Ed. by Barry McLaughlin, the Free Press, New York, 1969, p. 372.

and principles. These works are negative utopias, or dystopias ("bad place" in Greek). "Cacotopia" is synonymous with "dystopia".

But aside from these there are books which not only describe an undesirable world but also link its emergence to the very attempts to construct and implement a utopia. These books dispute and even negate utopia; they are antiutopias. One may debate which term should denote which phenomenon, but it is imperative to distinguish between them.

A negative utopia criticizes deviations from progress as seen by the utopians. And if its denunciations do deal a glancing blow to progress, it contains no radical negation of the latter. It is perhaps for this reason that a negative, often satyrical, utopia could exist side by side with a utopia within one and the same book. Conversely, antiutopia is a more or less pronounced negation of the very notion of progress, of the very striving to improve the world. And so the two phenomena differ quite substantially; to ignore this means to oversimplify the history of utopia, of the struggle of ideas and ideals.

The "parallel stream" Manuel refers to is made up not by antiutopias but by the negative utopia which was born simultaneously with utopia. And the works he mentions belong to the class of the negative utopia. Naturally, even some classical philosophers were skeptical of the attempts to improve man and society. But this skepticism could crystallize in the form of an antiutopia only given certain conditions which could not arise before it became clear that historical progress had a contradictory nature and that a striving to realize a utopia may entail far from pleasant consequences. This happened in the 20th century.

Some scholars who admit that antiutopia is a product of our times believe that it is rooted in the advances of science and technology. According to George Kateb, "antiutopianism ... is a crystallization of a number of ideas, attitudes, opinions and sentiments that have existed for centuries. And it is nothing but the development of technology and the natural sciences that is responsible for the crystallization that has taken place".[1] Other authors (Fred Polak)

---

[1] George Kateb, *Utopia and Its Enemies*, Schocken Books, New York, 1972, p. 3.

look for the roots of antiutopia in the political history of the modern age.[1]

Although in both cases authors speak of phenomena which have a bearing on the process under discussion, their approach appears too simplistic and superficial. Certainly, scientific and technological progress and political crises both are bound to influence the emergence of antiutopia. But the main causes were in-depth historical processes, above all the general crisis of capitalism and all its consequences. This crisis signified a gradual decomposition of bourgeois civilization which inevitably produced qualitative changes in bourgeois historical consciousness and led to disillusionment in "reason" and "progress" among certain social groups who felt they were now treading shaky ground. Before the very spirit of social utopianism (and not merely specific utopian ideas) was called into question, before the striving to attain social perfection encountered a skeptical reaction, before philosophers rejected utopia, progress and perfection on the grounds that the search for perfection led to destruction, bourgeois civilization had to enter a period of protracted but total and irreversible crisis.

In 1917 Pavel Novgorodtsev, a prominent Russian jurist and professor at Moscow University, wrote in his book *On the Social Ideal*: "Utopian hopes to find an ideal form of social organization have foundered. There is no political means which could give people immutable perfection of life once and for all.

"(1) We must abandon the notion of finding an Open Sesame which would show us the absolute form and point the way to paradise on Earth.

"(2) We must abandon the hope that in the near or distant future we might reach a blissful and happy epilogue of the earlier drama, the last and concluding period of history....

"The experience of the 19th century has undermined the faith in the miraculous power of political change, in its ability to usher in a heavenly reign of truth and good."[2]

This idea was subsequently echoed in different ways by many authors and philosophers, particularly Nicolas Ber-

[1] Fred L. Polak, *The Image of the Future*, Vol. 2, A. W. Sythoff, Leyden; Oceana Publications, New York, 1961.

[2] P. I. Novgorodtsev, *On the Social Ideal*, p. 17 (in Russian).

diaeff who expressed it almost aphoristically. "Utopias," this Russian idealist wrote in his essay "Democracy, Socialism and Theocracy", "seem very much more realizable than we had formerly supposed. And now we find ourselves face to face with a question which is painful in quite a new way: How can we avoid their actual realization?

"...Utopias are capable of realization. Life moves towards Utopia. And perhaps a new age is beginning in which the intellectuals and the cultured class will dream of methods of avoiding Utopia and of returning to a society that is not Utopian, that is less 'perfect' and more free."[1]

This was not simply one of the catch phrases for which Berdiaeff had a penchant, but an extremely succinct expression of the social mood certain strata of bourgeois society experienced upon entering a crisis; it was their social and political credo and, most importantly, the very essence of antiutopia. It was no accident that Aldous Huxley, an author of rare sensitivity to social change, used this quotation from Berdiaeff as the epigraph for his *Brave New World*.

Antiutopia expresses the *crisis of historical hope*, and the antiutopian is usually a *disenchanted utopian*. He would have loved to support the values extolled by many generations of utopians, all the more so because he himself harbors a utopian project which he hides guiltily. But the antiutopian no longer believes—is afraid to believe—that it is possible to create a free, happy and prosperous society. He is not only a disillusioned but also a despairing utopian for he is convinced that any attempt to put utopia into practice will lead to directly opposite results. And so he is against utopias and utopian experiments as such.

Critics of antiutopia justly blame it for some of the hostility toward utopia which emerged and became fairly widespread in the West in the 20th century and which contributed to the banishment of utopia from culture and political practice and to the spread of pessimistic, if not apocalyptic sentiments. I believe, however, that a purely negative attitude to antiutopia is as unjustified as the latter's purely negative attitude to utopia. After all, antiutopia is right in its assertion that attempts to translate utopia into

---

[1] Quoted in: A. L. Morton, *The English Utopia*, Lawrence & Wishart, London, 1952, p. 202.

practice very often lead to arbitrary and violent action against the laws of history, against nature and man and that therefore utopia should be rejected as a *practical* way of transforming society. Essentially, antiutopia soberly, albeit sometimes in extravagant terms, states the repeatedly proven fact that an arbitrarily constructed (and for this reason "perfect") model of society can usually be implemented only contrary to the natural course of developments—that is, also arbitrarily. Marx and Engels were well aware of this, and they resolutely opposed the practice of approaching social transformation as the realization of ideal (or perfect) projects constructed a priori. The founders of scientific communism invariably stressed that workers "have no ideals to realize, but to set free the elements of the new society with which old collapsing bourgeois society itself is pregnant".[1]

But the distinctly negative attitude of Marx and Engels to attempts at implementing social utopias *in practice* did not prevent them from appreciating the role of individual utopians in the shaping of socialist consciousness and culture and from making use of their legacy in elaborating a scientific approach to history.

When an antiutopian banishes utopia not only from the sphere of sociopolitical practice but also from the spiritual and intellectual sphere, trying to dismiss it as a phenomenon of culture, of consciousness, he, perhaps unwittingly, turns against the humanitarian principles, although their defense was perhaps the prime reason for the crusade against utopia launched by many other antiutopians. As a result, antiutopianism emerges as a sort of positivist tyranny which is no less dangerous than the tyranny of a utopian.

Let us now return to America and trace the genesis of the critical attitude to utopia.

In the opinion of some American literary critics, historians and sociologists, U.S. authors anticipated Yevgeni Zamiatin, Aldous Huxley and George Orwell, the classical threesome of European antiutopians, by more than a quarter century. They hold that the pioneers of this genre were Jack London, the author of *The Iron Heel*, and Ignatius

---

[1] Karl Marx, "The Civil War in France" in: K. Marx and F. Engels, *Selected Works*, Vol. 2, Progress Publishers, Moscow, 1976, p. 224.

Donnelly, a public figure almost forgotten today but very popular in the late 19th century, the author of several novels, including *Caesar's Column*.

"Obviously, *Caesar's Column*, though possessing definite characteristics of the utopian romance," W. B. Rideout, an American literary critic, writes, "stands more in the tradition of antiutopia, that tradition which has become characteristic of our own violent century and which has produced such books as Huxley's *Brave New World* and Orwell's *1984*. As a novel it is certainly inferior to either of these two; yet all three are alike in being extrapolations into the future of major forces that each author sees operating in sinister fashion at the present time."[1] M. Fellman, a U.S. historian, is even more outspoken in his claim that *Caesar's Column*, the peak of Donnelly's literary effort, marked the death of utopia and the birth of antiutopia.[2]

Before taking up Huxley's and Orwell's novels, one should examine these assessments of works by American authors. It is not a matter of precedence, for precedence here is nothing to be proud of, but of historical accuracy. There is no doubt that *The Iron Heel* and especially *Caesar's Column*, as well as several books written in imitation of these novels, recorded new tendencies in American social consciousness and a new stage in the development of the utopian tradition and in the attitude to it. But was Donnelly really the first antiutopian and his novel, the first antiutopia? Or, to put it differently, did the United States of the late 19th century really develop conditions which gave rise to the antiutopian phenomenon?

Caesar's Column is set in the United States of 1988. Gabriel Weltstein, a Swiss colonist from Africa, arrives in New York and witnesses the collapse of civilization, the inevitable result, the author emphasizes, of developments over the past 100 years.

"There was a golden age once in America—an age of liberty; of comparatively equal distribution of wealth; of democratic institutions."[3] The United States used to be a country of "universal justice" which meant "equal oppor-

[1] Ignatius Donnelly, *op. cit.*, p. XII.

[2] M. Fellman, *The Unbounded Frame*, Greenwood Press, Westport, 1973.

[3] Ignatius Donnelly, *op. cit.*, p. 45.

tunities for all men and a repression by law of those gigantic abnormal selfishnesses which ruin millions for the benefit of thousands". However, several shortsighted and selfish generations gradually spoiled it all. "Now we have but the shell and semblance of all that. We are a Republic only in name; free only in forms.... The very assertions, constantly dinned in our ears by the hireling newspapers, that we are the freest people on earth, serve only to make our slavery more bitter and unbearable."[1] The social classes have become sharply *polarized* and so have power and wealth, which have come alienated from the people and usurped by a brutal and mercenary *plutocracy* led by a handful of international bankers, with a few score dictating to the entire nation. "This is the real center of government of the American continent; all the rest is sham and form. The men who meet here [in the home of the Prince of Cabano, the leader of the plutocrats] determine the condition of all the hundreds of millions who dwell on the great land revealed to the world by Columbus. Here political parties, courts, juries, governors, legislatures, congresses, presidents are made and unmade; and from this spot they are controlled and directed in the discharge of their multiform functions. The decrees formulated here are echoed by a hundred thousand newspapers, and many thousands of orators; and they are enforced by an uncountable army of soldiers, servants, tools, spies, and even assassins. He who stands in the way of the men who assemble here perishes. He who would oppose them takes his life in his hands."[2] The plutocracy wallows in luxury, while at the opposite pole the workers are deprived of all rights and are doomed to poverty. Mistrust, suspicion and hatred are rampant. People "are suspicious, and properly so, of strangers, and even more so of each other".[3]

Donnelly paints a frightening picture of the *degradation of the personality* which afflicts this society at all levels. "The women, young and old, were much alike in some particulars ... their jaws ... were firmly developed, square like a soldier's.... The most peculiar features were their eyes. They had none of that soft, gentle, benevolent look ...

[1] *Ibid.*

[2] *Ibid.*, p. 62.

[3] *Ibid.*, pp. 30-31.

their looks were bold, penetrating, immodest....

"The chief features in the expression of the men were incredulity, unbelief, cunning, observation, heartlessness."[1] Here is the portrait of the leaders of the Brotherhood of Destruction set up by the desperate workers to fight against the system: "It was an extraordinary assemblage that greeted my eyes; a long array of stern faces, dark and toil-hardened, with great, broad brows and solemn or sinister eyes....

"The large heads at one end of the line were matched by the large heads at the other. A great injustice, or series of wrongs, working through many generations, had wrought out results that in some sense duplicated each other. Brutality above had produced brutality below; cunning there was answered by cunning here; cruelty in the aristocrat was mirrored by cruelty in the workman. High and low were alike victims—unconscious victims—of a system."[2]

Donnelly goes to great lengths to convince the reader that the situation in the America of 1988 is irreversible and can no longer be corrected by reform—it's too late! The only way out is an uprising of those below who would be glad to rebuild the world and to restore its former virtues but who are unable to perform anything constructive. The only thing they can do is to bring about *destruction, chaos, anarchy and death.* "The rude and begrimed insurgents ... do not mean to destroy the world; they will reform it—redeem it. They will not make it a world where there shall be neither toil nor oppression. But, poor fellows! Their arms are more potent for evil than their brains for good. They are omnipotent to destroy; they are powerless to create."[3]

That is precisely what finally happens in 1988. The people rise. "Like a huge flood, long dammed up, turbulent, turbid, muddy, loaded with wrecks and debris, the gigantic mass broke loose, full of foam and terror, and flowed in every direction. A foul and brutal and ravenous multitude it was....

"A sullen roar filled the air as this human cyclone moved onward, leaving only wrecks behind it....

[1] *Ibid.*, p. 15.
[2] *Ibid.*, pp. 148-49.
[3] *Ibid.*, p. 258.

"That which it took the world ten thousand years to create has gone in an hour."[1]

Having exterminated the plutocrats (together with a multitude of innocent people) the insurgents finally turn against one another. Caesar Lomellini, the president of the Brotherhood of Destruction, who distinguished himself only by erecting a column of 250,000 corpses over which cement was poured, is assassinated. The vice-president, having stolen 100 million dollars, flees by airship to Palestine where he "proposes to make himself king in Jerusalem, and, with his vast wealth, re-establish the glories of Solomon, and revive the ancient splendors of the Jewish race, in the midst of the ruins of the world". The dream of the insurgents was "to create order out of chaos and reconstruct society. But that dream is past".[2]

Donnelly's novel is valuable to the sociologist and the historian above all because it is a concentrated expression of the author's fears, of the trends in the development of American society at the end of the 19th century which, in his view, should be stopped so as to prevent the destruction of America and of civilization as a whole. Donnelly maintains that all evil is rooted not in private property (Bellamy's view) but first and foremost in *inequality and concentration of wealth*; not in the fact that a bourgeoisie exists but in the *concentration of power and the weakening of America's democratic institutions*, in the excessive gap between the classes and in the fact that entrepreneurs and bankers rob ordinary people, producers. *Caesar's Column* expresses the disillusionment and alarm of the utopian advocate of a "farmers' America", his warning to the ruling class to the effect that if it does not move fast to counteract the nascent antiegalitarianist trends and if it does not heed his advice, revolution will be inevitable and will destroy all.

Like many 19th-century authors, Donnelly ingenuously explains in his foreword what his novel is all about and who it is addressed to: "I seek to preach into the ears of the able and rich and powerful the great truth that neglect of the sufferings of their fellows, indifference to the great bond of brotherhood which lies at the base of Christianity,

[1] *Ibid.*, pp. 256, 257.
[2] *Ibid.*, p. 283.

and blind, brutal and degrading worship of mere wealth, must—given time and pressure enough—eventuate in the overthrow of society and the destruction of civilization."[1]

Donnelly, however, believes that the situation can still be salvaged, that *all is not lost*. His pessimism and criticism are directed not at utopians who try to squeeze society into the rigid framework of their constructs but at specific social and political groups and their policies. His position differs greatly from the stand taken by Aldous Huxley, George Orwell and other antiutopians of the 1930s and 1940s.

Donnelly openly admitted his dislike of Bellamy and the socialist ideas he advocated, a fact directly reflected in *Caesar's Column*. Viewed from this angle, his novel was not only a negative utopia but also a counterutopia (in relation to *Looking Backward*). Still, it remained alien to the antiutopian tradition for which the necessary conditions did not exist in 19th-century America—the very conditions which arose in Europe after World War I, after the fascists seized power in Italy and Germany—in other words, after developments which led critical consciousness to face problems America had not been ready to contemplate at the time. In the late 19th and the first half of the 20th centuries the United States stopped at the negative utopia, although the latter was represented not only by clumsy pieces like Joaquin Miller's *Destruction of Gotham* but also by serious works like Jack London's *Iron Heel*, let alone *It Can't Happen Here* by Sinclair Lewis.

While Donnelly warns against a plutocracy seizing power and, in the final analysis, against a revolutionary explosion, Jack London, taking a different stand (defending socialist ideas and advocating rule of labor) and writing at a different time (1908), warns against the danger of oligarchy and counterrevolution. Anthony Meredith wrote in his foreword to the novel: "The Iron Heel ... we feel descending upon and crushing mankind."[2] Like Donnelly, London tells the reader directly (but not so naively) that his goal is to warn of a danger that can be prevented. "What else than Feudalism could have followed upon the breakdown of that great

---

[1] *Ibid.*, p. 3.

[2] See: Jack London, *The Iron Heel*, Grosset & Dunlap, New York, 1917, p. XI.

centralized governmental machine known as the Roman Empire? Not so, however, with the Iron Heel. In the orderly procedure of social evolution there was no place for it. It was not necessary, and it was not inevitable. It must always remain the great curiosity of history—a whim, a fantasy, an apparition, a thing unexpected and undreamed; and it should serve as a warning to those rash political theorists of today who speak with certitude of social processes."[1] According to the novel, the Iron Heel finally (after 700 years of oligarchy domination) loses power to the labor movement which wins a worldwide victory. But the terrible nightmare of seven hundred years hangs, like the sword of Damocles, over the American people.

It Can't Happen Here appeared during the 1936 election campaign, when Franklin D. Roosevelt and his New Deal supporters clashed with their rivals, Huey Long among them, a man many democratically inclined Americans charged could become a dictator of the fascist type. In his novel, Lewis warned of the *danger of fascism* in America which could *lead to a new war, destroy democratic institutions, suppress personal freedoms* and do many other things fascism was capable of. Much of this was obvious enough from the German experience.

Lewis describes what could happen in the United States if the voters believed demagogues like Senator Berzelius (Buzz) Windrip (copied, in the unanimous opinion of the critics, from Huey Long, although he is mentioned in the book by name, as a different person) and helped him to become President of the United States. In his election speeches, Windrip spoke of a "Paradise of democracy in which, with the old political machines destroyed, every humblest worker would be king and ruler".[2]

After his arrival in the White House, Windrip proclaims a "*real* New Deal" which essentially means that "he should have complete control of legislation and execution, and the Supreme Court be rendered incapable of blocking anything that it might amuse him to do".[3] A personal dictatorship is established in the United States, all parties except "the

[1] *Ibid.*, p. XII.

[2] Sinclair Lewis, *It Can't Happen Here*, The New American Library, New York, 1970, p. 97.

[3] *Ibid.*, p. 126.

American Corporate State and Patriotic Party" are banned, labor unions are outlawed, censorship is introduced, labor concentration camps are set up to "help combat unemployment", and a reign of terror begins.

Lewis was no pessimist. Like Donnelly who believed that a plutocracy could be barred from power, like London who held that the rule of an oligarchy could be prevented, Sinclair Lewis was convinced that America could turn away from the German path if it voted for Roosevelt. This was obviously the immediate political goal of the author who was concerned over the future of America as a democracy.

And so one can conclude that neither Donnelly nor London nor Lewis nor their imitators approached antiutopia. They warned their country and the rest of the world of the coming danger but, I repeat, believed that democracy, freedom and other values they cherished could be saved. They did not oppose utopia because they still had faith in the very idea of progress and in its tangible results.

2. "Disillusionment with Progress" and Conflicting Attitudes to Utopia

No major negative utopias or antiutopias appeared in the United States during the war years. But that was then that the nation's social consciousness began to generate—with the help of immigrants from Europe, and especially from Germany—moods and currents which led to a critical opinion of utopia on the part of some American intellectuals.

The "decline" or even "death" of utopia was what highlighted these moods. "Our visions of the future," Kenneth Keniston wrote in 1960, "have shifted from images of hope to vistas of despair, utopias have become warnings, not beacons. Huxley's *Brave New World*, Orwell's *1984* and *Animal Farm*, Young's *The Rise of the Meritocracy* and, ironically, even Skinner's *Walden Two*—the vast majority of our visions of the future are negative visions, extensions of the most pernicious trends of the present. They are deterrents, cautionary tales: utopia has become counterutopia. The connotations of 'utopian' have similarly changed: the term is now unequivocally associated with 'unrealistic', with 'self-defeating', and, for some, with man's deepest and most prideful sins."[1]

Keniston presents a sufficiently accurate picture of the moods which spread in the West, including the United States, in the initial postwar years and which persisted up to the early 1960s. Proof of this includes the absence of serious and well-written utopias from the American literature of those years, and the "apostasy from utopia" on the part of certain philosophers and historians, particularly Lewis Mumford who turned into a utopiaclast in the 1950s and 1960s.[2]

These moods were also clear from the attitude to the books listed by Keniston, above all to Orwell's *1984*, which appeared in 1949, and Huxley's *Brave New World*, for which the author wrote his foreword in 1946. It would be no exaggeration to say that these British novels were as welcome among certain quarters of American society as they were among their counterparts in England and that they became organic elements of American culture. Moreover, reactionaries used these novels as weapons in the acute ideological confrontation of the Cold War. Orwell's book was exploited with particular zeal; it was interpreted as a purely anticommunist book, the reader being told that the totalitarian society depicted in the novel was a direct result of attempts to implement the "communist utopia".

It would be unfair not to mention that as early as the 1950s some (although few) American literary figures and social scientists pointed out that Huxley's and Orwell's works were ideologically and politically ambivalent and that they were interpreted in a rigidly one-sided way. As Erich Fromm wrote in his afterword to *1984*, "the warning is that unless the course of history changes, men all over the world will lose their most human qualities, will become soulless automatons, and will not even be aware of it".[3] Fromm called on the American reader not to be smugly certain that the book had nothing to do with

[1] Kenneth Keniston, *Youth and Dissent. The Rise of a New Opposition*, Harcourt, Brace Jovanovich, New York, 1971, p. 43.

[2] See: Lewis Mumford, *The Myth of the Machine. Technics and Human Development*, Harcourt, Brace & World, New York, 1967.

[3] Erich Fromm's afterword in: George Orwell, *1984*, A Signet Classic, New York, 1962, p. 257.

him, writing of enslavement and dehumanization as a danger "inherent in the modern mode of production and organization, and relatively independent of the various ideologies".[1]

That was a sign marking the beginning of a turn in some American intellectuals' assessment of both antiutopias (a turn away from their one-sided interpretation) and the state of American society. The turn itself came later, in the mid-1960s, when people suddenly saw an America of today or tomorrow in Huxley's and Orwell's novels. The Orwellian nightmares gave an impetus to the left radicals in their struggle against trends in the domestic and foreign policies of the United States in the latter half of the 20th century. Images from these books became catchwords these radicals used frequently to describe American realities.

The antiutopian feelings of the 1940s and 1950s were by no means accidental; they stemmed from a series of objective circumstances—first and foremost, the socially and politically differing phenomena of the times such as World War II and the traumas it inflicted on liberal bourgeois consciousness, the Cold War imperialism launched, and the anticommunist hysteria which, in the United States, took the form of McCarthyism. Finally, there were the increasingly pronounced and contradictory consequences of scientific and technological progress, the progress the social utopia of the late 19th and early 20th centuries had advocated so vigorously. All these were heterogeneous developments, but they all pushed in one direction, generating what Raymond Aron later called "disillusionment with progress" among Western intellectuals. This disillusionment was bound to affect utopia, with its faith in social (including political and moral) progress as its motive force (although this was not always recognized).

Still, by the mid-1960s it was already quite obvious that the "death of utopia" had been recorded prematurely and that the antiutopian trend had failed to take firm root in American consciousness and culture and to establish itself as a tradition. Utopia was alive. Having lived through a crisis, it reemerged, in a slightly different shape but with its essence unchanged. The proof was in the mass democratic movements which advanced social and political alterna-

[1] *Ibid.*, p. 267.

tives sometimes of a utopian hue, resurrecting the hope of creating a different, more humane world. This was also clear from what was happening in American literature.

The assumption here is that science fiction (or fantasy) and utopia are different things, that they reflect different phenomena. A utopia may be free from any fantastic elements, just as a piece of science fiction may be devoid of any utopian features. Here, science fiction means not only speculative fiction dealing exclusively with science but also science fiction concerned with technological or social matters: the term "science fiction" denotes not the scientific nature of a literary work or the degree to which it matches scientific accuracy (straight science fiction); it refers to the object of a given book, be it science, technology, or social, political or other processes. Certainly, science fiction may contain socioutopian ideals, just as a social utopia may use science fiction techniques—the path that authors of negative utopias or antiutopias may take.

Then, what was the genre of the hundreds of books critics described as antiutopian science fiction, negative utopias, or simply warnings? How can one assess, in relation to the subject under discussion, works that stand out among this mass, such as *The Space Merchants* by Frederick Pohl and Cyril Kornbluth, *Player Piano* by Kurt Vonnegut, Jr., *451° Fahrenheit* by Ray Bradbury, "A Ticket to Tranai" by Robert Sheckley and *Seven Days in May* by Fletcher Knebel and Charles Bailey?

Upon a closer examination, most of these and many similar works are better described as negative utopias than antiutopias in the strict sense of the term.

Expressing a critical attitude to various social and political phenomena, including world nuclear war, destruction of the environment, bureaucratization of the social fabric, limitations of human rights and freedoms, modern American negative utopias comprise a broad range of types. Among these, *antitotalitarian, antitechnocratic* and *antiwar* works should be singled out specially.

The notion of a "totalitarian society", which arose in American social consciousness and political sociology not without the influence by the European immigrants who came to the United States between the 1930s and the 1950s (including figures like Herbert Marcuse, Hannah Arendt, Erich Fromm and Thomas Molnar), was largely based on

European experience, above all on what happened in Nazi Germany. Projected against the background of postwar America, with its tendency to expand the functions and enhance the role of the state and with its crisis of traditional bourgeois individualism, this experience led to an image of totalitarianism as a system which was a repressive dictatorship of the whole vis-a-vis its parts: society oppressed the individual; the state, its citizens; and the organization, its members.

Of considerable importance as factors which contributed to the appearance of this notion were Huxley's and Orwell's novels, especially *1984*. The "Orwellian world" became a symbol of sorts of "totalitarian dictatorship" which frightened not only the American left but also conservatives and even certain right-wing groups, since in the United States their thinking was still shaped by individualist and antietatist values.

The influence of the European experience and its concomitant political interpretations were also evident from the fact that throughout the 1940s and 1950s the possible establishment of a totalitarian dictatorship in the United States was connected either with a socialist revolution—in the eyes of the right—or with a fascist coup—in the eyes of the left. In other words, this dictatorship was considered to be incompatible with the typically American political and legal procedures. Most Americans entertain this notion to this day. However, now it is being attacked as a primitive concept which does not fully reflect the political realities of today.

According to many liberal American journalists and sociologists, one cannot, essentially, rule out the establishment in the United States of a totalitarian regime of the "national type"—a regime which would take a "distinct road"—without a mass fascist party, without storm troopers or the use of the army. They maintain that a tense, stormy atmosphere and violent mass discontent would be all it would take—wary of the liberals, the masses would, without any storm trooper support, vote for some fascist demagogue who would seize power and "set things straight".

This was the pattern Sinclair Lewis used in *It Can't Happen Here*. A similar plot is present in *The R Document* by Irving Wallace. One of the protagonists—the director of the FBI—dreams of a totalitarian dictatorship in the United

States. And so he tries to push through the legislature—by-passing the President—the so-called 35th Amendment which would suspend (in actual fact, repeal) the Bill of Rights and would vest unlimited authority in the director of the FBI. Suspecting nothing, many states vote in favor of the amendment (the pretext is to strengthen law and all is in full compliance with the constitutional procedure), and only an accidental combination of events and an incorruptible Attorney General frustrate the conspiracy which could have led America to tragedy.

Today, such problems are discussed not only in novels but also in the academic community—witness, for example, the debate on the pages of *The Futurist* about the possibility of an "Orwellian world" in the United States.

How 1984 Came to America, a futurologist scenario by David Goodman, is set against such an ordinary and almost habitual sociopolitical background that the coming of "1984" looks frighteningly credible. "By the late 1960s," the scenario goes, "the increasing availability of fissionable materials and weapons-making information leads to escalating fears of 'atomic terrorism'. The intellectual community, journalists, corporate leaders, and politicians all warn that atomic bombs may soon spread beyond government control, but no one can devise a satisfactory solution to the problem.

"In the colleges, students are also discussing the private construction of atomic bombs and what the consequences of such an occurrence would be.... In one Eastern experimental college, a course is offered on 'How to Build an Atomic Bomb'."

Finally, a "group of idealistic students" lays its hands on the quantity of plutonium and produces a bomb capable of destroying a large city. They blackmail the government and advance a program of demands. Panic engulfs the nation. The President's aides insist that he declare an emergency. "Although the *National Emergencies Act of 1976* repealed many of the president's sweeping powers in time of national crisis, he is still able to issue binding executive orders good for six months provided he informs Congress of his intent." Therefore, Goodman argues in his scenario, "the president could still rule by 'lawful dictatorship', with rationalizations to come later". After long hesitation, he declares a national emergency, demanding restrictions on the freedom of movement and of the press, a ban on certain types of communications, and almost unlimited search powers for the police. He also proposes a "reassignment of troops and the institution of temporary martial law".[1] Pressure from the opposition is growing. Finally, the terrorists are caught, but the tension remains: everyone fears a repetition of the incident. The President addresses the American people with a plea for restraint. He asks them not to limit his emergency powers. He also wants the right to suspend the Bill of Rights.

One can easily see that the establishment of a totalitarian dictatorship as seen by Goodman is not connected with a violent rejection of bourgeois democracy. In his article "Countdown to 1984: Big Brother May Be Right on Schedule", published together with the scenario, Goodman explains that "Orwellian world" may be a natural outcome of the functioning of traditional bourgeois-democratic institutions. Within the framework of these institutions and without any visible deviation from the letter of the law (or against the law but without its open rejection) occur changes which, imperceptibly, push the West into "1984" and make American democracy so fragile and volatile that one tiny external impulse is enough to eliminate it as such. According to Goodman, "the social trends of the last 30 years have brought the West closer to *1984* than ever before, and these trends could rapidly accelerate under certain circumstances".[2]

"Doublethink" is the way of the Oceanians in *1984*. But it is already a feature of today's America, Goodman says: "A recent example was in the late 1960s when the Nixon administration overtly promoted domestic law and order and decried all forms of 'civil disobedience' while covertly ordering telephone taps, sponsoring break-ins, opening the mails, keeping the 'enemies' under surveillance, and committing other ostensibly lawless acts."[3]

Oceania is ruled by Big Brother, an omnipotent and omnipresent dictator who is watching each and everyone all

---

[1] *The Futurist*, Vol. XII, No. 6, December 1978, p. 354.

[2] *Ibid.*, p. 350.

[3] *Ibid.*, p. 351.

the time. But, Goodman maintains "with today's paternalistic government and powerful presidency, Big Brother may be somewhat diffused but just as strong".[1]

Total electronic surveillance is practiced in Oceania—and in the United States: "The surveillance of alleged subversives by U.S. government agencies has been documented by congressional testimony."[2]

In Oceania, people are conditioned to see and feel "the right way" so as not to subvert society. Newspeak, a special language, makes it impossible to semantically express a heretical thought. All, even family, relations among people who, in the opinion of Big Brother, could pose the slightest threat to the totalitarian regime, have been severed. But, Goodman argues, all this is a feature of American life too.

"The social trends of today clearly indicate a general decay of individual liberties, rational thought, personal privacy, and *self-determination*; a 1984-type future is getting closer every year. But the critics of 1984 are quick to point out that 'it can't happen here' and that 1984 certainly could not come true only five years from now. They maintain that our democratic beliefs run too deep to be destroyed by a predatory Big Brother.

"They are partly right. None of the social trends have yet reached the intensity that Orwell envisioned in 1984, and at the current rate of 'progress' an Orwellian future is definitely more than just five years away. Unfortunately the trends could speed up. Not one of Orwell's predictions is beyond the range of possibility, and almost any of the social and political trends described above could be brought to a head by just a *single triggering incident.*"[3]

Goodman's analytical logic clearly records both the crisis of bourgeois democracy in the United States and the crisis of democratic thought, the lack of faith in the ability of the existing cultural and political institutions to prevent society from sliding into antidemocracy, the fear of a large-scale terrorist act or a natural catastrophe which, he holds, can demolish bourgeois democracy. Goodman is especially alarmed by scientific and technological progress

[1] *Ibid.*, p. 352.

[2] *Ibid.*

[3] *Ibid.*

and the increasingly strong positions of the technocracy: he sees this as a sort of material base of a totalitarian dictatorship. This should be emphasized specially since the view that the threat of such a dictatorship is rooted in scientific and technological advances is not infrequently voiced in America. This view made itself felt, among other things, in the course of the discussion of Goodman's scenario and article in *The Futurist.*

"For the majority of the human race," wrote Joseph Maloney, an American systems analyst, "a society like 1984 is the most probable future. It probably won't appear within five years, or even within a generation, but the continued spread of high technology, coupled with the continual growth of population, guarantees the eventual establishment of 1984.

"A 1984-type society will not arise because of direct catastrophes, such as war, famine, and disease, caused by the growing imbalance between the earth's resources and its population. It will arise instead from the technologies that must develop to sustain large numbers of people at the standards of living they expect."[1]

The mass technophobia which springs from a fetishistic attitude to science and technology has, expectedly, given rise to an antitechnocratic and antiscientistic response in the sphere of consciousness and culture. Over the postwar decades, numerous books, including negative utopias, have appeared in the United States, critical of science and technology and aimed against their claims to omnipotence and their schemes to replace man by machine.

Player Piano, written by Kurt Vonnegut as early as 1952, still remains a classical example of an antitechnocratic negative utopia. The novel is set in the United States at the end of the 20th and the beginning of the 21st centuries, when Machine reigns supreme. True, to an outsider it could appear that "things really were better than ever. For once, after the great bloodbath of the war, the world really was cleared of unnatural terrors—mass starvation, mass imprisonment, mass torture, mass murder. Objectively, know-how and world law were getting their long-awaited chance to turn earth into an altogether pleasant and con-

[1] *The Futurist*, Vol. XIII, No. 2, April 1979, p. 115.

venient place in which to sweat out Judgment Day".[1] But this is only a superficial impression. Gradually, it turns out that man has paid a stiff price for prosperity.

Having guaranteed a certain minimum of material afflu-ence, the Machine has made man into its appendage. Con-trolling him fully, it has actually ousted him from society as something irrational and therefore absolutely redundant. Officially, power is in the hands of a small technocratic elite, convinced of its superiority over others and imbued with a "sense of rightness about the hierarchy topped by managers and engineers".[2] But even this elite does not en-joy the freedom of decision-making since ruling over all society, including the elite itself is EPICAC XIV, the man-made computer and the true master of the United States. There is even a joke, "the machine has all the cards". Lost in this world of machines, man loses his "feeling of ... dig-nity".[3]

Vonnegut demonstrates that such society unavoidably gives rise to protest—both by the mass of lumpens, a natural product of a technocratic society, and by some of the tech-nocrats themselves. No one knows precisely how machines and men should be managed, but everyone feels—and that is the main thrust of the book—that technocratic society is hostile to man and is doomed.

The idea that the technocratic world is inhumane and historically doomed permeates all antitechnocratic nega-tive utopias. But these books often distort the role science and technology do play in society. Taking them out of their broad social context and failing to detect their ambivalence, negative utopias frequently blame science and technology for just about all evils existing in this world. As a result, they make a fetish of the very forces they want to fight. That is why these books' positive significance is usually connected with their critical quality.

One of the reasons behind the criticism of technocratic ideals is that everyday consciousness often sees science and technology as virtually the chief culprits of the emergence of weapons of mass destruction and of the threat of a new world war. And war, especially nuclear war, is treated in

[1] Kurt Vonnegut, *Player Piano*, Macmillan, London, 1967, p. 6.

[2] *Ibid.*, p. 5.

[3] *Ibid.*, p. 80.

many modern American negative utopias as one of the greatest evils and dangers facing mankind. Significantly, negative utopias often use a devastating war either as a background or as the culmination. And, no matter how the cause of the war is interpreted or who is blamed for it (the accusations may range from anticommunist to antiimperialist), it is usually cursed as the destroyer of civilization and of man.

Fear of war is at the same time an indirect expression of fear of its source. Depending on the author's politics and intellect, this may be the military-industrial complex, a shortsighted government, the "Red menace" (sometimes transformed into the "Yellow peril", as in Peter Bryan George's "atomic utopias"), the right or the left.

The better-known antiwar negative utopias—like *Seven Days in May* by Knebel and Bailey—discharge the warning function traditional for negative utopias and antiutopias, and, given the present situation, are important in mobilizing public opinion for the prevention of a new world war.

In some negative utopias, antiutopian elements, sometimes muted and vague, can be detected. We may reject the world of *1984* as evil, Joseph Maloney writes, but we should realize, first, that this evil cannot be avoided and, second, that it is not as terrible or unfamiliar as it may appear at first sight. Essentially, life in a small town where each is known to all, where people live in a fishbowl and are at the mercy of custom and public opinion, differs little from life in an Orwellian world, Maloney argues. And so, while trying to delay the coming of *1984*, we should not despair when it does come. We would merely have to adapt to it, realizing that while it may not be to our liking, it is still not the worst of all possible worlds because its inhabitants at least have food, clothing, shelter and medical care.[1]

This reasoning, scandalizing the reader, displays a feature typical of modern utopian consciousness: the utopian ideal is becoming less and less remote. When an evil appears inevitable, the least of all possible evils appears as a positive ideal and eventually, it is no longer perceived as evil at all. The negative utopia, as a form of possible reality rejected today, becomes the utopian ideal of tomorrow. The distance separating the real from the possible and the possible

[1] See: *The Futurist,* Vol. XIII, No. 2, April 1979, pp. 115, 117.

from the desirable becomes infinitesimally small, the dividing lines practically disappear; it remains to be grateful for food, clothing and shelter and to hope that nothing worse will happen. Obviously, this is a covert manifestation of the crisis of bourgeois utopian consciousness, a covert rejection of utopia per se—although the fear that utopian ideals may be actually implemented (which surfaced in European culture half a century ago) is not yet in evidence; nor is there a conscious, philosophically substantiated rejection of attempts to build the "ideal society".

Still, it does not at all follow that there are no overtly antiutopian works in modern American literature. Take "A Ticket to Tranai" by Robert Sheckley, a well-known science fiction author. Marvin Goodman, the main protagonist, learns that "out past the Galactic Whirl" there is a utopian world called Tranai—"Tranai the Bountiful, a peaceful, creative, happy society, not saints or ascetics, not intellectuals, but ordinary people who had achieved utopia".[1]

After all sorts of ordeals and trials, Goodman reaches this Promised Land. At first he is delighted, but gradually he realizes the meaning and the price of utopia. There is no crime on Tranai—simply because criminals are not called criminals, and a man who has killed five people is termed a "potential criminal". There are "no police force or courts, no judges, sheriffs, marshals, executioners, truant officers or government investigators. No prisons, reformatories or other places of detention"[2]—because those in authority administer the law swiftly and easily, using rifles with silencers and telescopic sights. Arbitrary action and mistakes are ruled out because by definition and under the unwritten law, each person dispatched by the authorities is a "potential criminal". Tranai has achieved "a stable economy without resorting to socialistic, communistic, fascistic or bureaucratic practices", based on a distribution of wealth "without resorting to governmental intervention".[3] It soon becomes clear, however, that wealth is distributed and redistributed with the help of a blaster.

[1] Robert Sheckley, *Citizen in Space*, Ballantine Books, New York, 1968, p. 111.

[2] *Ibid.*, p. 114.

[3] *Ibid.*, pp. 114, 115.

In a word, Goodman had another think coming. "His mind was in a complete turmoil.... Was Tranai a utopia or a planetwide insane asylum? Was there much difference? For the first time in his life, Goodman was wondering if utopia was worth having. Wasn't it better to strive for perfection than to possess it? To have ideals rather than to live by them?"[1]

This is the clearest possible expression of the antiutopian's credo, the formula of antiutopia. Nevertheless, despite the fact that some literary antiutopias do exist and that antiutopian motifs do penetrate negative utopias and other literary genres, one would be justified to say that on the whole, the antiutopian tradition remains undeveloped in the United States. Eugen Weber, who holds this view, sees the reason for this undeveloped state in that while it has felt, perhaps even more acutely than other countries, the negative consequences of technological progress, the United States has not yet lived through the kind of social and political upheavals that have shaken Europe; a benevolent history is not the best environment for the rise of an antiutopian spirit. Americans are not yet really disillusioned with their political prospects. "They have produced utopian satires of the bitterest kind—D. N. Keller, *Revolt of the Pedestrians*; Ward Moore, *Greener than Grass*; S. Mead, *The Great Ball of Wax*,—but the dread and despair characteristic of anti-utopia appear only in the work of the 'technologists'—Bradbury, Vonnegut, Asimov, etc., writers who see the machines taking over; human personality, initiative, and fantasy lost or floundering in a sea of gadgets, experience garnered vicariously through electronic apparatus.... The mood of the American anti-utopia is just as despairing, the defeat of the individual is just as sure, but the end is attained by different means in plot and in treatment, which themselves reflect the author's different experience."[2]

Although Weber does not clearly distinguish between the negative utopia and antiutopia, he has grasped the essence of the latter, and, on the whole, correctly evaluated the development level of the American antiutopian tradition. "The utopian is either a hopeful critic or a hopeful rebel,

[1] *Ibid.*, p. 143.

[2] *Utopia*, Ed. by George Kateb, Atherton Press, New York, 1971, pp. 86-87.

because he has an alternative to offer.... The anti-utopian does not believe in alternatives: it is too late for that. He is defeated before he starts to write."[1] America has not yet lived through enough social and political upheavals, it has had the luck to easily solve the problems which plagued capitalist Europe, its faith in its abilities and historical destiny is still too great for a powerful, emotional and influential body of antiutopian literature to have developed in the United States.

Naturally, the undeveloped state of the antiutopian tradition should not be viewed as something meaning that American culture is inferior. One should remember that it is an ambivalent tradition. True, it does check the infiltration of political theory and practice by utopian concepts and it does stimulate greater realism. But its corroding skepticism leaves a twofold imprint on culture, since it breeds both pessimism and nihilism. So far, Americans are more idealistic than Europeans, with all this entails. However, things are changing now faster than ever before. The nation is growing increasingly aware that America has lost its "exceptionalism", and the possible range of historical adjustment is shrinking. This means that the contradictions America will in all probability face at home and abroad in the near decades will be increasingly acute. The 21st century promises many upheavals and great disillusionment for America; this is sure to affect the nation's consciousness and to generate, sooner or later, a more powerful and distinctive antiutopian spirit which will clash with utopian feelings and orientations and with practical attempts to implement new utopian ideals.

[1] *Ibid.*, p. 86.

Chapter V

THE LIVING UTOPIA

1. The Emergence of the Utopian Communitarian Tradition in the United States

America has failed to produce outstanding utopians like More, Fourier or Saint-Simon. It owes the justly prominent place it holds in the world history of utopia mostly to the utopian experiments it has hosted. No other country can boast as many communities established to implement utopian ideals. Their recorded history can be traced to the 17th century,[1] when the United States did not yet exist as a nation. This practice has lasted uninterrupted ever since, and even in the slackest of times, when it looked like the thread of the communitarian tradition was about to snap, a few tiny sparks of utopian communities still glowed in America to flare up again decades later.

It has always been typical of American utopians to regard utopian projects—their own, and sometimes others'—as specific plans of action which, given the necessary will and a favorable turn of events, could lead to success. And among them there have always been people (including immigrants from Europe) who regarded implementation of utopian communitarian experiments as something of special significance or even as their raison d'etre.

The scale of their efforts was growing because for a very long time, including the first half of the 19th century, America offered better conditions for utopian experiments than Europe or any other part of the world. Land was cheaper, and this was of considerable importance for people of limited means, a condition prevalent among architects

---

[1] See: Arthur Eugene Bestor, Jr., *Backwoods Utopias. The Sectarian and Owenite Phases of Communitarian Socialism in America: 1663-1829*, University of Pennsylvania Press, Philadelphia, 1950.

of utopian experiments. Almost throughout the 19th century, America retained holdovers of communitarian traditions (laid down at the time of the pioneers) with their orientation on collective property and cooperative forms of labor. Another important factor was that the practice of establishing utopian communities, especially on virgin land, fit well into the colonization of the West. Besides, the very fact that America was being settled by people of different nations and cultures made the country more tolerant of sectarian views (sectarian both in direct, religious, and in figurative terms) which were typical of utopian communities. The American ruling class, too, was more tolerant than its European counterparts of these communities— witness the attitude toward Robert Owen's propaganda and experiments in America. While laissez-faire was the underlying principle of material production, and political institutions did not yet present a definite, rigid system, it was tacitly recognized that utopians—both theoretical and practical—had the right to offer their "commodities" to society on the free market; in this case the commodities were the ideas and projects society was free to accept or reject, support or discredit. Of course, this tolerance on the part of the ruling class had its limits. There was also a line the utopian could not overstep, either in the formal, legal sense or in moral terms. This limit was recognition of the social and political system existing in America as lawful and rejection of violence. And so, the authorities offered no resistance to Owenite, Fourierist, and Icarian communities above all because the latter did not present a distinctly revolutionary image and because their attempts to realize a communist social ideal did not involve any open advocacy of a political overthrow of the existing system. One might generally note that none of the major European utopians or their followers who visited America or conducted utopian experiments there advanced a program advocating violent overthrow of the system in force. On the contrary, this system was regarded as the economic and social base for implementing utopian projects and the principles of the American Revolution, as fully consonant with utopian ideals, including socialist ones. This was the tone of the famous addresses Robert Owen made in the U.S. Congress on February 25 and March 7, 1825.

And now to the motives which were prompting Americans to establish utopian communities and experiment with principles and values going against the principles of bourgeois society with its individualism, free market and competition.

The motives were several. Of considerable importance was the fact that bourgeois social institutions continued to take shape in America throughout the first half of the 19th century. This was an incentive stimulating the spirit of constant search for the best possible model of society and its functioning (a spirit that could be traced to the American Enlighteners, above all to Thomas Jefferson) and, by the same token, the pioneer spirit of social experiment. But the chief reason was that the communitarian movement in the United States was motivated by social contradictions which were sometimes felt more acutely in America than in Europe.

Obviously, different factors motivated different founders of utopian communities. Some wanted happiness for themselves, others wanted it, eventually, for all and were convinced they were fulfilling a great mission. Besides, for some population groups, first and foremost for foreigners who were still outsiders in American society, and for religious and political dissenters, the utopian community was also a means of survival in an alien environment.

According to Lewis Mumford's classification, utopian communities are divided into two groups: those created to escape society and those set up to reconstruct it. Communities established by members of religious sects which had no missionary or messianic goals, or, say, Thoreau's Walden were classic escapist utopias. On the contrary, all Owenite, Fourierist and Icarian (Cabetist) communities were typical "reconstruction" utopias.

The utopian communitarian movement in the United States reached its peak in the first half of the 19th century, especially from the 1820s through the 1840s, when many communities which perceptibly influenced America's social and cultural fabric attained maturity.

The so-called religious sectarian communities, most of them established as early as the latter half of the 18th and early 19th centuries, were a special group among them, the more representative being Ephrata, The Shakers, Harmony,

Zoar, The Amana Society, Aurora, Bethel, Bishop Hill and Oneida.

Uniting people who fled religious persecution in Europe (chiefly in Germany), these communities had no desire either to test current utopian projects or to restructure American society according to utopian ideals. The prime and ultimate goal of religious sectarian communities was to preserve and protect their distinctive religious makeup, to establish what they saw as rules of communal life pleasing to God and based on the "true" interpretation of the Bible, and to prepare properly for the Second Coming. Some of these communities did expect their very existence to prompt the rest of society to follow in their footsteps.

Nevertheless, these were utopian communities—first and foremost because, functioning during the rise of American capitalism, they were based on the principles of collective property and social equality. This was explained by the scantiness of their means and by their religious credo; inevitably, this entailed a restructuring of all relations within the community on a utopian basis.

The utopian spirit was even more typical of the secular (Owenite, Fourierist and Icarian) communities which sprang up in the United States from the 1820s to the 1860s.

2. From New Harmony to Icaria

Owenite communitarian experiments were undertaken in the United States at the initiative of Robert Owen himself and under his direct guidance. The British utopian socialist followed closely the activities of religious sectarian communities in the United States. Their success, especially their economic success, made Owen optimistic. Another thing that encouraged him was his overall—and unoriginal—view of America. To him, "it was a *new* world, whose people had left behind them, when they crossed the Ocean, many of the worst features of the old. It was a world without kings and aristocrats, of civil and religious liberty, a world that, from a distance at least, and if one could shut one's eyes to the evil of slavery, seemed to offer something like equality of opportunity to all comers. And its Revolution, less than fifty years old, had established the first and as yet the only full political democracy in the world".[1] In 1824 Owen left for the United States, beginning his long American odyssey.

Virtually all researchers agree that New Harmony which Owen established himself was the most interesting as well as the most typical Owenite community in the United States (these communities totalled 10 to 15) and that it made a considerable impact on American culture.

Owen wanted New Harmony to be a model community displaying social relations in which man would no longer be "a slave to a TRINITY of the most monstrous evils that could be combined to inflict mental and physical evil upon his whole race". Thus he wrote in his *Declaration of Mental Independence*, proclaimed in New Harmony on July 4, 1826: "I refer to PRIVATE, OR INDIVIDUAL PROPERTY—ABSURD AND IRRATIONAL SYSTEMS OF RELIGION—AND MARRIAGE, FOUNDED ON INDIVIDUAL PROPERTY COMBINED WITH SOME ONE OF THESE IRRATIONAL SYSTEMS OF RELIGION."[2] In other words, he wanted to realize the socialist ideal he had cherished for many years. But Owen (and that was later true of Cabet too) had no specific working plan for translating that ideal into reality. Enrollment into the community was spontaneous: Owen's doctrine did not tolerate the creation of socialism for a selected few. On the other hand, this indiscriminate acceptance of members was the seed of the community's failure. Not only those who sincerely shared Owen's ideas and realized that their implementation called for hard work came to New Harmony, but also opportunists and outright swindlers eager to sponge off the "old fool". And so, for all of Owen's efforts and enthusiasm, New Harmony failed to develop the kind of unity of idea which played an important integrating part in religious sectarian communities.

To many of those who came to Owen he was not so much a reformer as a philanthropist; therefore there were few who were willing to work—the rest relied on his pocketbook. Besides, some Americans who were inspired by the socialist ideal refused to connect the image of a free social-

[1] *Robert Owen in the United States*, Ed. by Oakley C. Johnson, Humanities Press, New York, 1970, p. X.

[2] *Ibid.*, p. 70.

ist community with the need for hard work; they saw the latter as the curse of the world outside New Harmony. There was the illusion that merely replacing private property with public ownership and a religious system of values with a secular one would mean that the old life would give way to the new of its own accord. For this reason the community was constantly short of manpower, although it numbered some 900 members soon after its establishment.

Nor did Owen have any precise guidelines for managing the community's economy as an effective means of social regulation. The community was shaken by continuous splits and reorganizations. Actually, not a single social mechanism created in New Harmony worked; it turned out that the idea alone was not enough to remold men's minds and offset economic and organizational mismanagement.

However, New Harmony's cultural and academic achievements, upheld and promoted by William Maclure, Frances Wright and other outstanding figures of American culture in the first half of the 19th century, were so great that the community is still considered a mainstay of American science and culture. "From the very beginning," the Soviet historian M. N. Zakharova writes, "a school using Pestalozzi's methods was set up. Children aged 2 to 12 were educated, clothed and fed at public expense. They lived in special quarters, apart from their parents. Besides general education, vocational training and children's participation in productive work were also provided....

"In the evenings, lectures and discussions were held in New Harmony. Frances Wright sponsored a women's literary society, the first in American history. Josiah Warren presided over concerts of vocalists and instrumentalists. Weekly balls held in Harmony's former church were very popular with young people."[1]

Owen's and his followers' experiments paved the way for Fourierist communities which blossomed in the United States in the 1840s. At that time, Charles Fourier's ideas spread among Americans, attracting them mostly by the

[1] M. N. Zakharova, "Robert Owen and Owenites in the United States" in: *A History of Socialist Doctrines*, Moscow, 1976, pp. 195-96 (in Russian).

notion of "associations" interpreted in a distinctly American way. "Americans preferred not to wait for the conditions described by Fourier to mature; they lost no time in organizing phalanxes. Their precise numbers are difficult to calculate; John Noyes, their first chronicler, stressed that. He noted, however, that 34 communities were established in the United States in the 1840s. Albert Brisbane said in his letter to the Fourierists of Paris that by the autumn of 1844 there were 30 small associations 150 to 300 members each. Arthur Bestor, a serious researcher, updated the figure and wrote that 28 more or less big Fourierist phalanxes were set up in the United States between the 1840s and the 1860s. As to the membership, Noyes says that the figure 8,600 'might probably be doubled to represent the census of the obscure unknown attempts'."[1]

Just as New Harmony stood out among the communities created by Owen and his followers, Brook Farm rose above the other Fourierist communities. It offered a concentrated expression of major Fourierist principles—associated labor (based on joint use of the means of production and on a graded system of remuneration), associated everyday life, and a new system of education and upbringing. But, like other associations, Brook Farm demonstrated the weak points of Fourierism and its incompatibility with the conditions of bourgeois America. By the end of the 1840s Fourierist communities virtually ceased to exist.

However, "among the most interesting pages in the history of American Communism are those relating to the Icarian experiments. The records of patient sufferings, heroic devotion, and acrimonious feuds of these colonies cover almost half a century; they are full of pathos and instruction".[2] Instructive and dramatic their history is indeed.

Icarian communities were established according to the plans and under the guidance of Étienne Cabet, another 19th century French utopian, or his direct followers. Unlike Owen, who saw the communes as a way to transform existing society, and unlike Fourier, who regarded the

[1] M. A. Avdeyeva, "Fourier's Ideas in the United States" in: *A History of Socialist Doctrines*, p. 277.

[2] Morris Hillquit, *History of Socialism in the United States*, Funk & Wagnall's Company, New York and London, 1903, p. 121.

phalanxes as both sprouts of the new society and a way to its subsequent transformation, Cabet began by firmly rejecting the very idea of utopian communities. He held that Icaria—the utopian land he described in his *Voyage to Icaria*—should take shape not within a small enclave but throughout a whole nation and then spread to cover most, if not all of the world. Otherwise, Cabet maintained, the endeavor would be doomed.

"No need even for attempts to set up individual communities whose success will not do much good but whose failure, which is almost certain, will do great harm! Persuasion and only persuasion, until the masses adopt the Principle of Community! "[1]

Setting out his position, Cabet wrote, in March 1841, in the advance prospectus of his periodical *Le Populaire*: "We want no revolution, we want reform. We want to destroy the old only to replace it with the new which will be free from imperfection.... And we are profoundly convinced that all these happy results are quite possible and can be attained by force of public opinion.

"Proceeding from this, *Le Populaire* will be a democratic, reformist, socialist and, specifically, communist organ. It will demand community, but the sort of community established with the help of public opinion and after a transitional or preparatory regime. For this transitional regime it will demand democracy and reform, and the proclamation of the principle of community, growing equality, elimination of poverty, regulation of wages, uniformity of education, etc. Its guiding philosophical ideas will be justice, tolerance, morality and brotherhood."

Judging by his works, Cabet's anticommunitarianism was not the product of a profound theoretical analysis. It is doubtful that he understood that the ideals he proclaimed in his utopia were impossible to implement within a small community surrounded by a hostile world, that one could only start (sacrificing oneself for the sake of future generations and one's ends for the sake of the means to attain them) upon the road of implementing the ideals which could be realized only on a much greater scale, this great scale being the only way to identify the vast positive potential of the new social relations. It is much

[1] Étienne Cabet, *Voyage en Icarie*, Paris, 1848, p. 564.

more probable that Cabet reached his conclusions by following the efforts of Owen, Fourier and other utopians. Be that as it may, Cabet was adamant: no communitarian experiments.

In a few years, however, Cabet changed his views concerning the ways of establishing Icaria. In 1843 he proposed the organization of an experimental communist community. In May 1847 *Le Populaire* published his appeal in which he called on the French to leave for America and create a new society there.

Here is what Cabet was hoping to find in America, the principles and ideals he dreamed to realize in the Icarian community: "In Icaria we shall look for work and abundance ... well-being for our families as well as for ourselves ... a new World which will be the Kingdom of God and Justice.... Poverty and love of liberty is driving people everywhere to America. Let us go too, for we are children of France which is habitually considered the guiding star of the Human Race but for which we merely want to be servants and soldiers in the front ranks; let us go to found an Icaria for Liberty and Equality, let us realize the ideal of Philosophy, Religion and Brotherhood!

"And there, in Icaria, with our Icarian principles, what wonders and marvels! Nothing by chance, all by reason —One for all and all for one.—From each according to his powers, to each according to his needs.... From the first step, the very best roads, the most perfect cities and villages, the most magnificent workshops; perfection in housing, the environment, clothing, food, hygiene, education.... Community will be realized completely.... Community will begin at once; and within 20 years the human population will be educated and completely Communistic, a generation of children will be brought up for Communism, and Community will be developed and achieved, complete and perfect.... For the education of men, complete freedom of association and of discussion, all the means, books and necessary periodicals.

"Machines will multiply infinitely to give solace to man; purged of all danger and excessive fatigue, work will be easy, short and even attractive for all.

"The fine arts will have the greatest degree of development and perfection.

"In Icaria, no bankruptcies or worries, no court trials

or passports, no spies or gendarmes, no executioners or jailers.

"No one will be happier than others, no one will see anyone happier than himself."[1]

People responded differently to Cabet's appeal. Some welcomed his plan enthusiastically. Others, particularly the Communists grouped around *La Fraternité*, a journal founded by Charon and Lahautière, rejected it. Cabet appealed for support to the leaders of the German Workers' Educational Society (which played an important role in the organization of the Communist League), but they refused it. Their arguments, which they marshalled in the trial issue of *Kommunistische Zeitschrift* (September 1847), were prophetic:

"We are convinced that Cabet's plan to found an Icaria, that is, a colony based on principles of community, in America cannot yet be realized, and for the following reasons:

"(a) because all who emigrate with Cabet, while they may be ardent Communists, will be too steeped, through their upbringing, in the flaws and prejudices of modern society and will not be able to shake them off immediately upon their arrival in Icaria;

"(b) because through this, friction and discord will arise inevitably in the colony from the very beginning, and they will be kept up and fanned by the hostile and mighty outside society, as well as by spies of European governments, until they lead to a complete disintegration of the Communist society;

"(c) because most of the settlers will be handicraftsmen while those most in demand will be strong farmhands to open up and cultivate land; and for a worker to turn into a peasant will be not so easy as some appear to believe;

"(d) because the privations and disease which a change of climate brings will dishearten many and prompt them to leave the commune.—Today many people are for the plan, they see only its bright side and welcome it enthusiastically, but when harsh reality sets in, when all sorts of privations begin, when all the little creature comforts of civilization sometimes open even to the poorest worker in Europe disappear, then enthusiasm will give way to dejection among many;

[1] *Le Populaire de 1841*, No. 6, May 9, 1847, p. 298.

"(e) because for the Communists who recognize the principle of personal freedom—and the Icarians clearly recognize it too—community of property without a transitional period, a democratic transitional period in which personal property only gradually transforms into public property, is as impossible as for a farmer a harvest is impossible without sowing."[1]

Still, despite all warnings and arguments to the contrary, Cabet decided to act. A fund-raising campaign was launched, and in December 1847 the future colonists held a constituent assembly. Shortly before the inauguration of the society Cabet came to London to visit Robert Owen, who had by then returned from the United States after the collapse of his New Harmony. On Owen's advice, Cabet signed a contract with an American company which had purchased 10 million acres in Texas from the U.S. government; Cabet acquired over 1 million acres on the Red River. The company charged nothing for the land, but provided it on condition that the Icarian society take possession of it not later than July 1, 1848. On February 3, 1848 the first group of Icarians, 69 people, left for the United States to be followed, over the rest of the year, by several hundred others who traveled to their future paradise in groups.

Why did Cabet change his views of communitarian experiments? What drove him, a man with extensive political experience although sometimes without sufficient caution, to undertake such a risky venture, especially when Owenite communes were already a thing of the past and Fourierist phalanxes in America were falling apart one after another?

Perhaps the success of his novel played its part, creating, in the author's mind, the illusion that his idea was highly popular. Pressure from friends, ardent Icarians, must have made an impact too. But the chief reason was, in all probability, different. Cabet realized that for all the enthusiasm of his admirers, he had no chance of establishing Icaria in prerevolutionary France. And so, if he wanted to make mankind happy—and he did want it—he had no other choice but to go to America and start with a small Icarian community.

[1] *Kommunistische Zeitschrift. Probeblatt*, No. 1, September 1847, p. 7.

However, the venture ran into all sorts of obstacles from the very beginning. Failure in settling in Texas, shortage of funds, discord and health problems scared many people off, and by the spring of 1849, of all groups of settlers only less than 300 remained loyal to Cabet. They settled in Nauvoo, Illinois, where they managed to rent, on easy terms, some 800 acres of land, several houses and a few small businesses. "In February, 1850, the Icarians adopted a constitution which provided for the administration of their affairs by a board of six directors. Of these directors, the first was the president of the community.... The acts of the board of directors were, however, subject to the approval of the General Assembly, consisting of all male members over twenty years old."[1] Within a few months the community was recognized by the Illinois House of Representatives and later, by the Senate. Things seemed to be moving along well, and Cabet (like Owen soon after the founding of New Harmony) thought it possible to leave the commune for a while and visit France.

However, the administration system devised by the Icarians proved to be imperfect, and the consequences were not long in coming. The brief absence of Cabet, whose prestige was virtually the sole force holding the commune together, almost destroyed Icaria. At the same time, his personal authority increasingly hampered the commune's progress. Cabet, who wanted to be the Icarus of the community (in his book, Icarus was the leader and liberator of the oppressed), gradually developed dictatorial traits and a tendency to take all power in his own hands. This would have been natural in a religious sectarian community where an authoritarian system was interpreted from a religious standpoint and ideologically justified. But in a secular commune which proclaimed complete social and economic equality, established a General Assembly and advocated respect for popular sovereignty, dictatorial ways were out of place. Cabet could no longer effectively impose his will on the commune, while the commune could not keep Cabet in check. In August 1856 the community split into dissenting groups and in October, Cabet was expelled from Icaria. Together with his partisans (about 180 people) he moved to St. Louis and soon died there.

[1] Morris Hillquit, *op. cit.*, p. 130.

In 1858, after a series of failures, his partisans established a new Icarian commune in Chaltenham, near St. Louis. The colony did get started, but dissent finished it too.

A similar thing happened to the Icarians who remained in Nauvoo after Cabet's departure and then moved to Corning, Iowa. Here the split occurred between the older and the younger generations. Many young people, brought up in Icaria, were openly critical of the old guard who, they charged, abandoned the ideals they themselves proclaimed and operated inefficiently. "Many of them were new members who were deeply moved by the theories of Karl Marx and his International. Several had actually belonged to this organization, and others had fought at the Parisian barricades in 1871. These earnest young men were scandalized by the apostasy of the older generation. They demanded that all private possessions, valuable or worthless, should be given up to the community. The existence of private gardens and vineyards was a disgrace, encouraging vanity, enviousness (as was self-evident), and greed. Why were women not given equal political rights? Why was there no propaganda for communism outside the community? And why were new young members not admitted—as many as possible?"[1]

It all ended up in a rift between the young and the old. In 1883 a group of young Icarians left Iowa and moved to California, where a new commune, Icaria Speranza, had been established as early as 1881 and existed until 1886. The old guard organized what they called the New Icarian Community. This was a failure: in 1898 the community ceased to exist, thus ending the Icarian communitary movement in America.

Owenite, Fourierist and Icarian communities differed from their religious sectarian counterparts in their ethnic and social composition, in their attitude toward religion (as mostly secular organizations), in their lifestyles and level of prosperity. And—one should stress this again—they were utopias of reconstruction, not of escape. Michael Fellman writes that they were not conceived by their architects "as escape mechanisms from general society; they were intended to bring on the total reform of America by

[1] Mark Holloway, *Heavens on Earth. Utopian Communities in America 1680-1880*, Turnstile Press, 1951, pp. 207-08.

offering the perfect community where no alternative community existed in anything but embryonic form. Neither opposed to the current of American society nor alienated from it, utopian communitarianism was rather one expression, if an extreme one, of the possibilities for social reconstruction at that time".[1]

Indeed, throughout the first half of the 19th century, and even despite the crisis of the 1830s, American capitalism did not yet create conditions for a mass alienation from society which could mold utopian communities into the shape they were to assume over a hundred years later. Still, while emphasizing the precedence of the model function, one cannot lose sight of the psychologically important fact that the end goal of the members of utopian communities was to restructure American society on a socialist (communist) basis. In this they differed substantially from religious sectarian communities which wanted to establish a heaven on earth.

It appears, however, that none of the founders or members of Owenite, Fourierist and Icarian communities realized that America was not yet ready for socialism, that, at any rate, it was impossible to reform America in a socialist spirit—either through the establishment of communes or with the help of any other organizations, and that it took revolutionary means and appropriate historical conditions (absent in 19th-century America) to restructure any society. Nevertheless, their enthusiasm was all the greater and their faith in success all the firmer—until their ventures failed.

Despite all differences between religious sectarian and secular communities, both were "on the other side" of American society. In everyday life, members of these communities were to observe principles and goals which, reflecting their notions of genuine community and genuine relations, ran counter to the norms, principles and objective development trends of the society of their time.

Here are the principles and ideals American utopian communities tried to translate into reality.

First and foremost, it was the new type of property—

---

[1] Michael Fellman, *The Unbounded Frame. Freedom and Community in Nineteenth Century American Utopianism*, Greenwood Press, Inc., Westport, Conn., 1973, p. XVI.

public property—which, to be sure, was not completely alien to the American tradition. Some Americans (for example, Thomas Jefferson) recognized the need for private property on a nationwide scale while admitting the possibility of public property within small communities. Yet, it fundamentally contradicted capitalist civilization and at the same time was the root of the entire tree trunk of utopian values, institutions and relations of social equality and freedom from exploitation. In most communities, distribution of goods and benefits was organized not according to one's contribution or requirements but on the basis of "fairness", often interpreted as crude egalitarianism.

A new type of social institutions was taking shape in the communities. Although many were ruled in an authoritarian manner, attempts were nevertheless made to create administrative mechanisms based on the principle of popular self-government. Special attention was paid to the development of new family relations, and many different versions were devised—from a complete abolition of the traditional family to the so-called composite marriage which was practiced in Oneida and gave rise to severe criticism on the part of the community's neighbors. In any case, relations between the sexes were based in many communities on principles which were inadmissible for American society both for purely economic and for moral reasons.

Finally, utopian communities promoted a new type of personality whose goals and values differed substantially from those dominant in American society—a society which produced selfish owners of property, individualists who competed ruthlessly with others for a place in the sun.

3. Utopian Freedom and Historical Necessity

The record of American utopian communities offers a great body of information to discuss the relationship between theory and practice, ways to realize a social ideal and the role of utopia in the development of society.

Above all, this record shows that a utopia can be implemented on a limited spatial and temporal scale even when historical conditions for a complete and stable realization of its ideals throughout the given society have not yet matured. In other words, certain ideals and values arbitrarily created by the imagination and at variance with objective trends of social development can be implemented within a small enclave and can guide its functioning within a limited period.

In the 19th century, when U.S. capitalism was advancing swiftly, exacerbating social inequality, competition and individualism and turning man into an appendage of machines, there were islands in American society where people were trying to mold their relations according to the principles of brotherhood and cooperation, where work was no longer a curse, where there were no masters or slaves. For a short time, a social miracle occurred somewhere, alleviating despair with the hope that soon the world would become one big utopia making everyone happy, that the social ideal upheld by utopian socialists was attainable. In 1845 Frederick Engels published his "Description of Recently Founded Communist Colonies Still in Existence" and made the following conclusion: "Communism, social existence and activity based on community of goods, is not only possible but has actually already been realized in many communities in America and in one place in England, with the greatest success."[1] Using the sources available at the time, specifically the letters of John Finch, an Owenite and a traveler, in the *New Moral World*, Engels wrote that although members of these communities saw the world in a religious light, they managed to implement principles which were the aim Communists wanted to attain in society as a whole.

What attracted and inspired the young colleague of Marx was clear from his description, based on Finch's testimony, of the way the Shakers lived. "Each of these communities," Engels wrote, "is a fine, well laid-out town, with dwelling houses, factories, workshops, assembly buildings and barns; they have flower and vegetable gardens, fruit trees, woods, vineyards, meadows and arable land in abundance; then, livestock of all kinds.... Their granaries are always full of corn, their store-rooms full of clothing materials."

Material abundance is an important feature of life in communist communities, and Engels emphasized that.

"Amongst these people no one is obliged to work against

[1] Karl Marx, Frederick Engels, *Collected Works*, Vol. 4, Progress Publishers, Moscow, 1975, p. 214.

his will, and no one seeks work in vain. They have no poorhouses and infirmaries, having not a single person poor and destitute, nor any abandoned widows and orphans." This referred to the practicability of ideals like free labor and social equality.

"In their ten towns there is not a single gendarme or police officer, no judge, lawyer or soldier, no prison or penitentiary; and yet there is proper order in all their affairs. The laws of the land are not for them and as far as they are concerned could just as well be abolished and nobody would notice any difference." Here Engels stressed the absence of public authority, above all of the typically bourgeois organs of coercion.

"They enjoy, as we said," Engels concluded, "the most absolute community of goods and have no trade and no money among themselves"[1] —meaning that their relations were based on public property.

Today it is clear that Engels's article reflects both insufficiency of information and what a historian has termed "illusions of previous socialist thought".[2] But it is interesting first and foremost as a document which highlights the contemporary view of the American communities held by a man who was among the most progressive thinkers of the time, who was critical of existing society and already saw the key to social transformations not in communitarian movements but in social revolution, but who worked to devise a theoretical and practical substantiation of communism as a principle guiding the organization of social relations.

Engels underlined above all those features of utopian communist communities which were clearly to their credit: their attempts to organize life on the basis of public property, thereby solving many of the contradictions inherent in the very existence of private property. Utopian communities, Engels noted, had demonstrated that life could be organized on the basis of public property—something advocates of communism were trying to prove theoretically. The record of the American communities offered practical evidence which simply could not be missed.

[1] *Ibid.*, pp. 215-16.

[2] L. I. Golman, "Frederick Engels, Historian of Socialist Thought" in: *A History of Socialist Doctrines*, p. 9.

Later, when Marx and Engels formulated the principles of scientific communism and when the important thing was not so much to prove that communist relations and institutions could in fact exist as to identify the historical and material conditions necessary for their implementation, the founders of Marxism pointed primarily to the negative aspects of the utopian communitarian experience. They showed that the existence of public property as an institution in inadequate historical conditions was powerless to solve all problems even within the utopian communities themselves, and that the latter did not pave the way for transforming society as a whole. Engels wrote in 1866: "Our views on the distinction between a future, non-capitalist society and society as it is today are exact conclusions from the historical facts and development processes and, unless presented in conjunction with these facts and this development, are theoretically and practically without value."[1] Hence the criticism of all sorts of "domestic colonies" and "small Icarias"—and this despite the fact that the "small Icarias" were striving to observe faithfully the organizational principle of public property.

Indeed, the record of the American utopian communities proves that not only the scope of public property in the capitalist system but also its economic and humanitarian effects were limited. The emancipatory potential of the institutions of public property was small since at that time, in the first half of the 19th century, the capitalist mode of production had not yet exhausted all its possibilities, nor had it created a material and technical basis adequate to the new type of social relations. Public property could not ensure the realization of humanitarian, economic and moral advantages expected from it. Subsequent history confirmed that this realization was possible only on the basis of advanced productive forces and high labor efficiency. No wonder that members of most utopian communities had little likeness to the all-round, free people Owen, Fourier, Cabet and many other utopians dreamed about. Where economic success was attained, spiritual and cultural levels were usually low (except for the religious

[1] "Frederick Engels to Edward R. Pease in London," January 27, 1866 in: Marx, Engels, *Collected Works*, Second Russian Edition, Vol. 36, Moscow, 1964, p.364.

aspect). On the other hand, where special attention was paid to the spiritual and cultural aspects, as in New Harmony or Brook Farm, economic advances were small and the communities themselves survived for a few months only.

The American communitarian experience proved that realization of utopian ideals on a limited scale could not create a stable alternate utopian world (the dream of utopian experimenters) and that the establishment of a "living utopia" could not transform society radically or effectively. And, although communitarian experiments continued virtually throughout the 200 years of American history, it was a pulsating world, a phoenix of a world because most utopian communes were short-lived. Some disintegrated like New Harmony, others like Oneida or Amana, degenerated into capitalist enterprises, still others were in decline for decades and then ended up like New Harmony or Oneida.

While all communities ceased to exist sooner or later, their life spans were different. Ephrata survived for 172 years (1733-1905); Harmonian communities, for 102 years (1803-1905); Amana, for 89 years (1843-1932); Zoar, for 81 years; Icarian communities, for 48 years (1847-1895); Aurora and Bethel, for 37 years (1844-1881); Brook Farm, for 5 years (1841-1846); and New Harmony, for 2 years (1825-1827). Data on the duration of the communities' operation differ one to three years from author to author— as a rule, because the legal records formalizing a community's establishment or demise did not always coincide with the actual dates. Brook Farm, as a Fourierist community into which it was transformed in 1844, existed for only 2 years.

Religious communities proved much more durable than secular ones, especially Owenite and Fourierist. Does this mean that religion was the integrating and stabilizing factor of communal life? Or could it be that religious communities possessed some qualities extending their life span, yet nonreligious in nature?

It is common knowledge that religion possesses considerable integrating power rooted in its organizational, ritual and doctrinal elements, especially within a sect which is viewed by the outside world with suspicion or outright hostility and which has to continuously fight for survival, doing its utmost to block any deviation of its members from the credo proclaimed. Religion provides the community's members with a common purpose and an unshakable faith in the truth of the principles adopted. Besides, religious psychology is, in all probability, even more important than religious ideology. According to Candidus Hugo, an early student of the communitary movement in the United States, "there is good reason why religious inspiration plays such a prominent part in many colonies. Firm faith in the Bible as interpreted by an inspired medium, often the head of the community, is the very raison d'etre of many communities".[1]

But a secular doctrine can perform this function too— if it is properly organized in psychological terms and capable of arousing deep feelings and enthusiasm, at least within a comparatively small community. This means that the heart of the matter lies not only in religion but also in its concomitants which are, in themselves, devoid of a religious meaning but which, combined with religious faith, help to stabilize the community and keep its elements together.

In most relatively stable communities there existed a rigid hierarchy and a cult of the founder and leader. The important role of the latter can be deduced from the fact that upon his death some communities either declined rapidly and continued in a sorry state (although sometimes surviving for a long time) or disintegrated completely. For example, this happened to Aurora and Bethel which ceased to exist, respectively, three and four years after the death of their founder Dr. William Keil in 1877. Oneida turned into a company of stockholders soon after John Noyes, its founder, left it. The great stabilizing role of a charismatic leader is borne out by the record of many secular communes—New Harmony, held together by Robert Owen, or Icaria, whose pillar was Étienne Cabet.

A well-devised organizational structure and a smoothly functioning system of social management were typical of stable communities. Note that this does not refer to a "rigid" or "loose" management structure, that is, not to its flexibility or democratic nature but precisely to their smooth, orderly way of functioning. Where the administra-

[1] C. Hugo, *Die Vorläufer des neueren Sozialismus*, Vol. 1, Part 2, Dietz Verlag, Stuttgart, 1859, pp. 863-84.

tive system was haphazard, the death of the leader who held all power in his own hands and whose personal prestige checked centrifugal tendencies often spelled doom for the community.

Another typical feature of stable communities was the social homogeneity of their members. As a rule, they were peasants and handicraftsmen whose requirements, especially intellectual ones, were rather modest. It is important to add that many such communities were founded by foreigners (mostly Germans, but also Swedes, French, Russians and others) to whom survival of the community was often almost literally a matter of life and death.

Finally, most stable communities were closed societies. They were cautious and restrained in admitting new members, setting a trial period for them and strictly observing the principle of no deviations from a single faith. This was in sharp contrast to the admission to Fourierist and especially Owenite communities whose doors were open to all who wished to enter, and where social, ethnic or any other homogeneity was out of the question (with very few exceptions).

The features which destabilized the communities and contributed to their disintegration included, first and foremost, their social heterogeneity which led to gaps in the levels of requirements, education, culture, value orientations, etc. The higher the overall cultural level and the greater the gap in the levels of culture and requirements, the faster these communes fell apart.

Contributing to the disintegration was also the hostility of the social milieu around a community. In turn, the degree of this hostility depended on the degree of the community's radicalism, its social activity and its own hostility to the milieu. When a community's lifestyle appeared too dangerous—and everyday consciousness saw the danger not so much in the institution of public property as in "godlessness", "crimes against morality", "destruction of the family" and the like, that is, primarily associating it with religious and moral issues, and when its activities were too energetic and destructive, "society" took an active part in undermining and discrediting the community. This was what happened to Oneida which shocked American society by its practice of "composite marriage".

The succession of generations was a factor in the disintegration of those communities where marriage was allowed. This, incidentally, explains why celibacy was introduced in several communities and why the founders regarded it as a powerful integrating factor. The reason was not that it upheld the moral spirit, as it was often alleged, but that it prevented the birth of a new generation. If that was not the case, the children and grandchildren of the original colonists became community members not by choice or inner conviction, like their fathers and grandfathers, but by birth. And, although their socialization proceeded according to norms and principles which should have instilled in the younger generations devotion to communal life and to the interests which had guided the pioneers, the effort was often a failure, especially if the community maintained more or less close contacts with the outside world. The social organization principles and concerns of this world frequently proved more attractive, prompting the younger generation to abandon the commune and eroding the faith in the ideals which had inspired the original settlers.

Obviously, all these factors merely accelerated the collapse of utopian communities; the chief cause was the fundamental incompatibility of the communities' basic norms, institutions and relations with the norms, institutions and relations dominant in the outside world and rooted in objective sociohistorical trends.

Here one should note that most secular and even some religious communities were plagued by disputes (and consequent reorganizations) over loyalty to the doctrine or principles its members were to uphold. These disputes did more to erode than to consolidate the members' unity. They were not caused merely by the quarrelsome irascibility of some utopians but by basic differences of opinion which never failed to surface with the passage of time and which were connected with the search for the best ways for the community to function. These differences concerned property (specifically, the degree to which personal property and the means of production were to be socialized), organization of labor, distribution of the surplus product, contacts with the outside world and similar matters. "Dogmatists" refused to accept any deviation from the originally proclaimed credo (often formalized in the "charters" and "constitutions" of the communities), pointing out— and with good reason— that the realization of this credo was why the community was founded in the first place. "Revisionists" objected, with equally good reason, that without appropriate adjustments to the credo, both the community and the credo might simply cease to exist. Nevertheless, neither those who, after their communities split apart, reaffirmed a revision of the credo, nor those who remained rigidly loyal to its unadulterated version succeeded in realizing the original objectives consistently or fully.

In assessing, in overall terms, the historical role of the American utopian communities in the 19th and the first half of the 20th centuries and acknowledging their impracticability as economic, political and social enterprises, one cannot fail to see their role as an experimental model of social organization of great heuristic significance for social and political scientists and as an important factor in the development of socialist consciousness and culture in the United States—as emphasized in the program of the Communist Party, U.S.A.[1]

4. New Utopian Experiments

After the upsurge it experienced in the first half of the 19th century, the communitarian movement in the United States entered an almost 100-year period of decline. A handful of communities scattered across the nation "went almost unnoticed and involved a decreasing percentage of the population",[2] and their impact on the social fabric was minimal.

The situation began to change in the latter half of the 1960s. "Now, in the last ten years [from the mid-1960s to the mid-1970s], the process has reversed itself and communitarian experiments are attracting more and more people."[3] The absence of easily accessible documentary evidence, their short life span and their frequently semiclandestine nature make it impossible to accurately ascertain

[1] See: *New Program of the Communist Party, USA, May 1970*, New Outlook Publishers, New York, 1970, p. 116.

[2] *The Reform Spirit in America*, p. 595.

[3] *Ibid.*, p. 596.

their number in this or that period. Still, most American researchers agree that in the 1960s and 1970s from 1,000 to 3,000 utopian communities existed in the United States.[1]

The new upsurge of communitarianism coincided with the rise of mass democratic movements in the United States, but this was hardly a mere coincidence. The attempts to both transform American society and escape from it were rooted in the general critical attitude to the dominant institutions, relations and values. The humanitarian, political and social crisis was perceived all the more acutely because it manifested itself against the backdrop of economic and technological growth which technocratic consciousness connected with the possibility of overcoming at least the more pressing social contradictions.

Modern communities proved more numerous and more diverse than 19th-century ones. Herbert A. Otto, who studied the communitarian movement in the United States, estimated that in 1971 there were 16 types of communities differing in their leanings and objectives, including "agricultural" (based on the principle of self-sufficiency), "political" (uniting their members around a common ideology and a common political credo and subdivided by Otto into anarchist, socialist and pacifist), "spiritual/mystical" (which strove for inner perfection), "nature" or, more precisely, "environmental" (which advocated support of the ecological system and unity of man and nature), "craft", "art" and other communes.[2]

They were also classified by location (rural and urban), by their attitude to religion (religious and secular), by their organizational principles and by the type of relations existing in them ("authoritarian", anarchist, etc.).

The urban community was a new development without precedent in the past. It was usually a "big family" whose

---

[1] See: R. Hourriet, *Getting Back Together*, New York, 1971, p. XIII; David Moberg, "Experimenting with the Future. Alternative Institutions and American Socialism" in: *Co-ops, Communes & Collectives. Experiments in Social Change in the 1960s and 1970s*, Ed. by J. Case and R. C. R. Taylor, Pantheon Books, New York, 1979, p. 285.

[2] Herbert A. Otto, "Communes: The Alternative Life-Style" in: *Saturday Review*, Vol. LIX, No. 17, April 24, 1971, pp. 17-19.

members were united in their desire to create an "unalienated" atmosphere and ensure mutual assistance. Gathering by the fireplace after work, people of different ages and occupations (but usually of the same social background, color of skin—mostly white, and religious denomination) felt they were basking in the warmth of spiritual companionship and understanding.

As evidence of the increasing social and political alienation in postwar America, urban communities were a typical symptom of exacerbation in the crisis of the existing family relations and traditional institutions of socialization which no longer met the needs of either society as a whole or the individual. Essentially, by looking at the communities of the 1960s and 1970s, one could pinpoint the pain centers of America with sufficient accuracy. The decline of the cities, the disintegration of traditional family structures, the crisis of the success-oriented business and work ethics, the feeling that the technological world which was trampling nature and man underfoot was hostile and uncontrollable, as well as many similar developments—all this found a distinct reflection in the communitarian movement.

As before, the communitarians often turned to religion in their search for solutions to the problems they faced. But this time these were mostly esoteric Oriental religions, specifically Zen-Buddhism with its conspicuous mysticism which, compared to technocratic ideology and its social development projects, appeared to be geared better than Western religions to removing complex problems and establishing contacts between man and nature, man and the cosmos, man and man.

Not all communities of the 1960s and 1970s were distinctly utopian, that is, not all of them observed and preached values and orientations at variance with the objective trends and dominant values of contemporary American society. Lonely old people gathered under the same roof, young artists bent on setting up a cooperative of sorts and similar groups could not set for themselves any far-reaching sociocritical goals. Strictly speaking, however, even such communities did contain utopian elements since they countered the privately compartmentalized life of American capitalism with a collective element, albeit in primitive form.

Modern communities were born on the spur of the moment, through a spontaneous coincidence of interests among people of the same social background. And, while these communes comprised people representing virtually all age, social, occupational and ethnic groups, predominating in them was the member aged 20 to 30, of middle-class extraction, usually educated in the arts, dissatisfied with his job or studies, lacking a family and a stable income, and skeptical of society's ways and morals.[1] This means that in his social characteristics, the average member of the modern utopian community differed strikingly from his 19th-century predecessor.

As Moos and Brownstein point out, "the new communards generally had a much clearer understanding of the faults of the society they sought to abandon—materialism, spiritual bankruptcy, environmental decay, insane competitiveness, racism and militarism—than they did of the form the alternative communities should take".[2] Their organizers usually relied on the natural course of events which not infrequently, as developments soon proved, either destroyed the community or led it far astray from the original goals.

Few of the communities of the 1960s and 1970s were established to implement a definite utopian project, the way it was with 19th-century Owenite, Fourierist and Icarian communities. Twin Oaks, set up to realize the project advanced by B. F. Skinner in his *Walden Two*, was clearly the most colorful of them all. In 1966 a group of Skinner's followers gathered at Ann Arbor decided to organize a community based on behavioristic principles and described in *Walden Two*. This community, originally composed of 8 members, was established in Virginia the following year.[3]

The communities were usually small (a few score members at most) and fluid in their composition. In most cases the composition changed spontaneously: some left, others joined, sometimes visitors were accepted on certain terms

---

[1] See, inter alia, Rudolf Moos and Robert Brownstein, *Environment and Utopia. A Synthesis*, Plenum Press, New York and London, 1977, p. 41.

[2] *Ibid.*

[3] See *The Reform Spirit in America*, p. 600; Rosabeth Moss Kanter, *Commitment and Community. Communes and Utopias in Sociological Perspective*, Harvard University Press, Cambridge, Mass., 1972, p. 19.

for some time. For example, by 1971 up to 45 people, including some 10 visitors, lived at Twin Oaks, but of the 8 founders only 2 remained.[1] The communities mostly lacked a clear-cut organizational structure and reflected a broad range of lifestyles—from anarchistically free to rigidly disciplined and hierarchical (although the consensus is that the latter were few).

Among them there were, naturally, communities which, like Brook Farm long ago, were consciously striving to discharge a "model function". Describing his impressions of a visit to one of the "most stable and authoritative" U.S. urban communities of the 1970s, the Soviet sociologist Igor Bestuzhev-Lada notes: "The members of the Lyndisfarn Community are indeed united by a common idea. They feel as though they are in a Noah's Ark in an ocean of social reality unacceptable to them. And they would like to set an example for mankind by an attempt to save themselves from this reality."[2] But "model communes" were relatively few even in the late 1960s and early 1970s, when the new communitarian wave was at its highest. Mostly, they were cases of attempted escape from society into a "different life". People were fleeing loneliness and isolation; alienated, monotonous and backbreaking work, the mundane pursuit of success, money and creature comforts.

As in the 19th century, most new communes were short-lived; according to Moos and Brownstein, their life span did not exceed two years.[3] The causes of their disintegration were largely the same as a century ago—heterogeneous composition, no definite organizational structure, differences of opinion and economic difficulties. According to D. Moberg, "commune problems can be as endless as those families encounter and quite similar, but communes do not have the same proclivity to stick together. Illness, poverty, conflicting demands on limited resources, disputes between people earning money and those who aren't, and struggles for power over communal direction—all have contributed to the failures."[4]

[1] Rosabeth Moss Kanter, *op. cit.*, p. 19.

[2] I. V. Bestuzhev-Lada, "City, Family, Future" in: *USA: Economics, Politics, Ideology*, No. 5, 1979, p. 74 (in Russian).

[3] Rudolf Moos and Robert Brownstein, *op. cit.*, p. 42.

[4] D. Moberg, *op. cit.*, p. 285.

As in the past, what contributed greatly to the collapse of utopian communities was the hostility on the part of the neighbors who saw the activities of the communes not only as a violation of "law and order" but also as an assault on the norms and values underlying their own existence. This reaction of bourgeois society was natural because whether the communes tried to discharge "model" functions or not, whether they consciously advocated an anti-bourgeois alternative or not, they were objectively an alternative institution which stimulated critical thinking and fed the urge to leave traditional bourgeois ways behind. Yet again, utopian communities came into conflict with history and, yet again, were defeated.

The defeat was all the more painful because modern communes clashed with the bourgeois state, a powerful force not yet fully developed in the first half of the 19th century but blatantly repressive now. Walter H. Clark, a professor of religious psychology, says that "the laws, the police, and hostile neighbors constitute serious problems for many communes. They give rise to generalized paranoid ideas and a feeling of insecurity that weaken and poison the sense of community that ideally characterized such fellowships. Following the finest traditions of the Inquisition and modern police states, some law enforcement agencies have been known to plant spies and even *agents provocateurs* in communities. Understandably, measures taken to guard against such persons will have negative effects on the *bona fide* members themselves, not to mention the resulting breach between the community and the larger society".[1]

By the mid-1970s the communitarian movement began to wane. This coincided with the decline of mass democratic movements in the United States and other Western countries. It was time for stock-taking, for digesting and analyzing the experience gained.

What was the social ideal the new communities were trying to reach for consciously or unconsciously? What was the type of relations established objectively among their members? As Judson Jerome notes aptly, "the structures of the new communes are more like skeletons under the skin, which can be intuited and hypothesized, but remain

[1] *Utopia/Dystopia?*, Ed. by Peyton E. Richter, Schenkman Publishing Co., Cambridge, Mass., 1975, pp. 119-20.

implicit—to the extent that the communards themselves are often unaware of them".[1] Still, by summing up eye-witness reports and the evidence supplied by participants in communitarian experiments and by students of this social phenomenon, one can try to answer the questions posed.

For all the differences in their value orientations, the ideal which most communes were striving unconsciously to attain can be defined as an *unalienated society* in which man would realize his own worth and not be subjugated by things, other people, groups, organizations or the state.

People were dreaming of a community in which each could expect affection, empathy and understanding from others and be ready to respond in kind, without any fear of retribution for this kind of softness. In *Getting Back Together* written after the author's visits to several communes, Robert Hourriet recalls that in many, people were obviously eager to render material and moral support to others, to care for the sick, to help in raising others' children—in other words, to work selflessly for the common good.

People were dreaming of a community of free, creative labor which would enable each to assert his abilities and draw on man's inner resources. According to Herbert Otto, members of the communes he visited were unconsciously trying to introduce an element of play into their work, to make it "a form of joyous self-expression and self-realization".[2]

People were dreaming of a community where the purpose of life would be shaped not by external pressures but by "nonrepressive" inner motivations of the individual, where spiritual and not material incentives would dominate and where man could, as a result, feel freer than before.

People were dreaming of a community where man would reestablish "friendly" contact with nature as a source of not so much material wealth as moral purity, physical health and creative vigor. People were dreaming of a simpler existence free from a multitude of unnecessary things—that is, of setting up an uncomplicated and transparent social or-

---

[1] Judson Jerome, *Families of Eden. Communes and the New Anarchism*, London, p. 4.

[2] Herbert A. Otto, *op. cit.*, p. 17.

ganization in which each man could see all the social mechanisms at work and in which he could, competently and with justification, form his own judgment with respect to all developments and processes occurring before his very eyes.

"I came here because I wanted to simplify my life as much as possible," says a utopian commune member. "I had a lot of things to get rid of—a car, a hi-fi, a million useless things....

"I had done the political trip for a while, but I got to the point where I couldn't just advocate social change, I had to live it. Change isn't something up there, out there.... It's in here.... This is where I have to start if I want to change the whole ... system.

"We don't want to be in the materialist bag anymore, and we don't want to get caught up in the nine-to-five career bag, the two-week vacation, barbecues-in-suburbia bag....

"It was my dream to belong to a tribe, where the energies flow among everyone, where people care for one another, where no one has to work, but everyone wants to do something because we're all mutually dependent for our survival and our happiness."[1]

People were dreaming of many other great and small things, but the essence of the alternative underlying these dreams was clearly anthropocentric. The utopian community focused not on the state, not on society but on the individual, on the free and allround man as he could be pictured by those living in an alienated, mass consumer society.

This means that the social ideals which the communes of the 1960s and 1970s tried to translate into reality mostly stemmed from romantic, democratic and socialist utopias, although, as a rule, these ideals did not conform to this or that utopian type fully or exclusively.

Significantly, most modern utopian experiments regarded questions involving forms of property and the ways of distributing the surplus product and of organizing production—questions over which 19th-century utopians agonized—

---

[1] Keith Melville, *Communes in the Counter Culture. Origins, Theories, Styles of Life*, William Morrow & Co., Inc., New York, 1972, pp. 11, 12.

as minor, negligible and routine, to be solved in the course of routine efforts. This was not simply a sign of theoretical infantilism but also a direct consequence of the influence exerted by the consumer society which glossed over the issue of the system of property and relegated it to the periphery of critical thought. True, as the workings of a utopian commune were being "debugged", all these problems made themselves felt more or less acutely and demanded practical solutions. Still, the fact remained that the issue of utopian goals was discussed in isolation from the question of the system of property as a necessary condition for their attainment.

For some time, life in a utopian community could evoke in its members a feeling of psychological relief and moral satisfaction because it contrasted sharply with life in the outside world. Despite all financial difficulties, it was possible to create, for a brief period, a new atmosphere free from mercenary attitudes, from consumerism, hostility, competition, the fear of losing one's job and social status, and free from the interminable and pointless rat race. With the passage of time, however,—and if the community retained its viability—it simply had to tackle a multitude of routine, prosaic tasks concerning economic matters, relations among the members and contacts with the outside world. This gave rise to contradictions, problems and difficulties which were nonexistent in the world from which the members had fled.

Virtually no utopian commune of the 1960s and 1970s succeeded in realizing all the principles proclaimed with any degree of success or in establishing the results achieved as a feature of everyday life. (This does not refer to the typically religious communities whose life was influenced by devotion to religious dogma.) The actual communitarian practice was in many respects different from the ideal. Suffice it to cite the example of Twin Oaks, all the more so because its organizers had a clear grasp of what they wanted. According to a Twin Oaks member, "We raise our own beef, pork, and organic produce; supply our own dairy products; do our own repairs on cars, trucks, and farm machinery; are architects, carpenters, plumbers, and electricians; and produce income mainly through the manufacture and sale of handmade rope hammocks, but also through the sale of our own publications, typing services, miscellaneous crafts, and through some short-term work in nearby cities. There is no one leader. A planner-manager government is responsible for formalizing decisions reached by group input and consensus. A labor credit system helps us organize and share equally a constantly changing flow of work. All income and most property are held in common. Each individual's needs for food, clothing, shelter, and medical services are met by the community as a whole. Over time, Twin Oaks has evolved a unique culture that continues to grow. Cooperation instead of competition; sharing rather than possessiveness; equality in place of exploitation; gentleness, not aggression; reason instead of authority; an end to sexism, racism, and consumerism: these are some of the ideals around which our culture has developed."[1]

Agreeing that Twin Oaks closely resembled other utopian communities and was "a blend of planning and happening",[2] its inhabitants maintained that it was indeed behaviorist and that behaviorism should be interpreted more broadly.

It is easy to see that little was left of the project put forward by the commune's behaviorist father. A visitor to Twin Oaks wrote that had Skinner visited that laboratory he would have been very disappointed. Indeed, the community failed to attain its most important goal—to implement the "reinforcement" principle on which Skinner insisted—and its "behaviorism" was merely a signboard attracting numerous visitors and helping the community to keep afloat.

Deviations from the original ideal were all the more typical of many communities because their view of this ideal was vague; it assumed different shapes depending on the circumstances. "Freedom from alienated labor" often meant idleness. "Some collectively allocated labor; some survived through the efforts of a minority who chose to work; and some subsisted on welfare or outside contributions, preferring to avoid work altogether."[3] "Sexual liberation" often meant promiscuity which frequently resulted in tensions within the community; "relations of cooperation" degenerated into parasitism; "unity of man

[1] *The Reform Spirit in America*, pp. 600-601.

[2] *Ibid.*, p. 602.

[3] Rudolf Moos and Robert Brownstein, *op. cit.*, p. 41.

and nature", into orientation on preindustrial imperatives; and so on and so forth.

It would hardly be right to conclude, however, that these failures and deviations prove the essential impracticability of the principles themselves. Rather, the record of modern (and 19th-century) American communes proves the inadequacy of the methods used to implement these principles and of the conditions in which utopian experiments were attempted.

But the communitarian experience of the 1960s and 1970s was not confined to negative significance only. Like 19th-century communities, modern communes made a positive impact on American society—an impact we will be able to gauge precisely only later, when the overall result of their activities becomes more pronounced. Today, however, one can already state with sufficient justification that utopian communes played a noticeable role in the emergence of the new types of consciousness and the personality ("social types") which appeared in America in the 1960s and 1970s—not only because scores of thousands of eager and sometimes wayward young people who will live in the 21st-century United States have passed through these communities but also and above all because the new personality and consciousness "models" were tested precisely in these communities. In this regard the communitarian experience was a much more influential and constructive force than the theoretical constructs of Roszak or Reich who built them mostly on the basis of the experience accumulated in utopian enclaves.

Many American researchers point out that the communes have contributed to the emergence of a new cultural climate in the United States, expressed in so-called counterculture, and that they have helped in the creation of new cultural values which are objectively antibourgeois and are a factor in the disintegration of bourgeois civilization.

There is much truth in these statements. As an alternative subculture formed within nonconformist social groups, counterculture is a complex and contradictory phenomenon performing different functions. It springs from a variety of sources and is shaped by different mechanisms. While its more crude expressions hysterically rejected culture per se, that is, appeared as an anticulture, counterculture reflected a rebellion of petty-bourgeois consciousness not against culture as such but against the values and orientations of mass society, against the technocratic version of mass bourgeois culture. Hence the polemical attacks of counterculture against the philistine concepts of prosperity, wealth, success, against rigid morals and social conformism, as well as against the claims to omnipotence on the part of science which it regards as guilty of the mass culture phenomenon.

Of course, the counterculture of the 1960s and 1970s did not become a mass, real alternative to dominant bourgeois culture. Some of its elements even became part of the U.S. cultural establishment and were used by the ruling class to manipulate public consciousness.

At the same time, one cannot deny that this counterculture was a reflection of protest against the dehumanization of social relations, the bureaucratization of the social fabric, the growing alienation of the individual from society, etc. Keith Melville was right to note that while utopian communities and the counterculture they spawned could not tell one where one should go on from there or how to restructure society and its culture, at least they pointed to the real problems of American society[1] and thus discharged a heuristic and critical cultural function.

Today, when "new conservatism" is on the rise, one can easily get the impression that the trends which surfaced in communitarian experiments 10 to 15 years ago are finished once and for all and that the utopian quest for an alternative America is over, at least for a long time. But this conclusion would be a mistake. Although the number of communes has dropped sharply in recent years and so has their sociocultural role, the search for an alternative livestyle and alternative values goes on. As an example of the movement for a new alternative lifestyle one can cite the North American Movement for Voluntary Simplicity. Tomorrow this search may precipitate a new wave of utopian experiments.

[1] See: Keith Melville, *op. cit.*, p. 7.

This concludes my brief review of the American utopian tradition. I hope I have cited specific examples to prove that utopia played a substantial part in the emergence of American society, of its social and political values and institutions, of its consciousness and culture.

Utopia was not only a form of social criticism in America, but also a means of realizing the "promises" set forth in the Declaration of Independence and other basic documents of the American Revolution. In other words, to an American it was not only a challenge but also a legitimate form of the search for new social structures and new values, a form in complete accord with legitimate political practice. And so, while most utopian projects failed to materialize in actual fact, they did stimulate sociopolitical reform by discharging the function of a pressure mechanism.

Which way this or that utopia was trying to push society depended on its specific content, class nature and sociohistorical context. Generally speaking, any utopia is ambivalent and its social role, contradictory. Comparing the liberal and the Narodnik utopias which existed in Russia in the late 19th and early 20th centuries, Lenin noted that although the utopia of the Russian Narodniks was no more than a romantic dream "about abolishing wage slavery without a class struggle",[1] its actual functions in the then Russia were determined by the alignment of class forces and the priorities of the historical tasks facing the country. "When the issue of economic emancipation becomes as close, immediate and *burning* for Russia as the issue of political emancipation is today, the utopia of the Narodniks will prove *no less* harmful than that of the liberals.

"But Russia is still in the period of her bourgeois and not proletarian transformation; it is not the question of the economic emancipation of the proletariat that has *most completely* matured, but the question of political liberty, i.e. (in effect), of complete bourgeois liberty."[2]

From the viewpoint of the tasks most topical for Russia

[1] V. I. Lenin, "Two Utopias", *Collected Works*, Vol. 18, Progress Publishers, Moscow, p. 356.

[2] *Ibid.*, pp. 356-57.

at that time, the liberal and the Narodnik utopias discharged, objectively, different social functions, played different historical roles and, consequently, deserved to be evaluated and treated differently on the part of the contemporary political parties and social classes. "...The Narodnik utopia plays a peculiar historical role. Being a utopia in regard to the economic consequences that a new division of the land should (and would) have, it is an accompaniment *and symptom* of the great, mass *democratic* upsurge of the peasant masses.... The liberal utopia corrupts the democratic consciousness of the masses. The Narodnik utopia, which corrupts their *socialist* consciousness, is an accompaniment, a symptom, and in part even an expression of their democratic upsurge."[1]

Obviously, the historical situation obtaining in Russia in the late 19th and early 20th centuries does not resemble the one that existed in America at that time, let alone in subsequent decades. Still, Lenin's approach to the assessment of Russian utopias can serve as a methodological key to the understanding of the essence and social role of American utopias which arose in a different context, a key to the evaluation of utopian constructs appearing today and about to appear tomorrow.

In recent years, representatives of different political trends have been increasingly relying on utopia as a means of social activity in an effort to reawaken mass utopian consciousness and mold it into a constructive force. Suffice it to recall the famous "Letter to the New Left" C. Wright Mills published as early as 1960: "We are frequently accused of being 'utopian'—in our criticism and in our proposals.... There is truth in these charges. But must we not ask: what now is really meant by utopian? And: is not our utopianism a major source of our strength? 'Utopian' nowadays I think refers to any criticism or proposal that transcends the up-close milieux of a scatter of individuals: the milieux which men and women can understand directly and which they can reasonably hope directly to change. In this exact sense, our theoretical work is indeed utopian.... If there is to be a politics of a New Left, what needs to be analyzed is the *structure* of institutions, the *foundation* of policies. In this sense, both in its criticisms and in its

[1] *Ibid.*

proposals, our work is necessarily structural—and so, *for us*, just now—utopian."[1]

Herbert Marcuse, who tried to supply a theoretical justification of this thesis, wrote: "Today any form of the concrete world, of human life, any transformation of the technical and natural environment is a possibility, and the locus of this possibility is historical. Today we have the capacity to turn the world into hell, and we are well on the way to doing so. We also have the capacity to turn it into the opposite of hell. This would mean the end of utopia, that is, the refutation of those ideas and theories, that use the concept of utopia to denounce certain socio-historical possibilities."[2]

The appeal by C. Wright Mills evoked an unexpectedly wide response in American society—first and foremost, on the part of the left radicals with their extremist claim about the "end of utopia". But liberals, too, responded to it; they saw utopia as a means of solving the social and political contradictions of the modern world. As Daniel Bell wrote in 1962 in his foreword to the new edition of *The End of Ideology*, "There is now, more than ever, some need for Utopia, in the sense that men need—as they have always needed—some vision of their potential, some manner of fusing passion with intelligence."[3]

The 1970s gave a new impetus to utopian quests and experiments. Predictions of a cul-de-sac which mankind was to face in the near future (these forecasts were made by certain Western sociologists and futurologists, especially those involved in the drafting of alarmist reports to the Club of Rome) demanded that a search be undertaken for positive alternatives. The role of social utopias could appear all the more important because, as some of the alarmists stressed, the difficulties and problems American society encountered in the latter half of the 20th century were to a large measure connected with the absence of "bold projects". "...What the future is like depends on us now, that we are building

[1] C. Wright Mills, "Letter to the New Left" in: *The New Left. A Collection of Essays*, Ed. by P. Long, Porter Sargent Publisher, Boston, 1970, pp. 20, 21.

[2] Herbert Marcuse, *Five Lectures. Psychoanalysis, Politics, and Utopia*, Penguin Books, London, 1970, p. 62.

[3] *The Futurist*, Vol. VII, No. 6, December 1973, p. 266.

the future now," wrote Margaret Mead contradicting Herman Kahn and William Irwin Thompson. "And we have to realize that everything we say about the future is going to influence the future. And the picture we draw of the future is, therefore, tremendously important."[1]

That was when Alvin Toffler advanced his idea of organizing a "factory of Utopias". This referred to integrated groups in which representatives of different fields of knowledge and culture would, in the course of their communal life, work out systems of alternative values to open new vistas for different social strata. Traditional utopias, Toffler maintained, pictured simple, static societies sometimes even oriented on the past. But America needed utopias oriented on the future, on "superindustrialism" or the "third wave" society, as he later called the future.

But the 1970s were notable not only for the open appeal of left radicals and liberals for utopian quests and experiments. The dynamics of U.S. politics prove that while crisis developments within American society prompt part of this society to search for utopian solutions, they also stimulate a policy of protection and restoration which displays a critical attitude to utopia. This is especially so if champions of this policy gain control of the government, the way it happened in the United States in the early 1980s.

But even if the antiutopian trend should increase and persist in the coming years, history proves that this will not be "the end of utopia". First, because the so-called shift to the right, recently discussed so much in the West, is not comprehensive. Besides, the conservatives' failures to solve America's pressing problems may, after a while, give rise to a new wave of radicalism and stimulate a new utopian search. Second, no matter what the conservatives believe about themselves and assert publicly, conservative thinking itself is bound to reproduce utopian orientations and to generate social ideals and projects that meet all standards of utopia.

It appears that the contradictions of American society will continue to stimulate both utopian and antiutopian consciousness simultaneously, urging the rival forces to use all their intellectual resources either for perpetuating bourgeois civilization or for destroying it and building a new society on American soil.

[1] *The Futurist*, Vol. XII, No. 4, August 1978, p. 229.

NAME INDEX

A

Adams, John—52, 91
Akin, William E.—105, 106
al-Farabi—33
Arab-Ogly, E.A.—6
Arendt, Hannah—184
Aron, Raymond—183
Asimov, Isaac—25, 193
Avdeyeva, M.A.—6, 201

B

Bacon, Francis—16, 33
Bailey, Charles—184, 191
Bauer, A.—27
Bell, Daniel—112, 119, 121, 122, 125, 231
Bellamy, Edward—10, 16, 20, 21, 40, 43, 63, 88, 90, 94-96, 100, 116, 152, 178, 179
Bellow, Saul—116
Berdiaeff, Nicolas—172-73
Bestor, Arthur—6, 195, 201
Bestuzhev-Lada, I.V.—221
Billington, Ray Allen—37
Boguslaw, Robert—113, 114
Bradbury, Ray—116, 184, 193
Brisbane, Albert—90, 201
Brooks, Van Wyck—201
Brown, N.—138, 139, 143, 145
Brownstein, Robert—220, 221, 226
Bruce-Briggs, B.—115, 116, 122, 126
Brucker—21
Bryan, William Jennings—82
Brzezinski, Zbigniew—122

C

Cabet, Étienne—5, 10, 28, 91, 199, 201-07, 212, 214
Callenbach, Ernest—141, 144
Campanella, Tommaso—10, 21, 33, 94
Carmichael, Stokeley—169
Carpenter, Frederic I.—46
Carter, James—163, 164
Cartwright, John—35
Cavendish, Margaret—30
Charles II—31
Charon—204
Chase, Stuart—122-24
Chesneaux, Jean—33
Chizhevsky, A.—25
Clark, Ian—112
Clark, Walter H.—222
Clarke, Arthur—25
Columbus—176
Coolidge, Calvin—165
Cooper, James Fenimore—40, 89
Cotton, John—70
Coughlin, Charles E.—82, 83
Crèvecoeur, Hector St.
John de—60, 62

D

Dahrendorf, Ralph—116, 117
Danielson, N.F.—34
Darwin, Charles—121
Debs, Gene—90
Dodd, A.B.—96
Doig, Ivan—29
Donnelly, Ignatius—40-41, 76,

233

Owen, Robert—5, 10, 16, 20, 28, 33, 40, 91, 92, 196, 198-201, 205, 206, 212, 214

P

Paine, Thomas—52, 77
Parrington, V.L.—6, 56, 62, 70, 71, 75, 87, 95
Parrington, V.L., Jr.—6, 41, 43, 65, 70, 90, 104
Parsons, Talcott—117
Patrick, J.Max—6
Pease, Jane—66
Pease, William H.—66
Peccei, Aurelio—112
Persinger, Charles Edward—96, 97
Pestalozzi, Johann Heinrich—200
Phillips, K.—165
Phillips, Wendell—90
Plato—10, 12, 19, 21, 32, 114, 116, 125, 170
Platt, John—123
Plekhanov, Georgi—13
Pohl, Frederik—184
Polak, Fred L.—18, 49, 171

R

Rabelais, François—16
Reagan, Ronald—164-66
Reich, Charles A.—227
Rhodes, Harold V.—36
Rideout, Walter B.—175
Roberts, William—96
Roemer, Kenneth—6, 41
Roosevelt, Franklin Delano—56-58, 65, 180
Roosevelt, Theodore—57
Roszak, Theodore—227

S

Saint-Simon, Claude-Henri—10, 16, 33, 40, 92, 121, 195
Salinger, Gerome—116
Schlesinger. Arthur M., Jr.—41
Scott, Howard—65, 104, 106-08, 122, 126
Sevostianov, G.N.—74
Shakespeare, William—16
Sheckley, Robert—184, 192
Shestakov, V.P.—46
Shvyrev, V.S.—26
Sinclair, Upton—42, 90, 100-02
Skidmore, Thomas—40, 43, 93
Skinner, Burrhus F.—25, 43, 122, 127-31, 181, 220, 226
Sorel, Georges—47, 48
Sorge, Friedrich Adolf—34, 64
Swift, Jonathan—31

T

Terkel, Studs—166, 167
Thompson, William Irwin—232
Thoreau, Henry David—12, 40, 43, 84, 86, 88-90, 138, 140, 197
Tocqueville, Alexis de—35, 60
Toffler, Alvin—147-51, 232
Tolstoy, Lev—16, 77
Totomints, V.F.—147
Townsend, Francis—65
Tsiolkovsky, Konstantin—25
Turner, Frederick Jackson—36

U

Ustinov, V.M.—147
Utkin, A.I.—74

V

Vairase, Denis—33
Vaughan, Benjamin—72

PROGRESS PUBLISHERS

will soon publish

Recent History of the Labour Movement in the United States. 1965-1980

The present edition is a continuation of the two volumes of *Recent History of the Labor Movement in the United States. 1918-1965*, under collective authorship. It considers the complex problems of the working-class movement in the USA against the backdrop of domestic and foreign policy events from 1965 to 1980, and gives a general insight into the social and political development of the American woeking class.

Using abundant documentation, the authors reveal the main trends and most important features of the working-class, union, and communist movement in the US. The book shows what forms and methods of struggle American labour employs against monopolies. Their struggle demonstrates the inadequacy of bourgeois theories of "democratic capitalism", "the disappearance of the proletariat", and "income levelling".

The book is intended for experts in the field and anyone interested in the problems of the US working-class movement.

REQUEST TO READERS

Progress Publishers would be glad to have your opinion of this book, its translation and design and any suggestions you may have for future publications.

Please send all your comments to 17, Zubovsky Boulevard, Moscow, USSR.